VAGABOND

VAGABOND

Lerato Mogoatlhe

BLACKBIRD
BOOKS

First published by BlackBird Books, an imprint of Jacana Media (Pty) Ltd, in 2019

10 Orange Street
Sunnyside
Auckland Park 2092
South Africa
+2711 628 3200
www.jacana.co.za

ISBN 978-1-928337-69-0

Cover design by Palesa Motsomi
Cover image: Hamid El Nil shrine in Omdurman, Sudan
Editing by Megan Mance
Proofreading by Nkhensani Manabe
Set in Minion Pro 11/15.5pt
Job no. 003426

Printed by **novus print**, a Novus Holdings company

See a complete list of BlackBird Books titles at www.jacana.co.za

The freedom to wander from place to place and the possibility of knowing the world beyond what's around my corner is a seed planted by my maternal grandmother, Basetsana Mary Malebane, and my paternal grandfather, Rantswai Gabriel Mogoatlhe, who could only travel in their dreams. I dedicate Vagabond to them.

Contents

I

You are Home

24 June 2008

THERE ARE WAYS OF ARRIVING in a new country: You should know where you are going, have your first few nights' accommodation booked, be able to converse in the lingua franca and have a bottomless bank account – or enough savings to make cash the least of your problems. This is the way of the well-organised and the cash-savvy. I'm not this person. I arrive in Dakar at 3.30am on a 'dental floss' budget; I don't know anyone, and my seven-word French vocabulary doesn't include 'please help me'.

Go ahead and tell me I'm an idiot. I aim stronger words at myself as I leave the plane at Léopold Sédar Senghor International Airport. I fill in my customs forms as if my hands have never held a pen. An official comes over to help me with the daunting task of tackling page two, where I need to answer the horrific question of where in Dakar I will be staying.

The first plan I come up with is to head to a nightclub, but then I realise I'm yet to see a club taking in revellers with backpacks

1

the size of Mount Kilimanjaro. I anxiously watch it going around the conveyor belt until a guard comes over to ask if I have lost my bag. I put the backpack on a trolley and push it like I've never walked before, panicking with every step taking me closer to the exit, fending off touts and cab drivers. Dakar comes with two warnings: It's infamously expensive and brimming with conmen. Getting into a taxi to nowhere is not an option. The only thing I know about Dakar is that it's the capital city of Senegal, and that the country is home to Youssou N'Dour, Baaba Maal, Ismael Lo, and one of my favourite writers, Sembene Ousmane. I also know about President Senghor's concept of Negritude and that Gerard Sekoto spent some time in Dakar and Casamance.

I have no idea what I'm doing, only that I refuse to accept the image of Africa as the home of doom and gloom. I come up with my Plan B as soon as I spot a uniformed gentleman holding a sign board with the words 'Novotel Hotel'. I straighten my back – to appear confident – and hand him the backpack, warning that it's rather heavy. I'm the only passenger in the Coaster minibus. I plonk into my seat and wonder if a colleague who suggested going to Hillbrow when I told her about my plans to travel around West Africa wasn't onto something. Before Dakar, I had been out of South Africa for thirteen days on work trips to Swaziland, Zanzibar and Ghana.

'No money, no experience, no social connections,' I mumble to myself, 'and apparently no common sense too because who abandons their life and career for something they don't know?'

Just when my heart starts sinking, the radio plays Youssou N'Dour's 'Birima'. It's one of the most important songs of my life; the one I'd listen to and daydream about West Africa when I was still a student in 2003 – I know I'll be just fine.

Dakar has a great get-up-and-go energy even just before dawn. There's music from clubs and cafés wafting through the air. Cab drivers hang out topless on car bonnets or pavements. On some street corners there are already women setting up shop for their street cafés; firing up pots and unloading plates from trolleys pushed by young men.

'And you are?' The manager at Novotel asks with a smile that sparkles as much as the chandeliers hanging over us.

'L-e-r-a-t-o M-o-g-o-a-t-l-h-e. Lerato Mogoatlhe,' I reply.

'You're not on the system, miss,' he says after a few minutes.

'But my travel agent confirmed my booking,' I lie, hoping he'll let me hang out at reception until sunrise as the realisation that I have no idea what I am doing starts to sink in. Standing in that reception area and pretending to be a guest provides me with some momentary comfort while I collect my wits. He calls another 'good hotel' and asks the driver to give me a lift there. This hotel is several stars below Novotel's five, but at US$100 a night, it's still unaffordable. The night manager, Jean, makes more calls and sends me off to another hotel, promising to collect me there after his shift so we can look for an even cheaper place. My reasonable room turns out to be dingy with a sagging bed. The bedding looks like it used to be white. Now it's worn out and faded. The chair and table are solid but old and scratched and the roomy bathroom has a toilet that shifts with my body.

An upbeat Jean and our 10am appointment find me pacing around reception. I'm excited and anxious. I'm still frazzled by my disorganised arrival and the fact that I have no idea what I'm actually doing, but everyone I meet is friendly and kind. They greet me with wide smiles that make me feel welcome. It makes me believe that I'll be okay.

We find the promised cheaper place six kilometres away from the city centre in Yoff. Via Via guesthouse is set in a small courtyard. It's quiet, save for the Ali Farka Touré and Toumani Diabaté's 'Debe', another favourite, playing on Radio Pan Afrique. There's a hammock on the way to the five rooms named after tourist attractions like Gorée and Lac Rose. At the bar-restaurant, a middle-aged black woman sits alone, reading newspapers and drinking beer from a glass she covers with a coaster to keep the ever-present flies out. Some European travellers pore over guidebooks.

Via Via is on Rue La Fayette. At the top of the street, off the main road, is a bank where three boys look on with smiles, waiting to sell me fake Louis Vuitton bags, Chanel and Dolce & Gabbana sunglasses. An eye-level poster behind the bank sells dreams of instant riches showing a man leaping with joy, a lottery ticket in his hand. There's an apartment hotel and an office building with medical specialists. There are small shacks selling everything from car tyres to packets of Nescafé with a teaspoon's worth of coffee, one laundry basket's worth of washing powder, flip flops, newspapers, cooking oil, rice and powdered milk.

Like most of Senegal, Yoff is predominantly Muslim. Dakar is a party town but there are no night clubs and bottle stores in Yoff. The beach is the centre for relaxation. Mornings feature tourists frolicking in plastic-bag-infested waters, in between reading and tanning at the beach cafés. The cafés are compounds with bamboo umbrellas that you pay to use. The better-off cafés offer plastic mats and have restaurants and open-air kitchens where meals are cooked in large pots on fires made on the ground. In the afternoons, the beach is a sea of blackness, with swimmers, runners, a pair of girls working on their taekwondo and groups of soccer players with sensationally chiselled bodies. I can see why Dakar is famous for holiday flings.

My two weeks in Dakar are uneasy. I'm working as a freelance journalist – a first for me – and discovering that those cheques only show up in my bank account at the will and whim of the people who sign off invoices; I am also struggling to fit in. Other than my black skin, everything is foreign to me – especially the food culture. I've seen and heard about trays of food shared by many hands. I encounter one on my third day when musician Didier Awadi invites me to share a meal of white rice and a creamy peanut butter stew called mafé. I pass on lunch.

The biggest shock is the relentless sales pitch from the endless stream of entrepreneurs selling everything from cloth, jewellery and CDs to pans and coal. It follows me inside the colourful public buses called car rapide and finds me at restaurants and internet cafés. It joins me at tea invitations, usually at the third cup, when my hosts and I have talked long enough to count as friends. In the Sahel, tea is not just a hot drink, it is a social tradition that is brewed and served accordingly in three stages. The bitter first cup is likened to death; the second cup is mintier, lighter in colour and just sweet enough, like life. The final cup, like love, is the sweetest. Sometimes people just skip to the third.

I'm also struggling because I'm living according to the Lonely Planet guidebook, a manual which warns me to always watch my back. I go to the sites it suggests, visiting Lac Rose – thirty kilometres outside Dakar – and find the water dark brown instead of the vivid pink on tourism brochures. I explore the noisy and overcrowded Médina where Youssou N'Dour was born, go window shopping at the Grand Marché, spend an afternoon at Ngor island and go to Gorée island, where slaves were kept before being shipped across the Atlantic Ocean.

Gorée is a twenty-minute ferry ride from the city. Windswept, with coral-coloured buildings and baobab trees, it's beautiful. There are no cars, only boats bobbing on the beachfront as young boys play soccer or splash in the sea. Goats park themselves on a soccer field, and artists work in open-air studios painting sunsets, boats, village huts, women and children balancing water pails or logs on their heads. Some artists use glue and sand instead of paint and brush to create their work.

At the House of Slaves, a clay-coloured two-storey building, the guide raises and lowers his voice for effect while recounting history. The holding cells are dungeons where only slivers of sunlight come in through small openings. 'This is where our brothers and sisters and mothers and fathers were made to spend their last days in Africa. Can you imagine their pain and humiliation?' he yells at our group of mostly white tourists. He shakes his head and sucks his teeth. I roll my eyes at the theatrics. The white lady next to me is not the only person sniffling. This only makes the historian more emotional.

'After they were brought here, our people were shackled in ball-and-chain, and our women raped. I come here every day, and the pain is always the same,' he continues.

The sniffles get louder at the Door of No Return, where slaves last touched African soil. I ditch the group when their whimpers turn to tears. Nothing puts me off as much as white guilt about the past when the present is still racist.

The first time I feel like I'm creating my own experience is on a Tuesday afternoon when Fatuma and the rest of the female staff at Via Via invite me to a wedding. Everyone is caked in makeup and decked out in grand boubous, chiffon, silk and lace dresses, and towering doeks. The only men in the tent are the drummers, photographer and videographer. The bride is dressed in a body-hugging gold satin and organza ensemble that looks like it's inspired by TV dance competitions. Her already light complexion is painted in a lighter shade of foundation; her eyes shimmering with blue eye shadow. Her smile reveals gold-decked teeth. We dance to the beat of the sabar, the bride distributes cloth to her guests, and then we head inside where the scruffily dressed groom oversees feeding guests. We leave with a round tray of rice and mafé to share. I pretend that I'm tired to get out of eating from the communal plate.

November 2007

It's pay-day Friday night in Newtown, Johannesburg, and a department store is pouring cash as it does at the end of every month in the name of a music series. Tonight's party celebrates local hip-hop and its stars are performing to a frenzied public in between mingling in a VIP room that's crowded with mostly young, hip, party animals, media and marketing types, D-list celebrities, a kwaito legend, people who are famous for being famous, a handful of radio personalities and people who know people on the guest list. I'm paid to party as a music and entertainment journalist. My life should be fabulous. I meet stars and icons. I'm guaranteed VIP access to top music events. I've met Beyoncé and partied with John Legend in his suite. Yet I can't deny that this is just another insignificant moment in a life that's fast becoming a series of inane events.

My friend Siki walks back to our table with flat lukewarm ciders.

'Friend, you have your look,' she says.

The look is blank and distant. It's the look I have at most events lately. Whatever the occasion, I'm bored out of my mind being there. I have my look tonight because my mind burns with one question: Is this really all there is to my life, so predictable that I have been sleepwalking through it for months?

'I'm so sick of this,' I tell Siki. I'm tired of pretending to care about people's new albums and TV shows. I honestly don't give a damn who is dressed by whom and I'm over writing about other people's lives and dreams coming true.

I leave the party knowing what needs to happen. I need to listen carefully to the thoughts that have not left me since December 2006 when a media trip took me to Accra.

A few days after the party, I write on Facebook that I'm hearing voices.

'Make them stop,' I say.

'What are the voices saying?' another friend, intrepid traveller Adam Levine, asks in a direct message.

'They're telling me Africa – now,' I tell him. 'Then go. Now,' he writes back.

I leave South Africa seven months later, telling everyone I will be back after three months in West Africa. I start in Dakar.

My life in Senegal takes a turn towards the authentic when I run out of money two weeks after my arrival. I'm waiting for a cheque that's late by a week. It's not a problem as long as I can stay at Via Via, where payments are made at checkout. When I return to Via Via one evening, Fatuma tells me I have a day to move out – a group of diligent Germans booked out the guesthouse months ago. I go to the rooftop to cook up a plan. I'm buddies with a crew of four Liberian guys that I meet around Yoff – Jim, Ousmane, Eric and Solou, who says AIDS stands for 'America's Idea to Discourage Sex'. There's also Jean, the night manager I meet on the day I arrive here, but I'm not in the mood to live with a family and have to follow their rules. I go back to the restaurant and wait until only myself and Mustafa are left. He's a waiter and tour guide.

'Mustafa, I need a favour, and you can't say no,' I start. 'I don't have enough money to pay my bill tomorrow. Can I leave my laptop here until I can pay?'

He refuses. 'Do you remember what I tell you when we first meet?' It was on my second morning in the city. When I ask him how I can get to Gorée using a car rapide, he tells me that he is also a tour guide and offers me his services, which I find too expensive for someone who should be living on US$20 a day. He gives up on trying to be my tour guide and tells me to stop worrying about money.

'Here, you're home; you'll be taken care of.'

He says I can pay my bill when I have money without leaving my laptop at Via Via.

A thin guy who has been sitting alone all night comes over. His name is Amadou – black as coal with yellowish buck teeth that have gaps between them, a shaved head with a long, thick braid that hangs to just below his neck. His rib cage is visible under his yellow shirt. He's a tour guide and owns a beachfront café called Chez Amadou. He also has a white stallion he uses to transport goods around Yoff. He tells me I can stay at his house for free and for as long as I need to. I can't afford to refuse his offer.

His house turns out to be a bedroom at his mother's. The house has three bedrooms, a lounge with peach Gomma Gomma sofas, white lace-and-voile curtains with peach trimmings, and a well-polished room divider with a tea and glass set for guests. Amadou's bedroom has one wooden window facing the street. The bed is a thin double-bed-sized sponge. Décor is two souvenir art paintings. There's a small cooler box in which he happens to have two cold beers. The en suite bathroom has no shower or plumbing; I have to use the shared bathroom. To shower, I fill a bucket with cold water, wet my washing cloth and soap it; to rinse, I use a plastic jug to scoop water from the bucket and splash it over my body.

Our side of the beach has a view with piles of plastic bags and a well. But it's still a house at the beach; something I've never experienced. I move around the house like a ghost, afraid to run into Amadou's mother after I overhear them in a screaming match about what I'm doing at her house. Amadou moves to a back room in Chez Amadou. While other cafés have a lot of tourists, the only people at Chez Amadou are Amadou and his three friends. One room is a lounging area where they hang out eating peanuts, playing drums and drinking tea. The next is his bedroom. It's smaller than the one that has become my home. With three broken chairs, a hard mattress and no door, his generosity moves me to tears. Visiting Chez Amadou becomes my new daily ritual. We meet there just before sunset for drumming sessions with his neighbour, Africa, and his buddies. Dakar starts feeling like home.

My money comes in four days after I move to Amadou's bedroom, ending my stay in Senegal. I use my last Friday to pick up my Malian visa, book my train ticket to Bamako and go on a joyride around the city. The only person at Via Via when I show up to pay is Mustafa, dressed as always in loose-fitting navy-blue pants. When I thank him for helping me, he tells me to remember that I'm home, where I'll never be alone or want for anything.

At Chez Amadou, I hang out for the last time with Amadou and his friends. When it's time for me to leave, they lay hands on my head and pray for me. Amadou gives me a necklace: A wooden pendant hanging on a shoelace. It's 4am when he walks me back home. Watching me pack, he beams when I thank him for helping me out.

'You owe me 50 000 francs,' he says. 'And the necklace is 20 000.'

Over my dead body, I think. Not when he spent four days warning me about Africa's scams, not after wanting to march to Cissé's house when I tell him how Cissé, who has seen me on Rue Lafayette, where he lives with his family, walks me to the main road to get a taxi, jumps in with me and follows me around Dakar and to Ngor Island, saying that we happen to be running the same errands, only to claim that I owe him for services rendered as my guide. Amadou, it turns out, is just another conman running circles around me. Our fight is bitter; we hiss at each other. I throw 15 000 francs on the bed and give him back the necklace.

We are both losers when he walks out of his bedroom.

II

TRAIN TO BAMAKO

July 2008

THE MALI EXPRESS IS THE EASIEST way to get to Bamako from Dakar: Get a ticket a day or two before departure and catch the weekly train at Gare de Haan. The bare-minimum station, about three kilometres outside Dakar, isn't so much a station as it is a small office next to the rails. The platform is the ground outside the office. The train is infamous for never arriving at the scheduled time of 1.50pm. The waiting passengers sit on plastic mats brought for the journey while the area grows more domesticated with every hour the train is late. Some people fire up braziers to make tea or warm food. Kids chase a ball around the rails, their clean road-trip outfits – Barbie doll dresses for girls and shiny grey suits or mini boubous for boys – getting dirty. A mother gets up to bathe her child on the tracks.

The knackered train shows up ten hours later. To get on, I throw my bag into the train, then try to hoist myself up two rickety steps that sway when I move. There's a huge gap between the steps;

someone pulls me up while I crawl in on all fours. I dust myself off and find my cabin. I'm in a first-class cabin with Yusuf and his big brother Solou who were on holiday; Adama and his young daughters, Aicha and Aminata, who are in yellow chiffon dresses, back from visiting family. Our instant family is led by Khadija, whose ample size is in a black chiffon robe with a matching scarf covering her head. Her finger tips are stained with reddish blots of henna. The brothers are light travellers, with one duffel bag. Adama and his daughters have one large suitcase. I have my backpack and a duffel bag with books. Khadija has two extra-large suitcases. Our cabin is so small that our toes touch when we stretch our legs. The walls, handles, windows, torn green leather seats, bulbs – every surface – is covered in a thick layer of dust. We use twigs to keep the windows open. The previously white porcelain toilet at the end of the corridor is caked with dust and grime. It tilts away from its position when I use it. I make a note to only drink a few drops of water and eat the bare minimum to avoid using it again.

The Senegal leg of the journey passes through fields of baobab trees and small villages. In many of them, old women and children till the family farms behind their homesteads; the women digging with picks and hoes and the children gathering weeds. They stop to wave at us and sometimes the children run after the train. We stop for around ten minutes in some villages and close to an hour in towns. In Senegal, we stop in the town of Thiès; which until now is a place I know only through Sembene Ousmane's seminal novel, *God's Bits of Wood*.

We empty out of the cabins to look for food and drinks when the train stops in towns. Women stock up on cloth and groceries while the men make a beeline to the bush, where they kneel to pee. This gives them, and us, privacy. Food is baguettes, chips, fried chicken, grilled sheep – called mouton – and rice with stew. I stick to my decision to only eat one banana whenever I get hungry and, even though I starve, I also manage to avoid having to use the toilet for number two until I get to Bamako.

The longer the journey grows, the more Khadija piles the compartment with stuff, buying a sack of rice, three large smoked fish, a case each of Fanta Orange, Coke and water. When my cabin mates tire of stringing sentences together in broken English, we communicate by pointing at what we are talking about. This is how I discover that my feet are three times their usual size; swelled up by the heat and from sitting in the train for a day and half.

The villages in Mali are also built with mud and set along low, green hills. Khadija's trip ends in Kayes. As we get closer to Bamako, the number of mopeds that double as public transport increases. In one town, a shiny, significant-looking SUV is surrounded by mopeds like it's an official motorcade. It's just another ordinary traffic scene here, and a reminder that three weeks ago Mali was a dot on the map. I'm proud of myself but, right now, the heat that is spreading around my belly and up my chest to my temples is from nerves.

A swarm of men jump into the train when we reach Bamako. One of them gets into our carriage and takes our bags without talking to us. He works fast and silently, taking luggage from the cabins to the platform. I don't feel like having to figure out my way around a new place again; I almost ask Solou to take me to their house. He only leaves my side when I join my bags on the platform.

'Taxi, taxi?' several men shout at me at the same time. I'm going to Bamako-Coura. The first person who takes my bags to his taxi puts me in the backseat with two other people and takes me across a city that makes a strange first impression. Wide boulevards turn into muddy streets, roofs are held down by bricks, some windows are made with zinc, and cars share streets with grazing sheep. The taxis and buses are beat-up. There are no towering monuments celebrating independence from France or shiny, modern sky-scrapers; no visible construction in progress. The city is on the banks of the Niger River, but Bamako acts like it doesn't know. There are no waterfront cafés, sunset cruises or floating restaurants.

My guidebook says Mission Catholique is one of the best places to find a bed in Bamako. It's cheap, located close to the city centre and a favourite with backpackers. They haven't answered the emails I sent to book my bed in the dormitory, but I go there anyway, and find it fully booked. A local guy who overhears my conversation with one of the nuns offers to take me to another cheap place.

Hotel Lafia is a regular house that's been turned into a mixed dormitory with two single beds and four bunk beds, and a clean shared toilet that flushes. A group of guys is sitting under a mango tree with a small pot of tea boiling on a compact brazier. There's a tray with shot glasses, a packet of sugar, and mint leaves. 'Thé?' one of them asks. Tea? Maybe later. I need a shower and to walk until I'm no longer shocked by how beat down Bamako looks.

Bamako-Coura is a business centre. The Grande Marché spills out of a building into the streets around it. Every inch of space is taken up by people, mopeds and kiosks selling books, car and moped parts, soccer balls and soccer jerseys, stationery; name it, and they sell it at the market. Some streets are lined with women selling second-hand clothes, even bras, and others who sell bold and colourful wax-print cloth, called pagne. Young boys weave between the traffic, selling airtime vouchers. The hustling philosophy seems to be if you have something to sell, best you start working the city's streets. There are people with more pagne and airtime on sale. Others sell peanuts, bananas and oranges. One man has a metal basin with oranges on his head, long metal spoons used to stir big pots hang from his arm, and pairs of flip flops in his hands.

I keep walking, dodging cabs and mopeds, going sight-seeing, stumbling into a fetish market with monkey skulls and bound snake carcasses next to a mosque. I follow strangers to see the city through their daily life and end up at the riverside. An old man in matching blue-and-orange wax-print pants and a knee-length tunic plays griot melodies on a handheld radio. Griots are a caste of musicians and poets and the only people who entertained royal courts when West Africa was still made up of empires. Some musicians, like

Toumani Diabaté, Habib Koité and Mory Kanté, inherited music from their griot families.

Looking at the afternoon sun heading towards the horizon, Bamako starts feeling comfortable as I marvel at the strangeness of places that called my name.

In the morning, a woman turns the area in front of the beauty shop around the corner from Lafia into a food stall. A wide pan bubbles with oil and thick chips she turns with a metal spoon that has holes so the oil drains. A line of people waits their turn as she stuffs a sliced baguette with cubes of meat and chips, adding a splash of oil before wrapping the parcel with white paper.

I cross the street to a table with glasses and kettles. Its owner's kinky coils look like salt and pepper. His shirt is unbuttoned to reveal his navel. There's a tub of margarine, Nutella, a tin of Nescafé, cans of condensed milk, and teaspoons soaked in water that's gone cloudy from the milky syrup. Fat green flies cover the lace tablecloth he uses to shield the baguette.

He puts a teaspoon of coffee in the glass, which he fills halfway with the condensed milk. Blobs of margarine spread out on my bread when I bite into it.

'You're from South Africa? Tell me something: Why did you kill Lucky Deebee?' Lucky Dube is one of his icons. He doesn't believe that he was killed in a car hijacking gone wrong; someone wanted him dead. 'He was a big man with a big message for unity,' he says. His lament follows me around West Africa.

I enjoy Bamako for its people. They routinely walk across the street to greet me, offer me tea or lunch. I'm at a cybercafé when the boy next to me taps me on the shoulder. His screen is on Google Translate to help us connect beyond our language barrier. He takes me out for drinks in Hippodromo to welcome me to Bamako. Malians reach out to others as easily as the rest of us breathe. Take Oumou and Djeneba. I'm sitting at a corner table in an empty restaurant when they walk in. Djeneba comes over to invite me to their table. They want to share their meal with me. Even though she can tell by the empty plate in front of me that I've had lunch, she refuses to eat without me. As I discover, 'eat' is not a suggestion in Mali. It's an instruction. I move to their table for more chips, fried chicken and Castel, the favourite local beer. Oumou is from Bamako and Djeneba's family is originally from Niamey, Niger. She's visiting them from Chicago, where she works as a nurse. Djeneba wants me to stay with her family but I'm leaving Bamako tomorrow morning.

'Let's meet here at 10pm then,' Oumou suggests.

Bamako is home to Salif Keita, Habib Koité, Toumani Diabaté, Vieux Farka Touré, Oumou Sangaré, Amadou and Mariam and a galaxy of other internationally celebrated music stars who routinely perform in clubs around the city. A taste of this music is what I want. Instead, I join Djeneba and Oumou for a cab ride across town to the bar where they hang out on Friday nights. After wearing lipstick, girls' nights out are my favourite thing about being a woman. When we arrive at their spot, the barman brings out plastic chairs, a table and three Castel beers before hiding out at the bar. Djeneba peels open a box of cigarettes and Oumou takes one. They may be my mom's age, but they certainly aren't Dikeledi Mogoatlhe. We go through the pack and round after round of beer, snacking on the boiled eggs and peanuts we buy from a boy who walks into the yard. Our conversation gets raunchier with every puff and sip. They want to know about my love life.

'Sex life, honey. I have booty calls,' I reveal. We laugh at the one who wants to join me in Accra. 'As if I'd bring an old shag to a new region,' I add.

Oumou raises her glass, saying she only keeps her men around for sex. 'I have no other use for them,' she says.

We gossip and laugh some more before Djeneba asks me another question. This time, her mood is dark. 'Why did you kill Lucky Dube?' she says, repeating a question I will come to hear often around the continent. 'I cried for a week.'

She rummages in her bag and pulls out a *Best of Lucky Dube*

CD, ordering the barman to play it. It's on repeat for the rest of the evening. It's a simple but perfect night out under the stars. We stumble out of the bar drunk on Castels and happiness. I almost change my mind about leaving for Djenné in the morning. Visiting the ancient trading city and former centre of Muslim scholarship has been keeping my hope alive on days when my new life gets overwhelming. In these moments – and there are many of them every day – I remind myself that all roads are leading to me Djenné.

III

Magic Town

ON NIGHTS WHEN the pitch-black sky is lit by a million stars, and a full moon hangs so low on the horizon that it looks like you can walk to it, you have to hang out on a rooftop in Djenné. 'Then you will know why this is the most magical place in Mali,' Philip says. Malian tour guides will say anything to make you stay a while and spend more francs in their town. Philip is no different, but when it comes to full-moon nights in Djenné he's not lying. We're on the rooftop at my hotel, Chez Ali Baba, bonding over sweet mint tea. As Oumou Sangaré's song 'Ko Sira' fades from my laptop speaker, the sound of villagers chanting rises from below us, where a small group of men and women in traditional Islamic robes walk around the town's square singing blessings to Djenné.

Djenné was founded around 250 AD, rising to prominence in the sixteenth century when it became the centre of gold and salt trade and Islamic scholarship in the region. Take away the Land Cruisers and mopeds, and time seems to have stood still. People still mostly use wooden boats, called pirogues, to move in and out of the city. Houses are still built with banco mud and, to beautify themselves, women still stain their feet, fingertips and mouths with henna. They still wear gold rings in their septums.

Donkeys still carry goods around the town, and even though the square at the Grand Mosque has a broken bus and station wagons, the dial is set to ancient, with old men in pastel-coloured grand boubous herding flocks of sheep. And as they have been doing since the thirteenth century, the town's people come together after the rainy season to plaster the Grand Mosque with new layers of mud. Of all the mud houses and buildings that make Djenné a World Heritage Site, the Grand Mosque is the most awe inspiring, lording over the town with wooden marionettes that can be seen even before you enter it. The first mosque on the site was built around the thirteenth century, and the current one in 1907. It seats three thousand people and remains the heart and soul of Djenné.

For about a week after the rainy season, people organise them-selves into groups of women and children who bring buckets of water for the men to turn soil into mud. Afterwards, men and boys climb over the mosque using the sticks that jut out of the walls as a ladder. This ritual is as much about loving their heritage as it is about social responsibility: Djenné has to maintain its look to remain a heritage site. For families whose houses are part of its ancient legacy, this means keeping them exactly as they were one hundred and fifty or more years ago.

The further I get from Bamako, the more broken the English gets. Like every fourth guy in Mali, Philip claims to be a tour guide. It's a lie, but he understands English. For 15 000 francs, he takes me on a 'historic tour' of Djenné. Thus goes our tour: 'This is mud house, very historic', 'this is bogolan cloth, it's made with mud.' Bogolan, the ochre, russet, mahogany and amber coloured cloth isn't made with mud, it's dyed in mud. 'This is school for Islam,' he says when we walk past a madrasa, where pairs of plastic shoes have been left outside the door. Inside, young boys read Quranic verses on wood slates.

He rents a Land Cruiser for a trip about three kilometres out of town, to Djenné-Djenno, for more walking and pointing out of the obvious. Djenné-Djenno, he says, means 'little Djenné'. Like its big sister, it has mud houses. Old women and young girls pound millet in knee-high wooden mortars and pestles. He takes me to his grandmother's house and puts a franc note in her hands. She wears a doek and Fulani earrings to pose for me. We stumble on a stream of blood running through one of the streets. 'It's from the butchery,' he points at the obvious yet again to show me severed pieces of meat on the ground.

Our tour is saved by a public wedding with several couples saying I do at the same time. Brides are in lacy white wedding dresses and kitten heels covered with rainbow-coloured rhinestones. Their hair has been ironed and curled and their faces plastered with foundation that's two shades lighter than their real complexion. Earlobes sag from the weight of gold chandelier earrings that fall to their shoulders and twisted gold Fulani earrings the size of a large fist. They travel on mopeds. The women in the crowd wear multi-coloured grand boubous and long white skirts and tops. Their hair is slicked with gel, eyebrows thickened with kohl, and hands and feet painted with henna, including on their fingertips and toes, making them look like they were dipped in black paint. As is standard, earlobes, wrists and necks are heavy with gold jewellery.

Orange mobile network takes over the square in the afternoon to throw a promo party. The crowd is buzzing at first. Fists pump the air whenever the MC hypes by greeting them with 'Salaam Alaikum', instead of asking, 'can you feel it?' or asking them to say yeah. The crowd roars in reply with 'Alaikum Salaam'. Even when they're partying, West Africans remain true to themselves. The party is hot until three bikers rev into town, performing tricks that include high-speed chases, wheelies and driving in circles around each other. They're here to announce a free show at the sports ground, killing Orange's soirée. Philip and I follow the action to the sports ground. A few people watch from the wall around the pitch, in groups, or from the rooftops of nearby houses. There are about a hundred people, most of them young. Girls are hip in tight jeans and slogan T-shirts. Ears and wrists shine with gold, but this is not a special occasion, so the earrings, bangles and necklaces are low-key. The boys are in oversized T-shirts and baggy jeans that hang off their butts. All tricks involve driving from one end of the grounds to the other and spinning around the crowd.

Every Monday, since 'many, many years ago', as Philip speculates, hundreds of traders from Djenné, and the towns and villages around it gather around the Grand Mosque for market day, taking over the square to sell dried fish, clothes, pagne, rice, beans, millet, thick blankets, motorbike parts, beads, goats, chickens, tomatoes, peanuts and peanut butter, piles of second-hand clothing, spoons and pots, glasses, jugs and buckets, five-litre bottles of palm oil, fish oil, red onions, okra, potatoes that are still covered with soil, and pens and exercise books. There's even a box with a black strap-on dildo on display at a stall manned by two boys who fall over with laughter after flashing the box at me.

There are wholesale traders and those who are scraping by, with stalls that are marked by covering a patch on the ground with a pagne or grass mat to sell dried fish and little pyramids of tomatoes, red onions and wilting carrots. Butchers hang their carcasses in the open air, slicing the animal off piece by piece as and when people buy. Dusty kids chase each other and run after tourists to ask for cadeau – gift, in French. The market women bargain hard and fast, tucking shrivelled franc notes into knots formed at the corners of the pagne they wrap around their hips. 'This is just like they did forty-five years ago,' according to an old European couple I overhear at one of the stalls. They're in Djenné retracing steps they first made when their faces were still smooth and their bodies supple with youth. I want to be like them and find my way back Djenné.

I leave for the port city Mopti when traders pack up to get taxis to Bobo-Dioulasso in Burkina Faso. We cram into the narrow seats with our luggage and only stop for the last prayer of the day. We spend the night at the border, where I sleep on my seat while everyone slums it on the ground. Burkina Faso finds me with a bout of home sickness that I want to cure by getting to Accra as soon as possible. I spend one night in Bobo partying until morning at a club that plays Xitsonga disco music from South Africa, and go sight-seeing in the morning before trekking to Ouagadougou to apply for my visa to Ghana. I pass time with what's becoming usual trips to the market, museums and other sights. I've never been as happy in West Africa as I am stepping inside the bus to Accra.

IV

SUN, SAND AND SEX

Accra, December 2006

MY FIRST TRIP TO West Africa, the region of my obsession since reading Chinua Achebe's *Things Fall Apart* at fourteen, is a media trip to cover a charity fashion event. The four days in the city go by in a blur and we mostly move around in a group. We go dancing and hang out at Golden Tulip Hotel's pool drinking cold Star beer. We go to an orphanage outside Accra for the customary mix-and-mingle between the press and the poor.

Still, Accra gets under my skin with the loud high-life music that's played everywhere, the fellows who drip sex appeal, the old men dressed regally in togas, the beaming smiles everyone flashes when we make eye contact, the first taste of plantain, the first sip of sweet hibiscus juice, and the laughter that ricochets around the city.

Everything I see and do enthrals me. When we stop to buy water at Koala supermarket in Osu, my spirit feels out of balance; there is something different about the experience that I can't immediately put my finger on. I realise later that everyone who works at the supermarket is black: The manager, packers, cashiers and security guards who don't want to see our receipts or peek into our shopping bags at the exit.

Accra feels so good, things that should offend me make me laugh, like the men at Boomerang nightclub assuming I'm a prostitute. This I discover after asking another guy who hits on me why all the men approach me like they're sure I will say yes to them. 'You're wearing a mini skirt and you were dancing on the stripper's pole.' Ordinarily, I'd tell him off for thinking that my existence as a woman is as a nun or a whore. Tonight, I grind my body against his and laugh at him, and with him.

We go to Makola market on our last morning to buy ankara cloth. I leave with three prints and a tie-dye kaftan I buy for a rip off at 100 000 cedis. It's the first dress I wear that makes me feel drop-dead gorgeous. Watching a colleague buy gold from a stall on the road – a setting I don't associate with buying jewellery – I realise that I don't want to leave Accra. As I tend to do when flirting with fate, I make a pact with God: I'm moving to West Africa if I see a Woolworths store.

We drive past a Woolworths store less than a kilometre later. On our way to the airport in the afternoon, our driver Joseph suggests that we stop at Labadi Beach. We don't have a lot of time, he knows, but a trip to Accra is incomplete without going to its premier party spot, he insists. Labadi is made for people-watching, with its bars and cafés, and people sporting incredible beach bodies. There are drummers, hot boys with thick chains around their necks and acrobat dancers moving between tables for dance shows.

There are grills fired up with sausages, mobile manicurists, people hawking second-hand swimwear, boiled eggs and groundnuts, and hustlers selling knock-off CDs of Alpha Blondy. One of them pushes *The Best of Lucky Dube*, a Brenda Fassie compilation, Yvonne Chaka Chaka's *Thank You Mr DJ* and Rebecca Malope's *Greatest Hits* into my hands. Lovers stroll hand in hand, beach boys flirt with tourists, and heavily made-up girls wrap themselves in the arms of very old white men. The smells of the sea, ganja and sausages waft in the air, and as Joseph rounds us up, Lucky Dube's 'I've Got You Babe' blasts from a stage that's being set up for a party. We run to a circle forming next to the stage and dance our hearts out. I've forgotten what it feels like to be delirious.

Accra, August 2008

I arrive from Ouagadougou just after midnight hoping the Young Women's Christian Association has a room for me. The night watchman, as guards are called here, is not in the mood to entertain me. No one is allowed to enter the premises after 10pm.

'You'll have to come back in the morning,' he says, with his head peeking out of the gate.

'I don't have anywhere to go,' I say.

'Try a hotel,' he counters.

'I can't afford it,' I confess.

'That's too bad. There is nothing I can do.'

He tries closing the gate. I block it with my foot and push my way in.

'I don't think you understand me. I don't have other options – you will not turn me away from this place. Besides, who stays at YWCA unless they're desperate?'

He doesn't help me with my backpack, and says nothing when I trip on my skirt, fall on the concrete path and graze my knee. He doesn't slow his brisk walk down now that I have to hobble. 'Don't move,' he says, shining his flashlight on a steel bench where I sleep until the residence opens. I spend my first night back in Accra hoping that the big rats running around don't crawl up onto me.

My stay at YWCA goes downhill from here. Morning breaks, and even though the dormitory is open, and the young Christian ladies start their day, I remain on the bench until the matron arrives at 9am. The ladies file past me without a word. This is not the Accra of 2006, with the smiles, laughter and akwaaba – welcome in Twi – that follow me everywhere. The yard has over-grown grass and weeds. The outdoor kitchen is a wall-less structure held together by poles and a zinc roof; you use a brazier to cook. The empty rooms at the back of the dormitory used to be a nursery, with pictures of cars, trains, toys and the alphabet painted on the wall.

The nursery becomes my go-to place to hide from the hymns and the loud, Holy Spirit-infused prayers that can be heard everywhere at the YWCA but here. There's a hall that holds prayer meetings for about two hours every evening, and a church service that lasts all morning on Sundays. And then there's the office block, where the matron spends most of her days policing our morality. The YWCA in Accra is the most miserable, soul-crushing place I know, thanks in no small part to the matron.

I find her waiting for me on the veranda of the office block, her hands on her waist. She has a medium-length permed afro and is dressed to please Jesus in a long black A-line skirt, a three-quarter sleeved white shirt, and black kitten heels.

'Good morning,' she says in a sweet, almost sing-song way. 'I hear you visited us after hours? I understand your circumstances, but the rules are very clear and we don't break them. We don't allow alcohol, men are not allowed in the dormitory at all; they are not allowed anywhere on the premises after seven. No guests are allowed after eight and gates close at 10pm,' she says.

I look around her office to stop myself from back-chatting. The posters of aid organisations and campaigns against violence and child abuse are more comforting than she is. 'Remember the rules,' she says on my way out: No sex, no fun, no boys or living like a regular student. They should change the name to The Christian Association for the Infantilisation of Young Women.

The dormitory is worse than the rules. There are six rooms that sleep three and four inmates each. I feel the springs through the thin mattress. We use shared bathrooms with wet floors and toilets that always harbour a piece of crap floating or stuck around it. The basins have a rusty streak from the permanent droplets of water leaking from the tap. There's a bare lounge with a small TV and some chairs. Silence reigns.

For a residence full of young women, the mood at YWCA is sombre, which is a pity, because in Ghana, even funerals are boisterous; with music and dancing to celebrate the dearly departed. I'm in a room with Rose, a Togolese girl who is in Ghana to study English. I'm reeling from the difference between the Accra of my nostalgia and my current experience. Shy and reserved, Rose keeps to herself and clings to me as much I hold on to her. Her English is as scratchy as my French, and we mostly listen to Oumou Sangaré's music and talk about how much we love it. Our cell of two grows to three when Diana joins us. She's a forty-five-year-old business woman from the Volta Region in Eastern Ghana. She's in town for a wedding.

'I'm too old for this nonsense,' she says on her second evening. She flings her legs off the bed and tells me to wait for some time while she makes a plan. About an hour later, we have a bottle of red wine.

'We're too old to be told what to do,' she says, laughing until she starts coughing. We raise our glasses towards the matron's office.

'Here's to sex, drugs and Rock 'n' Roll,' I say. We laugh until we cry and nickname the matron Jesus' bride.

Ghana is obsessed with God. In the morning at markets around the city, shopkeepers start their days by blasting gospel songs. 'Oh Nyame,' I overhear one man say tenderly, as if he is talking to his lover. Nyame is the Akan word for God. Businesses have names like Blessed Hands Beauty Salon, Saviour Phone Shop, Innocent Blood cold store, as butcheries are called. There's a God's Time Unisex Boutique, Stay Blessed Real Estate and Leap of Faith Catering Services. Consequently, the only man whose name is mentioned loudly at YWCA is Jesus. He is everywhere at the hostel. Where other girls their age may have posters of sports and pop stars, the inmates at YWCA cover their walls with tributes to Christianity and the Blessed Child; with Bible verses and posters of Jesus. 'Did you remember to thank Jesus todei?' a note in the bathroom asks. 'Did you remember to ask Jesus to teach you how to spell?' I hiss back.

With its position on the shores of Korle Lagoon, Jamestown should make for a pretty picture. It does – to some extent – with a lighthouse that affords sweeping views of the area. The beach bursts with brightly painted boats. People go about their life; smoking fish in griddles or disappearing into its streets. Jamestown is the grittiest place I have been to. The houses are stacked in small spaces and the smell of crap from overflowing communal toilets hangs in the air. I meet Johnson at the lighthouse and take him up on his offer to show me around his neighbourhood. We end up at his house, where I hang out with him and five other guys, drinking palm wine. They spark a joint; I eat sugar cane. Johnson keeps getting up to follow a slow but steady trickle of people who walk into his shack. They all walk out after about thirty minutes – sometimes more.

'Hey, come inside,' someone says to me. An orange flame glows in the dark, followed by thick white smoke spiralling upwards.

'You want a hit?' he asks, offering to share his heroin.

'We thought this what you are here for,' he says when I decline. I leave Johnson's a few minutes later.

I meet John on my walk to the road to get a tros tros to Adabraka. He has been following me since I left Johnson's drug den. He stands with his thin torso leaning outwards. He puts his left arm across his chest.

'I hear you're from South Africa,' he says; no greetings, no smiles, no akwaaba. He strokes his chin with his right hand.

'Why did you kill your own brothers?' His soft voice rises with anger. His brother works on the boats in Cape Town. He hasn't been able to get hold of him since the xenophobic attacks that left sixty-two people dead. The attacks were in Johannesburg.

'I guess I'm just worried, you know, I hope you didn't kill him.' I don't know what to say; there's nothing I can say, so I just listen in silence.

'Anyway, akwaaba, we don't hate Africans – you'll be fine.' We part with a hug.

In the evening, I lie in my bed with a throbbing headache and joints that feel like they're being hacked at. I'm shivering, and my body has goose bumps, but I'm also hot. Beads of sweat form on my forehead. I've spent the day walking around the city, visiting museums, the art market and the Kwame Nkrumah Memorial; maybe I'm sick from choking on the heat and exhaust fumes. Rose brings me packets of cold water and tries to get me to eat some rice and canned mackerel stew. 'Your eyes,' she says, her own round, becoming bigger. I gasp when she holds a mirror to my face. They're bloodshot-red. I pop aspirins and pass out.

When I eventually wake up, I take baby steps to the internet café. It's about three hundred metres around the corner from YWCA, but I stop often until my breathing calms. P-Square has just released their breakout album *Game Over*. The single, 'No One Like You', is on full blast and repeat. The volume makes me dizzy. I surrender to the tears I've been suppressing. I feel lonely and defeated; I bit off more than I could chew by thinking I could just uproot my life to wander around West Africa. My friend Sarah-Jane has also moved countries, to Belgium. She's been travelling since her teens. She uses her Friday off work to talk to me until my tears and grunts turn to laughter. She reckons I need a holiday; a place with Rastas, where I spend my days reading on the beach and cool tropical nights swaying to reggae. I leave for Kokrobite two days later.

September 2008

I get a tros tros from Adabraka to Kaneshie station, where minibuses that connect Accra to the coast are found. The station feels like a place that's holding its breath, trying to contain hundreds of people with their luggage and families, and just as many buses and minibuses. Hawkers walk around the station selling water, biscuits, juice, slices of pineapple and watermelon. Tros tros keep to Ghana's taste for bright colours, especially along the coast, where houses are painted lime, fuchsia, yellow, pink, red and other animated colours. Minibuses to these places are mostly yellow, white, red, green and blue. Drivers have assistants who collect money, called Chalé, like a lot of boys and young men are called here. Chalé looks like he's between sixteen and twenty-three. He keeps one eye on the road while calling to customers and taps a coin on the door to tell the driver when to stop. He's the link between the passengers and the driver, whose only job is getting us around.

A slow one-and-a-half-hour trip from Accra, Kokrobite is a great first-stop on my travels around the coast. Nature gives the village views of the Atlantic Ocean on one side, while hills dot the horizon with their green tops on the other. To this, people have added houses that look like candy floss with white-washed pink and green homes. As always, there's a Lucky Dube tune blasting from somewhere. I'm at Big Milly's Backyard; chosen for its beach-front location and a guidebook review that promises lots of Rastas and lots of partying.

Walking into the compound, the first thing my eyes land on is the bar. The tables around it have mixed groups of people who look cool in shorts that show off athletic legs. Girls with previously pale skins that are now brown have flowing hair and strings of beads on their wrists. Even hotter local boys and men hang on their arms. I find a seat at the counter and introduce myself to Noah, the barman on duty, by declaring that I drink orange juice with vodka. It's my first time living at a beach that's deliciously tropical.

I waddle back to the bar, where Noah adds personality in the form of a double shot of vodka to my orange juice, and make friends with a Liberian guy called MD; he of the smoothened accent, dancing eyes, wide smile, and a flair for conversation. MD is the type of fellow who has everyone he meets at hello. He knows it and he works it. A few people come over to him and, by extension, meet me. Kofi looks like a taller and hotter version of Thierry Henry; Francis's dark black skin glows in the light. He lives around the block and performs here as an acrobat on weekends. He looks interesting, with cowrie shells dangling on the thick dreadlocks that fall into his face. The rest of his 'locks are tied in a bun that makes it look like a carrot top. Alex is on a break from her life in Australia and is working as a volunteer legal representative. Alex's cousin lives in the overland truck that's parked in the yard with her man and dog. Darren is from Australia, I think. He's turning the house next door into a guesthouse. There are several people I meet and greet without leaving my chair. We holler at each other and jump into each other's conversations. The place reverberates with laughter. This is the Ghana I fell in love with.

Ready to check in at last, I walk past the bar and some chalets to the office, where the manager, Uncle Thomas, has only one rule for guests: 'Have fun and feel free to ask for whatever you need.' I'm at the Loft. It's a six-bed dormitory with bamboo walls that come up to the waist. The beds are sleeping sponges in boxes that have been sectioned-out with planks. Mine is the third from the space that constitutes our invisible door. The rest of the décor consists of mosquito nets, and six wooden boxes we lock our stuff in. I can't sleep – nothing new there – but for once it's because the open wall helps the breeze carry the sound of the waves to me. I'm from Mabopane in the north of Tshwane. Back home, every effect of apartheid's housing policies is still intact, especially the lack of scenery. I feel like a tropical queen, and I'm paying less than R100 for the pleasure.

Monday: The fishermen are the first to start the day, just before dawn, when they hum and chant slowly as they push their boats out to sea. It sounds like spiritual music. The beach falls silent again until before sunrise. The area in front of Patrick and Paul's gallery has been swept, and their shop is ready for business. 'Daybreak Africa,' Patrick says when the sun finally peeks out through the clouds. I go back to my bed and sleep until mid-morning, when I take my shower. The one I use stands alone, behind some rooms. It's open-air, with high bamboo walls and a bamboo door and requires drawing water from a well. I wind down the lever so the bucket can get to the bottom and pull it back up and I feel like I'm walking on air: I love turning previously new or weird experiences into comfort zones.

By mid-morning all shops on the beach are open. The stalls at Big Milly's have been laid out with beads, hats and crafts. Week days have a slow pace. People who aren't at school are at work, or hustling for work. Every third guy I meet seems to be Kofi or Kwame. 'What's up with that?' I ask Kwame number five. The Akan people name their children after the day on which they are born. Monday's sons are Kodjo, and daughters Adowa. Tuesday has Kwabena and Abena. Those born on Wednesday are Kwaku and Aku. Nana-Yao and Nan-Yaa are born on Thursday. Friday's children are Kofi and Efua, and the weekenders are Kwame and Ama on Saturday, Kwasi and Akosua on Sunday.

I'm Efua the beach bum in the morning, hanging out at Father Ben's bar. He sells packets of gin and sodas from a small shack that can't take in more than two people at a time. Drinks are served on a counter that has two stools. The drinks are cheap, the company of guys who have shops here great and the view of the sea fantastic. All the men here have dreadlocks. Most importantly, the men's dark bodies ripple with muscles that have been honed by a lifetime of pushing boats and pulling nets swollen with fish, arms chiselled by carving wood and playing djembes, legs made sinuous by soccer. These sculpted bodies also come from pumping iron and doing push-ups against one of the logs on the beach. They give Kokrobite an oversexed vibe that makes holiday flings part of the experience.

I order a black coffee with two sugars and take this moment in. A woman walks across the beach carrying a tray of fish on her head by balancing it on a cloth that's been twisted into a flat bun. A girl comes over to sell sugar cane and boiled groundnut. Life is sweet and the living easy. We call it 'irie' on this side of the beach. There's always a fat joint going around and hiplife playing on someone's cellphone.

Tuesday: Hell has broken loose. Calamity of Nollywood proportions has befallen me – there's a python on the loose. I live in a glorified bamboo hut. Who the hell loses a freaking python? Francis just looks at me and smiles. 'Don't worry. It probably went home.' Yeah-bloody-right.

Rewind to a few hours ago, in the mid-afternoon, when Francis is napping on the hammock with his pet baby python, Princess, coiled around his leg, he says. Next thing he knows, he wakes up in the early evening to realise that his python is missing.

'No need to worry,' Uncle Thomas says when I ask him to move me to a chalet until Princess is found. 'We know her, and she has never harmed anyone.'

Wednesday: Francis wants me to come over to his place for lunch to see how friendly his favourite pet is. Not even in his wildest dreams am I hanging out at a house that has a python. I repeat my daily routine of hanging out at the beach with my crew of boys named after days of the week, listening to Blakk Rasta's ode to Barack Obama's impending election as America's first black president, and Bob Marley. When I get bored of the beach I move to the bar. A boy I've never seen is at the top of the coconut tree, throwing some to his friend on the ground. As usual, Trinity, the bubbly three-year-old whose mom sells cloth and beads at Big Milly's, is giggling and running around the bar. She calls me 'Sister Lee'.

Thursday: She jumps out of the cab as soon as it stops next to the overland truck, running to the bar with outstretched arms.

'Hakuna matata,' she shrieks. Noah plays the song; Helen throws her hands in the air, her feet rising and falling, like Ladysmith Black Mambazo without the rhythm. It's a good thing I can stop myself from laughing out loud. Noah repeats 'Hakuna Matata' until Helen pushes her hands upwards, occasionally wiping the sweat off her face with the back of her hand. 'It's good to be back,' she tells me before I ask. She's a Brit who lives and works in Nigeria. She used to live in Accra, where she found her much younger husband. They come to Kokrobite for a holiday every year. Helen always announces her arrival by dancing to 'Hakuna Matata' from *The Lion King*.

Big Milly's bar is definitely the place to be from 4pm on Fridays, when the curio tables are laid out around the entrance and around the bar. The stage, beneath the Loft, has speakers in every corner. The weekenders arrive in cars and cabs and only check into their rooms after a few drinks. Weekends are a full house at the Loft. The beach turns into a market that also sells bikinis and Bob Marley sarongs, along with drums and paintings of sunsets and coconut trees. When night falls, everyone goes to Big Milly's bar for live entertainment. Francis jumps around the yard leading a troupe of dancers and flame throwers. Their act is followed by live drummers.

The bar is full, like it will be on Saturday night for the weekly reggae night, when the stage is decorated with neon lights, and a band performs reggae hits that always include Bob Marley and Lucky Dube's music. There's a white poster at one of the beach shops that says 'Rastafari keep fit Sundays'. The theme plays out in a game of beach soccer with the weekenders. The teams are mixed, but the boys are all different shapes and sizes of the hottest bodies I've ever laid my eyes on. They strip into swimming trunks for a cooling dip in the sea after the game.

I'm on my way to take a shower when MD, at his usual Sunday afternoon position at the bar, which keeps his all-seeing eyes on everyone's movements, calls me over. 'Lee, I want you to meet my friend.' His friend, Shola, is in navy-blue dad jeans and a white high-collar shirt. His skin is dark and beautiful. He's forty-seven, Nigerian and flirtatious.

'MD tells me that you are travelling around Africa?' he says.

'Hardly, Ghana is number four.'

MD takes over the introductions. He's been to twenty countries in Africa. He has lived my dream.

'Can I offer you a drink?' Shola quips.

'I drink Star, but you're buying, so South African wine please.' The wine menu has a choice between two South Africans wines, both bottled for Tall Horse.

We move our flirting session to Accra, where he takes me to dinner in Osu. I don't have cute clothes and I've been out of my red lip gloss for a month; I can only hope my cleavage will distract Olushola from looking above my chest. We get a cab to Osu with MD, who is still committed to his role as a wingman. I have been missing Joburg and my fabulous, sponsored lifestyle as an entertainment journalist. I want sushi, I want champagne and cocktails, and for Shola to pay for it all.

Monsoon is a Japanese restaurant that overlooks Oxford Street in Osu. Unfortunately, it doesn't open on Sundays, so we go up the road to Frankie's. It's a burger and chips joint on the ground floor, with a more formal set-up on the first floor. I order prawns and salad and a Long Island iced tea. MD leaves after one drink.

Shola brings out his West African male charm; removing the shells from the prawns before putting them in my mouth. I'm not completely shocked when I feel a moistness between my thighs. I am, however, floored to discover the drops of blood when I wipe up after peeing. My period is going to be here any minute now. Meanwhile, I need to get laid; now that I think about it, my body needs it. I have to go back to Kokrobite, to get my boxes of Lil-Lets tampons. 'I'm sure we can find them at any pharmacy,' Shola says, setting us off on a joyride around Osu and Cantonments, where we stop at every pharmacy that's still open. He insists on leaving me in the car, from where I watch him forming circles with his thumb and index finger, putting his free index finger in the hole, pulling it out, pushing it in, and so on. We finally find a box of Tampax, and head over to his hotel; he wants to shower before our first night out together.

We go to a club that only opens on Sunday nights, arriving just after 11pm. Other than the shining black tiles, dim blue lights and massive couches in the VIP area, another thing I notice is how empty it is. 11pm is too early to be here.

I lead us to a corner couch, he orders champagne, we quaff and talk until the night starts, and getting to the loo means squeezing myself between people. I have not partied in West Africa since my first time in Accra in 2006. Back then, I was too stuck to the stripper's pole to notice that people don't buy alcohol in single units of shots. If you're drinking a Smirnoff Storm you buy a six pack, if you want a double shot of something you buy the whole bottle. This I discover when the waiter brings another bottle of champagne with a bottle of Belvedere vodka, to make something Shola calls a Sex Bomb.

'Just as well, seeing as there can't be sex tonight,' I coo.

The last time I had vodka I woke up with my dreadlocks on my bed stand. The Belvedere is passed to the group of girls next to us. Well after midnight, the club is on fire; the crowd buzzing on bottles of Moët and Hennessy dashed with Red Bull. Girl squads are decked in minis that fit like a second skin, their high-heeled legs commanding attention. I feel plain in my old green dress and yellow pumps that are starting to fall apart from trodding Kokrobite's stony paths.

I sit in the corner boring the hell out of my date, whose groin is currently rubbing up on the girl shaking her bum against him. P-Square's 'Do Me' has turned the club into something like a sex party.

I make a note to buy new shoes, seeing as Shola and I are definitely becoming an item. I love flings that move fast: We're on holiday, we're horny and into each other – of course we are going to end up in bed. We spend the night at his hotel in Cantonments.

The first thing Noah says when I arrive back at Big Milly's is that Shola has already called three times. I don't have a phone. I make calls on Friday afternoons when I go to the internet café to check emails. I decide to make him wait until then. Not Olushola. He's back that very night with my best friends Moët & Chandon.

I join many tourists around West Africa's coast whose tropical life is fuelled by lots of sex. There are couples in real relationships, but in Kokrobite sex is a sport. Over time, I become the team captain, and go on a sex spree that leaves several people angry at me for playing them. But first, Shola. I enjoy his mind and listening to his wild stories about life in Lagos and California. And while I love the champagne lifestyle that comes with dating him, I don't like that he wants to upgrade me from the Loft to a private chalet or how irritable he gets when my buddies hug me. We're on the deck at Monsoon with MD and Malcolm one afternoon when Shola sends Malcolm to the coffee shop below, where there's a stall with cell phones. He has had enough of only reaching me via the phone at Big Milly's.

I like Shola for fun and for practical reasons like getting me a phone – now I will be able to talk to my next fling, Eliasu, whenever I want to. I met him back in my YWCA days but my fever cancelled our date. Seeing him in Kokrobite a few weeks later puts him back on my radar. I keep Shola for our champagne lifestyle, and play with Eliasu for his woolly locks, taut ass and great sex.

Things get weird between Shola and me when he goes to Dakar and Abidjan for business. He wants me to move into his hotel while he's gone, so his usual cab driver can take me to the places we always go. My list of travel rules has three items: Arrive with no expectations, leave with nothing that doesn't fit into a bag, and always use a condom.

Shola's business trip is my moment to pay some attention to Eliasu, more so as I will be moving to Cape Coast, his home town, when I leave Kokrobite. I don't want my other lover's driver's eyes on me, so I decline Shola's offer and remain in the village where I pass time with my occasional shag, Kodjo. Life in Kokrobite doesn't change. The waves are still my night song. Fishermen wake me up before dawn with their chants. I hang out at the beach, read, nap, eat, visit Kodjo and his friends most week nights, and have vodka-soaked parties on Fridays and Saturdays. One Sunday, two guys I've seen around ask me to join them for a joint on one of the verandas at Big Milly. The one closest to the entrance shifts to make space for me on the cushion. He moves something that looks like a round snakeskin bag.

'What's that?' I'm still at the entrance.

'Just my snake,' he says.

'What the fuck, man? What is it with you guys and the damn pythons? Call me when you're aren't playing with snakes.' I'm scared of snakes and the only reason I put Princess around my neck at the Reggae party and asked people if they liked my scarf is because vodka makes me do crazy things.

October 2008

I'm on the balcony at the internet café to send work emails when my mom calls. My body starts feeling weird and her words are suddenly annoying. 'Mom, please stop talking.' I hang up before she can respond and lean against the wall. A sharp, stabbing headache flashes across my head. My ears are hot, but my arms are covered in goose bumps. My knees burn with pain, like something is hacking my bones.

I'm with Kwame, the sixteen-year-old boy who has been following me around from when we met on my first day at Big Milly's. He's a sweet kid who likes Blakk Rasta and soccer, and I've got used to him being my shadow. He carries my laptop and walks ahead of me. The plastic bag I'm carrying has my lunch – a rice and bean dish called waakye, egusi and fried fish. Walking to and from the internet café, between the palm trees, usually puts me in a sentimental mood, when I talk to myself silently about how good it feels to be here – in Kokrobite, in Ghana; West Africa. Not this afternoon.

At Big Milly's, the bar staff are setting the scene for the Friday-night party. Speakers have made it from storage to stage, waiting for sunset, and people hang around at the bar. I unlock the wooden box with my things to take out my medical bag and the malaria test kit in it.

The bag is still on top of the box, with the plastic bag containing my food, when I wake up on the Saturday morning. I don't wait for the two stripes to appear on my test kit before taking out a box of my malaria treatment. I knew it was malaria from the moment it hit me, during the phone call with my mom. It's the kind of pain and sensation that I've never had before: Weak, dizzy, disoriented and more painful than period pains. Kwame is at the bar waiting for me to wake up. When I tell him what I have, he tells me to drink lots of water. 'You're going to vomit a lot.' I spend most of Saturday with my head hanging outside the Loft, spewing thick yellow goo.

My head feels hot, my body swings between being so heavy I can't even move my lips, and so light it feels like I'm floating. While everyone is jamming to reggae, I dream about shadows trying to pull me from the bed, and technicolour spider webs. I have short spells of hot flushes punctuated with cold shivers that run up and down my back. My bedsheets are drenched in sweat. And so goes my first experience of malaria. It makes Shola even more convinced that we need to shack-up at his hotel. He's hardly in Accra for more than a few days at a time, so I put my cards on the table: This is just a shag. I'm not in West Africa looking for a true romance story.

When I'm back to normal after four days in bed, I get a minibus to Elmina and Cape Coast, where I visit the former slave castles – trips that fail to make me sad or put me in a reflective mood about history. If anything, I get annoyed whenever a guide takes us to the Door of No Return, saying how blessed we are because, unlike our ancestors, we can make our way back through the door. The biggest sham I know is saying never again, and crying over slavery when millions of Africans live in abject poverty. I go on these visits because I feel compelled to, not because I want to.

So, it's with great pleasure that I pack my bags for Takoradi to look for transport to Ivory Coast. I arrive just before sunset, opting to rather look for the first taxi out of town than wait another day for a bus. The taxi I get claims to be leaving 'any moment now'. As if.

I'm too cheap to get a hotel room I'll only use for a few hours. Besides, this is Ghana. There's always music blaring hiplife from dusk until dawn. I leave my bags inside the taxi and follow a guitar riff to a chop bar across the road from the taxi rank. There are several other chop bars next to where I'm sitting. Patrons sit on plastic chairs and down bottles of Star beer. As always, Lucky Dube plays from one of them. It's my cue to dance my heart out and catch someone's, anyone's, attention. Giving people something they can talk to me about is one of the tricks I use to make friends.

A group of four male friends invite me to their table and, later, to one guy's house.

I start feeling uncomfortable when we leave the main road and go into a dark alley. I don't mind strangers, but I must always be in a position to walk back to wherever I need to go.

'I have to turn back,' I say.

'Are you feeling uncomfortable?' one of them asks. He doesn't wait for me to answer. 'I understand, but let me tell you something, my sister. You need to relax a bit. This is not South Africa. We are not going to rape you.'

I'm relieved, and realise that I have been carrying a lot of my old life with me. I'm as cautious as I have to be in South Africa. I don't walk alone at night and I don't wander off with men I don't know to places I haven't been to in day light.

I spend the rest of my evening at the taxi rank, and drag my bags back to the bus station in the morning. Now that there is lots of transport available, I want the comfort of a luxury bus that leaves in a few hours over the convenience of using a taxi that leaves for Abidjan in a few minutes.

V

YOUNG, BLACK AND WASTED

Abidjan, October 2008

THE CITY'S SKYSCRAPERS ARE rising so quickly you'd think there's a competition between property developers. Bumper to bumper cars and human traffic make some parts of the city centre hard to walk through, especially when people pour out of offices after work. The fashion sense here is a cut above the rest – tailored suits, fine pinstripe that's barely noticeable, and the sheer diversity of the outfits worn as daily wear. It looks like a trip to the opening of Parliament. The most lasting impression Abidjan makes is that of being a city that used to be a forest not so long ago; even as the light from buildings close to Ébrié Lagoon twinkle on its surface. Everywhere, the mounds of earth are covered in grass, trees and thick vegetation. Plumes of black smoke hover above the backed-up traffic out of Treichville.

Now that he can't turn back, it's time to let the cab driver in on my problem. I arrive at Elubo border between Ghana and Ivory Coast with an expired visa. The border official says I have to go back to Accra unless I give him 'something small'. I open my bag in front of him to find the small change he wants. The man almost puts his hands in my bag to get to my cedis. He takes all the money I have on me. 'You see, I need enough for my colleagues as well and there's plenty of them,' he lies when I protest. A girl who has been watching us breaks into fits of laughter when the official kisses me on both cheeks after taking my money.

I arrive in Abidjan with US$5 dollars between me and a pay cheque that's already a week late. Mohammed finds me outside the office at the bus station where the bus driver leaves me while he explains to his boss how, instead of paying for the Ivorian leg of my trip from Elubo to Abidjan, I propose he holds on to my passport until I have cash. From the group of cab drivers circling me, I let Mohammed take my bags and I say nothing, other than 'Village Ki-Yi', until we are stuck in traffic. He switches the engine off to save petrol and turns his long, lean body towards me.

'My name is Lerato,' I tell him. 'What's yours?'

'Mohammed,' he says.

'Well, Mohammed, here's the deal – prostitutes don't have sex for free on the job and cab drivers don't give lifts, but the thing is, I don't have money to pay you,' I declare.

'I understand. You pay when we get to Riviera?' he asks,

'No. I can only pay you in a few days, if you're lucky. You don't know me, but I'm not going to run away with your money.'

'What do you mean you can't pay me?' Mohammed asks.

'I don't have any money on me,'

'You can ask your friends in Riviera to help you,' he suggests.

'They're not my friends. I'm going there to look for accommodation,'

The only person I know in Abidjan is Werewere Liking, the Cameroonian artist and co-founder of Village Ki-Yi, a Pan-African arts collective I read about in Adam Levine's *Wonder Safaris*, about his travels around Africa. Werewere doesn't know me.

When we get there, Mohammed eases the car up the gravel

driveway into Village Ki-Yi, the Iroko tree in the middle of the compound is standing as tall and domineering as is described in the book that brings me here.

Four people stand around Mohammed, listening to his final shot at getting paid. One of them wears square spectacles with lenses as thick as the bottom of a Coke bottle. He tells Mohammed that they're just as confused by my arrival. I simply show up, ask for help and let my life become someone's chore. Mohammed leaves on our agreement to call him when I get paid.

I wait at an office for the general manager, rapper Ben Mpeck, who walks into the room hairstyle first; a sharp mohawk that looks blow dried to its last inch. Werewere is out of town. The problem with arriving unannounced instead of, say, sending a message beforehand on Facebook, is that my room is dirty and there is no one to clean it. Ben's really sorry that I will have to sweep it myself, if I don't mind.

My room is a one-bedroom flat in the living quarter next to the office. The bedroom is narrow, fitting in a three-quarter sponge and three yellowish shelves. The wide lobby that leads to the main door has a round table and matching chairs. Next to this is an empty lounge. My favourite thing about the room is the bathroom, which has a shower I can stand under to wash, and a toilet I can sit on and flush. I have not had a private bathroom in four-and-a-half months.

One of the best things about living on the road is never having to perform domestic chores – that's just not something I've ever taken to. I'm the type of person who honestly believes that making a bed every morning, only to mess it up later, is obsessive-compulsive. Tonight, I unfold my bedding, airing my two sheets before wrapping the first one, fitted, over my bed, tucking every corner tightly so it doesn't move when I'm sleeping.

I sweep the thick layer of dust off the concrete floor and mop it. I'm so happy about having my own space, I wash the shelves until the water I use to rinse my cloth is black. I also unpack my backpack, folding my eight-piece wardrobe onto one shelf.

There will be no stepping over a trail of clothes and books on the floor and definitely no dirt, not even an invisible layer of dust, at *my* place.

In the morning, my room vibrates with beats from drums playing somewhere, making me fall – no, roll – out of bed. It's time to start my first day in Abidjan. Village Ki-Yi under a clear, sunny sky is a half-moon amphitheatre that faces a museum adorned with masks and statues that have exaggerated features. Ki-Yi, the Cameroonian Bassa language word for ultimate knowledge, is founded with the singular aim of turning life into art, so that every aspect of life at the village feels like an ode to creativity. The outside walls of the main building have coral blue stripes and zig zags. There are white circles and dots and the floor on the veranda has black and white triangles. From its beginning in 1985, Village Ki-Yi has been home to artists from around Ivory Coast and West Africa; some come here as kids. To live here as an artist, I discover, is like taking your spirit to its Pan-African home where East, Central and Southern Africa meet in West Africa. As it does for most hours of the day, life this morning is focused on performance and rehearsal, giving the impression that the only living thing around is the black and brown puppy that thankfully stays away from me.

Other than her plays, Werewere also writes books, including her English novel *Amputated Memory,* which has been called a modern-day *Things Fall Apart.* Abidjan can wait, I have a novel to read and Ki-Yi also has a marquee, as outdoor bars are called around here. One of my favourite things about life around the continent is its simplicity. The marquee is at the property's entrance. It has a fence on the side that faces Carrefour Riviéra Cité Universitaire, the roundabout that has a permanent cloud of smog over it from the perpetual traffic jam. The marquee has plastic chairs and wooden tables, and a shack at the entrance that doubles as a bar and kitchen. A new kitchen is under construction. For now, food is served by two women who come here around lunchtime to sell rice and sauce.

I sit at a table at the back and settle into the large wooden chair that gives me a view of the marquee. I order a Fanta Orange to go with my intention of spending the morning discovering what makes Werewere an award-winning author. *Amputated Memory* never makes it out of my bag. Instead of my Fanta, the waitress brings a one-litre bottle of Bock beer. The two uniformed gentlemen at one of the tables say bon jour. They would also like the pleasure of my company. I move to their table and discover that other than being traffic officers, they're avid beer drinkers who believe that the right time to have a drink is when you feel like it, and right now, they feel like Abidjan's favourite beer, nicknamed Drogba. The superstar is the face of the brand and, just like him, it has a strong kick. We spend four hours drinking and trying to get me to memorise what they say is the only French phrase that matters in Abidjan: Je veux boire bière. I want to drink beer.

When it's time to leave they call for the bill, but instead of paying, one of them goes to the street to set up a road block. He returns after ten minutes with money he collects as bribes, and uses it to settle our bill for eight bottles of Drogba. The beer kicks me back to my room where I pass out for a few hours. I never make it out of Ki-Yi. I'll do better tomorrow. Then again, with US$5 to my name, staying at home seems like the perfect plan. My money comes in three days after my arrival. As promised, I call Mohammed to let him know that I can afford to pay him, and arrange to meet at the bus station. He agrees to meet, but refuses his payment. He doesn't know if I'm brave or a clown for travelling on faith and prayer, he says. Whatever the case, he's glad he could help me.

In the coming days, I begin to sense a creeping loneliness starting to eat away at me, even with my daily outings to different parts of the city. Then it hits me. I may be surrounded by people, and meeting more every time I leave the house, but I don't have girl friends; no one to hit the club scene with or giggle about flings and schemes with. I buy a teddy bear that I cling to all night after a day of literally eating my loneliness away. The feeding frenzy starts in the morning, at the roundabout with the woman who sells bread, chips and fried meat. I wash it down with homemade passion fruit juice that's more sugar than fruit or water. And so it goes, with fried plantain and fried chicken sometimes before lunch, and sometimes rice and meat with sauce from the vendors at the taxi station across the road from Village Ki-Yi.

There are stalls of deep-fried plantain called alloko, and I'm a midnight guest at the Lebanese café that only serves shawarma and chips. I interchange this with grilled meat I buy from a man who sells from a braai stand made from a zinc water drum cut in half. Salim buys a whole sheep every morning, selling it piece by piece in portions for 500 francs and upwards. Abidjan's buzzwords seem to be food, fashion and fun. I don't know about fashion, but I certainly take to the food and the fun once I get a taste of Abidjan by night.

It starts on the afternoon I walk into a restaurant that has the flag of Ghana hanging at the entrance. It's a medium-sized room with six tables that seat six people each. They don't sell Ghanaian food. The menu of fried chicken and fish and chips also includes onion-based chicken yassa and thieboudienne – the spicy national dish of Senegal. The yassa is bland, and the thieboudienne isn't spicy, but what the food lacks in flavour, the owner, Kristle, makes up for with her personality. We hit it off from our first meeting. She sits behind a white, arm's-width counter next to the door, from where she watches me take a seat at a table outside. There's a bottle of Guinness and a glass covered with a coaster in front of her. Tina Turner is on the CD player. I love Ghana and Kristle loves South

Africa. She has been in living Abidjan for three months to learn French and to try her hand at being a restaurateur in a city that has one of the largest appetites in the region.

We bond over our insatiable need to live for the night. Every evening starts with our usual lie, that our walk through the streets covered in coal dust to the shack that sells ginger moonshine is the beginning and end of it, only to stumble out of Vieradrome just before the city starts its day; partying like Abidjan is not on curfew. Kristle loves Vieradrome for the pool tables and the rounds of games she wins against whoever dares to play against her. I'm here for the red walls, and mirrors that run from the ceiling to the floor so ladies in three-inch minis and towering heels can look at their behinds shaking to zouglou hits. The dance floor heaves with grinding bodies whenever 'Bobraba' plays; it's slang for ass. Winding the booty is the only move in its dance routine. When Kristle is ready to dance, it's only to one song; always on special request. She locks my arm in hers to the deejay booth. 'Mon ami,' she says to him, 'We have a guest from South Africa.' She pulls me closer, so I chime in with the usual line. 'I really miss home. Please play "Vulindlela".' People pull me off the dance floor to ask me to translate the song.

Then along comes Kevin; just the right ingredient to add to my *Sex & the City* lifestyle. We spend a lot of time together on what he sees as dates. I consider them a prelude to the shag I'm after. It comes a few days later at his studio apartment, also in Riviera Deux. We're on a cream leather couch when Lucky Dube says 'It's Not Easy', his hands are on me at 'Different Colours, One People'. My mouth is on his at 'Back to My Roots'. My top joins his shirt on the floor at 'Feel Irie'. We move to the bed with 'Prisoner' in the background. The condom goes on his dick with 'Remember Me' and we get going. I don't know why I use sex as entertainment when I can't have it without hearing my mother's voice. 'Always use a condom, and don't fall pregnant if that's not what you're planning on.' I was fifteen. But that's my mom for you – the most practical person I know. That conversation always plays in my head when I have sex; use a condom.

And I do, always. I go for regular HIV tests, I protect myself, and I make no exceptions to this rule. Mom's words are in my head minutes into the action. I look to see if the condom is on properly. Kevin smiles like a kid caught being naughty. The condom is on the floor. I push him off me. I could lose my shit on Kevin and let him discover that, like Angelina Jolie, I have the temper of a cobra. And I am angry as hell, but it's with myself. I'm part of a generation of young Africans who have had millions of dollars poured into drilling safe sex practices into our heads. It's not enough to know my status or use a condom. Maybe there comes a time, and now could be that moment, when I think seriously about what it means to be sexually active in Sub-Saharan Africa, where HIV infections are still high. I need to change my attitude. If my next HIV test comes back positive, I only have myself to blame.

Lucky Dube is on 'Ding Ding Licky Licky Bong' when I walk out. 'I took a wrong turn in life,' Lucky sings when I close the door – what the fuck just happened? I've always been curious to know what the most definitive moment of my life would be. Would my aha moment be an act of love or desperation? Would I be high on life, or on my knees in desperation? None of the above. This moment has tyres screeching and cars hooting and exhaust fumes that sting my eyes. There's a young girl running errands, with a brazier in her hand, looking fancy in a green and navy pagne skirt and a matching top. Life is moving on perfectly fine. The street vendors who take over the roundabout at Boulevard Mitterrand set up shop. The guy who sells porn DVDs has already packed his table with covers of soft and hardcore porn. The tomatoes at vegetable stalls are still in a pyramid, and the street still smells like used oil, fried chicken and grilled fish. I bury the incident at the back of my mind and go to Kristle's for our evening ritual.

November 2008

The Fondation Félix Houphouët-Boigny building in Yamoussoukro is as grand as the man it's named after. The first president of Ivory Coast had a taste for over-the-top buildings, turning his run-of-the-mill home town that's more dust than tar into the home of the Basilica of Our Lady of Peace. It's the world's biggest church, bigger than St Peter's Basilica in Rome; with a US$300 000 000 bill. The Fondation Félix Houphouët-Boigny building is lowkey in comparison. Still, with its marbled interior, it is elegant and showy; making it the go-to venue for grand events in Yamoussoukro.

Tonight, Salif Keita will be on stage with Aïcha Koné: One of Africa's biggest stars on stage with the Ivorian singer who inspires the same frenzy in her audience as Beyoncé does to her Hive. I'm with Setou, a Burkinabe dancer who trains and performs with the Village Ki-Yi Mbock. We're the only people who aren't dressed up. Setou's in jeans and a tank top. I'm in a long skirt and a hoodie. Our drabness stands out when the venue fills up. Middle-aged couples are in his and hers grand boubous. A couple in brown and gold boubous walks past us. He's dressed in fitted pants with thick gold embroidery on the hem, and a tunic with matching embroidery around the neckline. She's in a wrap skirt and a top with bell sleeves, covered with gold patterns that look like the letter 'Z' written in cursive. A group of three women make an entrance head-gear first, their sky-high doeks dwarfing all others. Ivorians are vain, and never leave the house without dressing to impress. For special occasions, Ivorians dress like they'll be walking a red carpet with the eyes of the world on them. The dress code befits the artists' stature.

The show is running on African time and starts two hours later than the 7pm advertised. It's definitely worth the wait. Proceedings kick off – literally – with the three zougoulou opening acts. Zougoulou music still sounds like noise to me, but I lap it up anyway and join the audience to rumba and tango and gyrate our hips like they are made of liquid. The mood is electric.

Africa knows how to party, West Africa sets the roof on fire, and Ivory Coast is the after-party. By the time Aïcha Koné gets on stage, after her son Tchaga's performance, we're in a frenzy.

Aïcha's beautiful, with a soft, round face and eyes that command attention even from across an auditorium. Covered in a white shawl, she sings like an angel and performs with drama and emotion. We swarm the area in front of and around the stage. We swing left and right in step with each other; the aim is to move, not sweat. We are Aïcha's toys, breaking into fast-paced dances when she tells us, holding on to a partner or anyone close when she says so.

Salif Keita's band walks to the stage first, each person behind their microphone and instrument. Conversations stop mid-sentence when Salif walks in and takes his place at the front, in the centre of the stage. Dressed in a white bazin tunic and pants, he kneels before us and puts his hands together. 'Bon soir,' he says softly. Good evening. 'Aniche?' he continues in Bambara, before switching back to French to thank us for being here tonight. He stands up and clasps his hands to his heart, and bows his head towards us, before sitting on a chair to start the show off with an acoustic solo set. Our silence is reverential. He puts his guitar down after three songs and walks towards his band before turning back to face us. He shoots his hand in the air, and the party finally starts. The aisles turn into a dance floor again.

I saw him on stage in South Africa in 2004, where he floated to the stage on angel wings to receive his Kora All-Africa Music Lifetime Achievement Awards. His performance is short, but even among many other stars from around the continent, Salif Keita shines brighter than all of them; every performance of his an affirmation that he is a gift from the gods. What makes tonight special, I realise, is that Salif is at home, and there's a difference between being with your people and strangers, no matter how welcoming they may be. Your people know you beyond face value.

The crowd walks towards the stage in a single file to leave notes of francs, some of them in wads, at his feet. He leans towards those who want to pin their money on him so they can do so. When more people stand on the steps leading to the stage, he signals the bouncers to let them through. He gives over his body to them. They kiss his hands and fall to his feet. This is why I know he means it whenever he stops singing to tell us, 'Je t'aime, I love you', his voice softening; the soaring voice that's taken him around the world several times over turning into an intimate whisper.

Salif turns the last part of his show into a heart to heart sermon on love. He asks us to take a seat. He scrutinises the crowd until he finds who he is looking for, starting with the small girl he calls to the stage. In this moment, the only person who matters is the little girl. 'Good evening my darling, what is your name?' he asks. He gives her time to answer him between each question, so she knows that this is a conversation of equals. He turns his whole body to face her and speaks to her away from the microphone. They cling on to each other afterwards. Salif does this with every person in the audience who has albinism. Satisfied that he hasn't missed anyone, he turns his attention back to the crowd and tells us, 'We are one. We are all human. We must love and respect one another.' People with albinism are still killed around Africa in the cruel belief that their bodies make powerful magic potions.

The show ends and Salif goes back to his dressing room. He spends an hour entertaining the growing crowd that's followed him there. I follow them and wait for my turn to meet him. Once again, people fall at his feet instead of shaking his hands, which they kiss. He clasps their hands into his when they get up, offering long embraces and kisses on their cheeks. He spends about five minutes with each person. When my turn comes I imitate everyone by falling to his feet and kissing his hands, hoping for an on-the-spot interview.

'There's no time,' he says softly.

'Tell me one thing: Why would you defy your lineage?'

West Africans are deeply traditional and still hold on to the ways of their ancestors. As a Keita and descendent of the founder of the Mali empire, king Sundiata Keita, Salif shouldn't be a singer. That's the role of the griots, like Habib Koité, who still inherit music from their forefathers.

'I would have gone crazy if I didn't become a musician,' he says, and excuses himself to talk to a woman who has just walked in with her child. Salif's attention never returns to me.

I find Setou hanging out with his band outside their bus. 'We're waiting for you, hop in,' she says. What starts out as a lift back to our hotel ends two days later. The show is moving to Bouaké, and we are invited to tag along. Bouaké is one hundred kilometres from Yamoussoukro. It's Ivory Coast's largest city after Abidjan. Salif travels here in a private car, and even though I never get my moment to interview him, Bouaké helps me to know him better. We arrive on Sunday afternoon with hours to spare before showtime. Salif has already settled in at the lounge when I arrive at the hotel the band is staying at. Groups of fans wait their turn to speak to him; some have albinism, others, like Coulibay, Cissé and Idrissa, are legless and armless from polio. The legless crawl with flip flops on their arm stumps, their bodies swinging them to their hero.

'I love him because he makes me feel important,' Idrissa tells me after meeting his hero. 'I can feel his love.'

Tonight's show is held in a field. It's free, and it looks like the whole town is here. Some watch the event from rooftops and walls. The band tunes instruments, and the vocalists sing until the quality sounds like an album after a final mix – perfect. The only seating available is several hundred metres from the stage, where plastic chairs are lined up behind couches reserved for VIPs, who are dressed in their finest bazin ensembles. Aïcha's set is followed by a duet of 'Mbife', with Salif. He doesn't kneel this time. Instead, his hand on his heart, he greets and thanks the people of Bouaké for coming. 'Are you ready?' he asks before raising his fist in the air. He's a party animal tonight, bouncing and strutting around the stage. He's on fire and we're feeling the heat. The VIPs get on their feet and slow-step to the front of the stage. The power goes off. Salif keeps singing and his band performing, their sound as perfect as ever. The power cut lasts for several songs. When the lights come back on, people throw money at his feet and over his head. We leave with the band on Monday morning for Abidjan.

Back in Abidjan, the Kevin episode refuses to remain buried in the dark corner of my mind, and I still have to chase after payments. My emotions refuse to be anything but dark, making me wish I could get back on Prozac after flushing them instead of fully engaging with the clinical depression I was diagnosed with at sixteen. I hit rock bottom once again and think about running back to Jozi – a decision that makes me spend the evening crying in the dark in my room. I roll off my mattress to start packing, picking clothes up from the floor, putting leftover food in the bin, and cleaning the bathroom.

As I do every day, I sit down to listen to Habib Koité's album, *Afriki*. The Malian is my favourite artist. His music feeds my soul. When 'Nteri' plays, it feels like my soul is making a transcendent prayer. I close my eyes when 'Fimani' plays so I can feel maestro Kélétigui Diabaté on the balafon; it feels like sitting at God's feet. 'N'tesse' has me up and swinging back and forth. My movements become robotic and comical for 'Massake', which makes me playful. I picture myself in a bellowing boubou, dancing with a group of women in equally big dresses, when 'Namania' plays. I'm in the desert when 'N'ba' plays – it makes me want to go to places that are far away. I listen to *Afriki* until I find my answer. I need to start over.

My sister, Lesego, has been calling me an ocean of emotion all my life. I have to feel deeply or experiences don't carry any value. I don't want my stay in West Africa to only end at me being here and ticking off a list of tourist attractions. I want to start over because I want this to be the story of my life and not just an adventure I go on. I want West Africa to recreate me so that when I return home, I will tell the story of my life in two chapters: Before and after West Africa.

Habib Koité is headlining the Festival of the Desert in two weeks; I'm going back to Mali. When I apply for a two-month visa at the Malian embassy, the woman handling my application offers to add four months, on the house. The catch is I have to spend the first half of 2009 in Mali. 'You never know what will happen,' Madame Diarra says. It's the best gift I have ever received.

VI

TIMBUKTU

4 January 2009

I'M SCURRYING AROUND the bus station in Sogoniko, Bamako, looking for a bus to Timbuktu. Darting between battered taxis and overenthusiastic touts peddling tickets to Accra, Lagos, Nouakchott and Niamey, I meet a tout who tells me the truth: There are no buses to Timbuktu. I tell myself not to panic. Sure, not even people around me have a faint idea of where I'm going, but how hard can it be? As it turns out, getting to Timbuktu is not a world-famous joke for nothing. I finally find what I'm looking for with a bus company that I'm told is not among the most reliable at the station, but it's the only one leaving Bamako for Northern Mali this afternoon.

It's always a slow trip in Mali. This Sunday is no different. The bus fills up after two hours. The waiting lounge is a rusty, three-sided shack with wooden benches and a TV showing R. Kelly, Celine Dion and Luther Vandross videos. Young boys walk in and out selling airtime, soda, juice, dolls, toy cars, batteries and handheld radios. When I refuse to buy fake Chanel and Gucci sunglasses or a palm-sized green Quran, one boy shakes his head. I'm buying something whether I like it or not. I give him 700 francs for white plastic prayer beads. The bus arrives at 3pm. Four men pile the roof with luggage, carefully stacking suitcases with sacks of potatoes, onions, rice, chairs, tables and chickens bound at the feet, before tying ropes around everything so it doesn't fall off.

The bus driver looks at his clipboard.

'Diarra, Diop, Keita, Kouyate,' he says, calling out surnames one at a time, ticking them off as he goes. 'Coulibaly, Diallo, Cissé, Mog, Moku – no, no, no,' he stumbles, scratching his head with the pen.

'Mo-go-a-tlhe,' I say, laughing at his confusion and effort.

He laughs with me and goes back to calling out surnames that roll off his tongue – Ba, Keita, Samake. I tiptoe over suitcases, worn white sacks filled with more rice and produce, and luggage packed into plastic bags with pictures of the Eiffel Tower, Big Ben and the Statue of Liberty – Paris, London and New York written across them – to get to my seat. Mali is hot and dusty, and public transport is always overloaded with people and goods. Even so, children get dressed up for trips. A boy in a shiny silver suit clambers over the seats with two girls in chiffon and lace dresses.

We leave on time, at 4pm, only stopping to pick up and drop off people. We stop twice for prayers, when the bus gets off the road to park next to four others and two cars. Some passengers wash their faces, arms and feet, and roll out their mats to face Mecca for Maghrib and Isha, the sunset and night prayers. Those who are not praying stock up on water, oranges, cookies, pieces of grilled goat, bananas, papaya, pineapple and groundnuts. Back in the bus, the driver plays Wassoulou music, named after the region of its origin in Southern Mali, along the borders of Guinea Conakry and Ivory Coast. Someone cranks up the volume for a Bambara talk show, another radio plays griot melodies and the guy on my seat plays Akon on his cellphone.

Travelling around Mali is connecting with the meaning of isolated destinations. The country is a series of vast, empty spaces, punctuated by small towns and even smaller villages, dimly lit by small kerosene lamps shining on small tables with fire wood, smoked fish, sweet potatoes and cassava for sale. It's dawn when I'm told to transfer into a bush taxi. We're in Mopti, the transport hub that connects other regions in the country to Gao and other parts of Northern Mali. This is where you catch boats to Timbuktu and Djenné. I move to a previously white, fifteen-seater bush taxi that looks like it hasn't been roadworthy in decades. The door bears multiple scars from being welded too many times. Seats made for three hold five bodies. We keep wiggling around to make room for more passengers and their luggage.

The engine doesn't so much start as it coughs like a TB patient to take us to Douentza. We travel on a potholed road, through long stretches of fields with sunburnt shrubs. Occasionally, the feeling of being in the middle of nowhere is interrupted by a herd of camels, cattle at a watering hole or a shepherd sleeping under a shrub, secure in the knowledge that his flock is too beat down by the sun to stray. A phone rings. A wrinkled Tuareg man dips a hand into the pocket of his light blue boubou, and out comes a maroon Samsung still shiny with newness.

Everything in Douentza is dusty: There's dust on the children who sell water in two hundred and fifty millilitre plastic packets, on two boys who walk over to me asking for pens, on the oranges and bananas sold at the roadside, and on the tables and chairs at the restaurant where I leave my bags to keep looking for a car to Timbuktu. Clouds of dust rise whenever a car or bus goes by, settling on our bodies, bags and food, and on the flock of sheep on top of a bus. I walk to a group of Europeans hanging out in three SUVs parked under a tree. The SUVs are taxis to Timbuktu. A driver says my seat will be US$70 but I think he's charging me like I'm a European. I accept that West Africans will always inflate their price tags for travellers but I refuse to pay like I earn in dollars and euros; I am, after all, 'at home'. I go back to the restaurant, where my bags are being watched over by Amadou and Modibo, whom I meet in the bush taxi. They're going to sell CDs and paintings at the festival. I ask them to buy my ticket for me, which they pay 15 000 francs for.

'We'll leave soon, Inshallah,' our driver says, even though our car is full. Inshallah is Arabic for God willing. It's also the biggest cop-out in Islamic countries, in my opinion. Instead of committing to anything people say it will happen if God wills. I've been on the road for two days since leaving Abidjan: We are not leaving when Allah wills. I nag the driver until he says we'll leave in thirty minutes.

Amadou sits with the driver, Modibo is at the back with another tour guide and everyone's luggage. An old couple in safari khakis is on the seat behind the driver. I'm behind them with a Swedish woman who is 'sorry' to announce that Africans are liars. She didn't pay US$100 to share the ride with people who aren't the old couple. 'Is it because the people are poor? That's not an excuse to lie,' she hisses in a tirade that lasts more than an hour. There are one hundred and seventy kilometres between Douentza and Timbuktu. I bite my tongue and will her to shut up. This trip will end if my tempter explodes.

The closer we get to Timbuktu, the more barren the landscape becomes. We're in a convoy of seven SUVs. We stop for drinks in Bambara Maoudé, a village with one street. People climb out of the cars wearing wide smiles; Nikon and Canon cameras pointing at mud houses with no doors. There's a nameless restaurant with a plat du jour of mushy rice and a thumb-sized piece of meat served with the water it was boiled in and a fine layer of dust. Across the road is a kiosk that sells warm sodas and cold Nescafé.

In the car, I keep asking the driver when we'll get to Timbuktu. 'Soon,' he says.

'When exactly is soon, my friend?' I demand.

'In about two hours, if the car doesn't breakdown,' chimes in a tour guide.

'Why would it breakdown?' the Swede asks.

'You just never know,' Amadou pipes in, making her renew her tirade. We fall silent again. The car finally stops on the banks of the Bani River. Even here, the West African entrepreneurial spirit reigns. A woman sits next to a brazier frying cassava chips and fish. Small kids dressed in dirty, torn T-shirts sell water and sodas. They run up to us offering to pose for a gift of money or pens. Across from us, two boys push a cow into a pirogue. We buy peanuts in paper cones and take pictures until our cars can get onto a ferry.

The sun sets on the flat horizon, turning the river and the villages on its bank gold. A young boy pushes a pirogue with a stick that's longer than the boat. A woman sits in the middle with her baby on her back. It's a beautiful moment worth the self-torture of going to Timbuktu by land. We get back into the SUVs and convoy on to Timbuktu, where the river fades into the sand of the Sahara Desert. The darkness blacks out my arrival, which starts with following Amadou, Modibo and Abu, a tour guide we meet next to the market, where the SUV drops us, to a hostel. Abu's friend owns it; he'll negotiate a cheaper rate for me. Time goes by with no sign of the tenant who has the only key to the dormitory. Plan B becomes sleeping at Abdoulaye's house. He's Modibo's friend. Abdoulaye's blue-black complexion is lit up by his cellphone, Akon's 'Mama Africa' squeaking from it. Abdul and I go home on his red and blue chrome moped while Amadou and Modibo walk there. The moped barely holds its own against the desert streets. I lock my hands around Abdul's body; afraid of being the fat girl who falls off a moped.

For tour guides like Abdul, Timbuktu's lack of budget accommodation is another way to earn cash; letting out rooms, beds and camping space. His other tenants are an American student studying in Accra called David, who is also attending the festival, and a French couple. Abdul's place has one bedroom and a lounge that turns into our dormitory at bedtime, when the three settees turn into beds. The couple sleeps on the floor. David, Amadou and I are on the settees, Modibo's in the bedroom with Abdul and his friend Abdi.

The room goes back to being a lounge in the morning. The settees are joined by a TV stand with two shelves with laminated brown finishing. The top shelf holds a small black TV that shows grainy pictures. There's a French-English dictionary on the bottom shelf, a dog-eared copy of Paolo Coelho's *The Alchemist,* and the *Autobiography of Malcolm X.* Abdul also keeps a copy of the Holy Bible, even though he's Muslim. Abdul should be making money to buy more bricks to extend the house but he refuses to charge me and lets David pay what he can afford. He acts like a butler, serving a breakfast of coffee with sugar and powdered milk and a flat round bread called takoula that's baked in dome-shaped mud ovens built in the front of some yards. The takoula crunches with sand.

David offers to show me around town. We start at Sankore quarter, walking slowly through the sand, past donkeys and old men in flowing robes. All houses are built with mud bricks. Children loiter around, like the little boy in maroon sweatpants covered in dust, a trail of dry snot tracking down this ashen face. Occasionally, a young boy or girl walks up to us to say hello. Everything is the same colour as the desert it rises from. Flat roofs are dangerously close to dangling electric lines that look like they can spark at any time. Donkeys trudge through sand with high loads on their backs, and mopeds and cars hoot when approaching intersections, alleyways and street corners. The streets are a jumble of weird angles. Compounds are littered with jerry cans, firewood and pairs of women minding children or cooking, or groups of students reading the Quran. Houses still have traditional gates of heavy wood, with metal decorations and handles.

Timbuktu still looks as old as it is, even with the SUVs and electronic shops that sell flat-screen TVs and DVD players. Markets around the region are a loud mixture of music, people haggling over prices, and women walking around with piles of cloth balanced on their heads. At Badjinde market, the loose-fitting pink, yellow, lime, blue, orange and other bright cotton wraps worn by the women are as loud as it gets. I ditch David when he runs into friends from Accra, and head to Bibliotheque Al-Imam Essayouti, where some of the ancient manuscripts are kept. The Bibliotheque is across the street from Djinguereber mosque; built in 1327 at the behest of Emperor Musa Mansa on his way back from Mecca. The mosque is closed for renovations, and the grey loudspeakers that call the town's men to prayer on Fridays are silent. Green treetops peek out from behind the mosque. The horizon has shrubs that look as light brown as the desert. It's also the colour of the sky. 'I'm in Timbuktu,' I say out loud, pinching myself.

I should be looking for a media pass to get out of paying for my festival ticket. Instead, I walk around town over and over again hoping to meet Habib Koité. My walks, like my presence, are infused with wonder and magic, even when I follow a man walking behind his donkey to see how many times he will make a growling sound from his throat before a glob of spit juts out of his mouth. I accept every invitation for tea and grilled meat, and become Abdul's shadow at night. Abdul takes me out for dinner at a rooftop restaurant at Badjinde market. The night is jet black, making the stars look like they're shining brighter than they do in other places. We dine on riz avec sauce tomate – rice with tomato sauce.

Our full house at Abdul's breaks up on Thursday morning to go to the festival. Abdul's going on a friend's bakkie. The trip is a bargain at 3000 francs, but I'm not in the mood to slum it. I go to Hotel Colombe to use their flushing toilets and to look for solo travellers to share a car rental with. I order coffee and strike up a conversation with a woman sitting by herself. She's an Israeli learning music in Bamako, music festivals are her holy grail. Her guide negotiates an African rate of 7000 francs with the driver of their SUV. Our trip stops at the market where I buy a second-hand wind breaker and a blanket and stop by the ATM for extra cash.

Essakane is a small village about two hours out of Timbuktu. It has a smattering of houses in different stages of crumbling, with missing door frames and walls that look like they were abandoned midway through the process of building them. An eerie silence keeps the village in a comatose state. The trip is uneventful other than for the cars getting stuck in the sand. At the festival site, I stand on dunes to catch my breath; taking in hills of soft white sand that burn from the scorching sun. I make my way to the media camp, where the publicist's only regret when I ask for a media pass is that they don't have a mattress for me, only a thin sleeping mat. I share the tent with two journalists from America and Argentina. The site has sections for sleeping – divided into camps for the press, artists, a conference area and accommodation for everyone else – bars and restaurants, bathrooms with showers and toilets, the market and the main stage area.

Before becoming a world event that brings more than thirty thousand people to town, the Festival of the Desert was the traditional meeting of the Tuareg tribes of the Sahara. Even with roots and families in villages like Essakane and towns like Timbuktu and Gao, Tuaregs are nomadic at heart and still follow a way of life inherited from ancestors who roamed the desert with their camels and livestock. Get-togethers like this one are the fabric of their social life.

The festival remains true to its heritage. Men and boys are dressed in bazin boubous, their faces wrapped as always in indigo cotton turbans called tagelmust. Women drape themselves with flowing robes; their heads gleaming with gold accessories. Walking past the stage, I see Harouna Samake tuning his kamale ngoni; Salif Keita's making a surprise appearance. I huff my way to the entertainment area to look for a good time. A short, very black man in a khaki suit and straw hat jumps at me, planting a kiss on each cheek.

'Mon cherie, join us, please,' he says, his right hand clasping my left.

His name is Djibril. He and his friends Cherrif, Omar and

Adama have boxes of Marlboros and bottles of whiskey on their table; of course I'll join them. We barely understand each other – I don't understand French, still, and Djibril's English is worse than my French. I pretend to follow their conversation; laughing when they do and contributing by talking about how amazing the festival is. Our table falls silent, their eyes and bodies turning to face the same direction. My jaw drops when I see who they're looking at. He strolls between plastic tables, smiling at everyone who greets him. Habib Koité hugs everyone and sits opposite me. I walk over to him and fall at his feet the way people here do when they meet at icon.

'That's not necessary,' he says, laughing.

'Habibo, this is our great friend from South Africa, Lerato,' Cherrif says.

'Lerato, this is our friend Habib.'

Habib envelopes me with a long embrace and follows me back to my chair. He never leaves my side. He translates the conversation for me or starts one between us, encouraging me to use the growing French vocabulary that still struggles to roll off my tongue. He holds my hands and shares secret jokes with me. More people join our table, some for a few minutes to greet Habib. I'm with my favourite artist and he is hanging onto every word of my seriously broken French; he thinks it's amazing that I'm travelling Africa.

'I hope you're hungry,' he says after a while, pointing at an old man bending over a sheep. One sweeping slash and the sheep stops bleating. It bleeds out into a hole the old man digs for this purpose. He hangs the carcass on a tree to skin and gut it before putting it on a spit fire. When it's ready, he slices it, and we eat with takoula. Habib and I leave the gang to watch Salif Keita. He holds my hands to help me move up and down the dunes and offers me water whenever I stop to catch my breath. The area around the stage is already full. There are rows of people sitting on the ground at the front circled by the standing crowd. Habib is tall enough to see from the back; I'm happy as long as I'm with him. He uses his star power to cut through the crowd to take me to the front. My life is a fantasy – I'm with Habib Koité at a Salif Keita performance, and the band wink and smile when they spot me in the crowd. We go back to the gang after the performance, where the party moves inside. Whiskey and beer make way for tequila shots, and the music goes from barely audible to full blast. The deejay makes my night when he plays 'Bobraba'. It always inspires the most skanky-ass dance moves; I lay them on Habib, laughing, downing shots, dancing, becoming friends.

The festival by day is an open-air market with food, jewellery and fringe performances. A woman sits on the ground beating a drum, occasionally dipping her hand into a calabash with water, which she splashes on the drum's hide. Other instruments in the performance are the clapping hands of three women in black chiffon wraps and cornrows styled with gold disks. A Tuareg boy in matching tan tunic and loose pants stands centre stage, his short arms spread away from his body. He jerks his shoulders and neck in rhythm to his left leg, which he holds in the air at a forty-five-degree angle. He breaks his gaze with a grin at the end of his performance. Four coned, black leather hats lined with cowrie shells peek out from the top of a dune. I follow them, and discover that they belong to musicians who chant around the site and play a musical instrument made with calabashes. One hat has round mirrors, another is decked with blue, yellow, purple, pink and lime cowrie shells. There's a camel parade and a traditional sword fight dance, with men moving slowly and gracefully in their grand boubous; my first time in the Sahara Desert remains one of the most enchanting times of my life.

Timbuktu empties out on Monday afternoon with the last of the tourist-packed SUVs leaving. The town falls back into silence that's only broken by the five daily calls to prayer and, sometimes, Mory Kante's 'Sabou' playing softly from one of the houses next to Djinguereber mosque. I stay until the end of January based on a rumour that Nelson Mandela is coming.

'If it's true, it will be the biggest event in the history of Timbuktu,' Abdul says.

Life absorbs me into its fabric. I start my days around 5am to feel the breeze before the sun comes out to remind my body that I'm in the desert, where days are incredibly hot and nights extremely cold. Filling a blue ten-litre bucket with water from the tap marks the official start of my day with a shower, when I walk through the doorless opening in the wall that divides the yard into his and hers sections. Hers belongs to Abdul's sister Aisha and her two children. I always carry lots of water to the toilet because I still can't use the hole-in-the-ground toilet. My piss still trails down my thighs. My poop always misses the hole; when I get the runs, it splashes around the toilet, so every trip to the toilets is followed by cleaning it and showering again. Abdul still refuses to tell me how much I owe him for sleeping at his house, where I now occupy his bedroom.

'We are family,' he insists whenever I nag him about my bill.

Abdul doesn't want me to buy food, preferring that we make an equal contribution of between 2000 and 5000 francs depending on what he can afford. We eat a set diet of plain rice and watery brown stew with two cubes of meat or small chunks of liver. On days when he barely has money, and there's lots of them, we eat plain rice with spinach that's chopped so fine it looks like it's been ground. Our family of six includes his friends, Abu and Mustafa. Mustafa is an English teacher and Abu, who always swims in his clothes, is a hustler like Abdul. He comes during the day for lunch and is back at night to sleep.

Our street corner is marked with a tyre stuck in the sand. Our landmark is a nomad's camp with a knee-high bamboo house fenced with dry shrubs. The land beyond the camp has an unfinished building, a dumping ground covered by black plastic bags, and a soccer field with poles that don't have a crossbar. Life is centred around social connections, my people are still Cheriff, Alou and Djibril. I meet another Abu, who commands attention from his wheelchair most nights at Amanar bar, on the edge of the desert. My night time circle includes Florence, the Italian archaeologist on a field trip, and a German man who has been trekking from Mauritania to Timbuktu in his Land Cruiser since 2005.

Life is predictable, with the occasional dust storm and, as Abdul's house becomes my home, my body starts settling into my life as a wanderer. I now shower in the morning and in the evening instead of every time I use the toilet. As if there has been a call to action, the community turn into my French tutors. Abu doesn't let a moment pass without teaching me basic French words, pointing at objects and translating my actions. The man who always gives me a bite of the grilled meat he sells doesn't consider it a visit without tea. Water, tea, mint, sugar, eat, sheep, fire: Eau, thé, menthe, sucre, manger, mouton, feu. My greetings are becoming more conversational. When people ask me how I'm doing, I respond as they would, telling them ca va bien, demi or empe; if my cup of wellness is full, half or empty. Life feels old, even with ATMs that work all the time, a fast internet connection and a DVD rental shop with *Desperate Housewives*, *CSI* and *24* box sets.

A young boy follows me home one morning on my way back from buying tadjala and packets of Nescafé and powdered milk for breakfast.

'I'm Mohammed,' he says, wiping his hand on his clothes before shaking mine.

He sits cross-legged on the floor and switches on the TV. This starts a pattern of coming over at will; sometimes to talk, but often just to hang out. Mohammed is eight years old and lives three houses away with his mom and sisters. He's always on the street chasing a plastic ball with a group of his friends. He seems to be everywhere I go. I run into him at the Flame of Peace monument, where he explains that the three thousand guns stuck at its base are from the Tuareg rebellion. He shows up at one of the office containers at the site that's becoming the Ahmed Baba Institute of Islamic Studies and Research. If I'm there while the sun is out, chances are Mohammed is close by. He comes over one morning for breakfast – which now includes him – to invite me for afternoon tea at his house. His bemused mother lets me into the yard, while he storms in twenty minutes later. He got engrossed in playing soccer. He apologises for being scruffy and puts on his tagelmust to look decent.

'Please come in, you are welcome,' he says, leading me to a shed.

He makes a fire and gives me a camel leather pouch with two handles; telling me to press in and out so that air blows onto the fire. 'That's very good.'

We drink our tea in three stages – a strong first cup with lots of mint that's as bitter as death, a milder second cup that's as bitter-sweet as life, and finally the lightest, sweetest cup.

'It's as sweet as love,' he winks.

By this stage, his sister has called two of her friends over, and their baby brother has crawled off their mother's back to join us. Walking me to the gate with his friends, he asks me to bend down and lean into him. 'Bisou?' he says with a grin. I plant a kiss on his cheeks and lips. 'A demain matin, mon amour,' he says, confirming our morning appointment.

More than anything, I love Timbuktu because it's only here that I can spend mornings reading *Malcolm X* and afternoons at Bibliotheque Al-Imam Essayouti looking at the ancient manuscripts that are considered the most important after the Dead Sea Scrolls. The only ones on display are in a glass table in the middle of the room. One of the them is a thick, perfectly preserved Quran handwritten in Arabic script with gold ink. Some manuscripts only have intricate designs, others have writing with decorations around their frayed pages. Manuscripts that are not on display are in a wood cabinet with mesh doors.

It's not just the students who wrote. Political and religious leaders wrote laws and decrees and responses to counter decrees. Ethicists wrote about extending women's rights to free them from being reduced to belonging in the kitchen. Cases were made for and against tobacco. Even tea was turned into poetry. Friends and families wrote letters and recorded genealogy and family history; all articulately and beautifully written. There are manuscripts with titles like *The Key to the Wings of Desire on the Knowledge of Arithmatic*, about mathematics and calculating inheritance. *The Joyous Companion of Those Whom I Met of the Maghribi Men of Letters* is about the author's encounters with writers from North Africa. *The Rights of the Prophet* describes in detail the life of Prophet Mohammed and his genealogy going back twenty-one generations. It was sold for twenty-four grams of gold.

Families also passed them down from generation to generation. Their collections are held in private libraries at their homes. I visit a family library for an intimate encounter with history. The small room is typically Malian, and especially Timbuktian in its simplicity. The only furniture is a table covered in a maroon tablecloth. The decorations on the walls are paper print outs praising the virtues of knowledge. 'Writing is spiritual geometry,' one of them reads. The manuscripts are arranged into neat piles on the table. They look their age, with faded brown pages that have holes and burns around the fringes. There's a clay pot with twigs and sticks – these were used as pens, but they are not the original tools that wrote the family's scrolls – and a cured sheep skin with some writing. It is full of holes but I can still see some of the words on it. Sheep skin was used before paper became widely available. I hold a manuscript; brittle, it's the most fragile and precious thing I will ever touch. With so much of our history erased and rewritten to depict us as savages, the manuscripts of Timbuktu are an eternal reminder that Africa is the cradle of civilisation.

The Saturday of Nelson Mandela's arrival dawns, and Timbuktu becomes a ghost town. All the shops are closed. The road to the market and the soccer field are empty. Greetings end at 'good morning', and the slow gait that defines walking here is replaced with hurried steps to Sankore mosque. Crowds have already formed a circle around the field opposite. Camels and mules are dressed in bells and colourful leather pouches. Boubous shine with newness, and women are wearing so much gold jewellery the desert sparkles with it. Kids stand in the front row waving South African and Malian flags. Nelson Mandela is not in town. The recently ousted president of South Africa, Thabo Mbeki, is here to inaugurate his presidential pet project with his replacement and Jacob Zuma's placeholder, President Kgalema Motlanthe, and political VIPs who include Minister Manto Tshabalala-Msimang. Their host, President Amadou Toumani Touré, is proudly West African in a grand boubou. They walk around the building for some time before standing in front of the plaque that bears one of the most prolific scholars of his time, whose legacy transcends time. Born into a family of lawyers and judges and raised on a diet of reading and reciting the Quran by his father and uncle, Ahmed Baba had already established himself as an intellectual in his thirties, writing fifty-six books and a collection of sixteen thousand manuscripts for his private library.

The party moves to a field where the VIPs sit in a tent to watch Thandiswa Mazwai singing 'Nizalwa Ngobani' into a scratchy microphone. Her stage is a rug on the ground. When the show ends, and the town goes back to normal, Abdul drives me to the edge of town where I gatecrash the VIP lunch. The only person manning the entrance lets me in without a fuss. Lunch is chicken and lamb served with couscous and takoula. A cooked camel carcass is on a table in the middle of the camp. The presidents sit in their tent sipping mint tea, watching a group of musicians sitting in a semi-circle on a dune with their camels behind them. A melody rises and the only kid in the crowd stands up and starts dancing, his index finger wagging to the beat. It's the kid from the Festival of the Desert; my young friend Mohammed.

I leave Timbuktu a week later with Abdul to go to the town of Savare, where we meet friends who are also on their way to Ségou for the Festival sur le Niger. Held on the banks of the Niger River for five days at the end of January and the beginning of February, the festival attracts thousands of people from around the region and the world. Every hotel room in town is booked; family compounds and the flat rooftops of houses close to the river's banks turn into camping grounds. Street corners turn into jam sessions, drummers and musicians put on impromptu shows, and offer lessons that end with a sales pitch to buy djembe drums, kamale ngoni – a stringed harp made by stretching goat skin over a calabash – and a twenty-seven-key xylophone called balafon, which dates back to the thirteenth or fourteenth century. Craft shops around town turn into artsy spaces with exhibitions and more music lessons. Restaurants turn into pop-up nightclubs or host traditional dancers and dance shows. It doesn't matter whether I'm front row at the main stage or on a random walk around the town, it's impossible to disconnect from the festival. Walking around town one afternoon looking for food, I'm swept up by a crowd gathered around a masquerade with stilt dancers and spirits wearing masks that have sculptures on their crowns.

Another time, on my way to Hotel Joliba for a daytime party, I end up following a group of marionettes. Here they are not toy-shop-sized puppets with painted outfits, they are real-life, giant human caricatures, controlled not by pulling strings but by walking on stilts. When the dust of the marionettes settles, the air explodes with gun fire from a street parade put on by the Donsow. The Donsow is a brotherhood of hunters that has existed since the seventh century. They're re-enacting a hunting dance, walking in slow leaps and occasionally bouncing towards the crowd with guns pointed at the sky. Trailing the Donsow are griots humming in a trance-like state. This year's bill has artists from Senegal, Niger, Guinea, Mexico and Portugal. The line-up includes Coumba Gawlo, Mamar Kass, Les Amazones, desert queen Haira Harry, Oumar Koita, Bassékou Kouyaté and the town's icons, Super Biton de Ségou. The star of the show is Oumou Sangaré, who arrives like the superstar she is in a Hummer that's surrounded by a motorcade. She drives it slowly so her adoring fans and the hands they stretch out to touch her car can have their moment.

Later when she strides on stage, her actions say, 'Show me how much you adore me and I will give you the time of your life'. She smiles and giggles and pouts her lips playfully. Everyone dances and sings along. The most beautiful moment for me is when she starts greeting the audience by name. At first I think it's a new song with many names until I realise that she gets hysterical screams every time she demands love from Mohammed, Amina, Amadou, Oumou, Aminata, Ibrahim and other Muslim names that are as common as Lerato and Vusi in South Africa. Other than the music, happy hangovers and glimpses of ancient Bambara culture, the festival introduces me to Olga, Abbas and his lover Miriam. Abbas and Olga's friendship turns Bamako into home.

VII

NUMBER 227

February 2009

I'M WALKING DOWN A street in Bamako-Coura when Cissé waves me over to sit with him and his friend Prince outside his kiosk. The brazier is glowing with red coals and a bubbling pot of mint tea. By the time we get to the third cup, I know that Cissé's favourite politician is George W Bush and that Prince has a room to rent at his apartment. The building has four floors, each with a bathroom-cum-toilet that I have to hold my stomach in to use. It's five footsteps wide and smells like crap and disinfectant. Prince's corner unit on the second floor has a wrap-around balcony decorated with the flags of Mali and his homeland of Senegal. The only time Prince talks to me is when he offers me tea. The only time he shows some personality is when his country's tennis team visits for a game against Mali.

Bamako hasn't changed since my visit in 2008, but I'm different. I have a life now. It starts with Olga, and the happy hours on the bamboo couch under a mango tree at the back of her house listening to French love songs and Angélique Kidjo. Olga introduces me to Peter, an artist from Ouagadougou. Through him and our nights at Bla Bla Bar, I meet a Danish NGO worker whose circle includes a Senegalese dancer who introduces me to Jacque, originally from Paris. Jacque's four-bedroom house in Hippodromo has a pool, and housemates who include Ngozi from Lagos. I sleep over whenever I miss a double bed, fresh linen and fluffy pillows.

When Abbas calls to say Miriam is in hospital with malaria, I visit her because they're the kind of people who would do the same for me. It is during one of these visits that Abbas invites me over for lunch at their new place in Djicoroni Para, where my first impression of Bamako being a beat-down city comes back as his moped dodges big mud paddles and kids washing in bathtubs in the middle of the street. The open drains on the streets bubble with black goo and plastic bags. We stop at house number 227. It's a large four-bedroom flat with two kitchens, a lounge, two typically un-inviting bathrooms and a lounge. Abbas leads me in through a room that's divided into two using a wooden screen. In the foyer, we walk past a very bony guy lying face-up on a thin single mattress. Samba's right knee and hands are in bandages. His long, yellowish teeth protrude. He looks like breathing hurts him, let alone talking.

There's also Jilly, with a head of thick dreadlocks and a body he has to bend to walk through the door. Mbaye looks like a healthier version of Samba. The Sene brothers live with their female cousin Astou. I sit next to a bow-legged boy called Champion, whose sixteen-year-old skin is scarred by the zits he can't help but pop. We're joined at the balcony by a couple from Paris. Doreen is an art student in her last semester of study in Bamako. Her man Pierre blushes when Abbas says he's in Bamako to babysit his relationship lest a local take his place in Doreen's bed. Another tall man bends his body through the door. Charles is a guide from Senegal. By the time Astou empties the contents of her pot into two large metal dishes, there are ten of us; five at the table and five others on stools to eat their lunch on the floor. We dig into the food, eating together in every sense of the word. The five hands in our plate turn into three, then two. Mine keeps going until all that remains are specks of rice. I've had thieboudienne many times; Astou's turns me into the lunch guest that never leaves.

Jilly is another reason I move in. It's April, when temperatures soar to 40° Celsius. Sleeping in has become impossible and the rooftop of Prince's building is overcrowded. There's always room on Jilly's rooftop of one more person. The roof has two sections with a small wall between them. Each side is about twenty steps long, and six lunges wide as I discover in a few weeks. I find a spot for my sponge among those belonging to Jilly, Charles, Mbaye and Samba and their neighbour Omar, who sleeps here every night during the hot season. Abbas and Miriam sleep on the other side of the roof even though, like Astou, the French couple, Jilly and Mbaye, they have a bedroom to themselves. At any given moment, there are no less than ten people who call number 227 home.

You call it overcrowding, we call it 'social living'. Your first obligation is to your community, not just your family and friends. It's the reason Jilly has an open-door policy. I move in at the same time Astou's sister, Oumou, visits from Dakar.

Everyone has a connection of some sort. The French couple know Samba, Charles and Jilly know each other from Dakar, Abbas and Jilly met in Lomé, Togo's hard-partying capital. Mohammed from Guinea Conakry, another broken body looking for a place to mend, is friends with Abbas. The stream of visitors includes Doc, a male nurse with a broad, flat nose that overshadows his other facial features, even the broad smile and thick lips. He comes over every evening to hang out on the rooftop while Champion brews mint tea and Jilly lords over the remote control from his traditional stool. The TV is always on the Euro soccer league, *CSI New York* or *24*, his favourite show and the inspiration behind his mongrel's name Bauer, which everyone pronounces 'Bo-u-er'.

There's also light-skinned Mohammed, who only dresses in grand boubous; Harouna, who wears regular pants with wax tunics; Seray and Mustafa. Mohammed the herbalist loves showing off a picture taken at a field somewhere in Banjul, with a crowd watching him charm a puff adder. Adama from Benin sells shoes from door to door and is a regular lunch guest. Adama the drummer and dancer is introduced with the warning that he is a bit of a clown. He comes over to sleep on the roof. There's also King from Freetown. He has lived in Accra and Dakar, where he first crossed paths with Jilly. King is obsessed with God, custard and Brenda Fassie. He's in the habit of dropping weird one-liners like 'your best servant is your hand' when I ask him where he gets his laundry done. Moussa comes back from Kankan, where he's been working. He's dating Fana, who helps to clean the house in exchange for food for Ibrahima, her son. She's a skeleton when we meet. There are other guests who stay for a few days in between. They include Aisha and Fatima, who are in the business of buying bazin in Bamako and selling it in Dakar. They sleep in the lounge; a room Jilly only unlocks for special guests. Even then, we aren't allowed in. A family of three takes their place for several weeks.

With this many people under one roof, everyone imitates each other. Astou and Oumou do like Adama from Benin and throw cowries to tell fortunes. Abbas starts running when Moussa does. Seray and several others start praying in keeping with Moussa's devotion to prayer times. Doreen goes wild with bazin and pagne clothing; Miriam and I follow suit.

It's fun until Miriam takes up music. 'I can't live without music' is her catch phrase. It's followed by the clearing of her throat, the soft humming of a melody and then a full throttle song. Her favourite question is 'you want I play something?' followed by strumming. She clears her throat, then howls: 'All we need is love. And peace. Love. Love. Yeah.' She passes her weapon to her man and asks him to strum 'No Woman, No Cry'. This is her cue to freestyle, yelping 'don't cry mama Afrika. Farafina. Yes, Mr Bob Marley. Afrika. Mali. Fara-fina.' Miriam turns the roof of our communal home into something close to hell. One night, she takes out her djembe and starts to wail as loud as ever. We cringe. She bangs the drum harder. 'Music takes me to a deep place,' she says. That place is painful. I peek at the note pad she always has in case she gets inspiration for lyrics:

'Every time best way is the truth. Sometimes it's hard but always is the best because no real feelings. When we talk about love can broke many things. Feeling me good in spirit is the first thing. After feeling me good with my brothers. Time is going and I want to enjoying all the way. Free your mind and don't confuse yourself. Love is love.'

'I prefer my own lyrics,' she says.

Her depth makes enemies of us and of instruments alike: A drum, a flute, a guitar and the kamale ngoni. The ngoni sounds like heaven in the hands of a maestro. Miriam makes it sound like a crime against humanity. Even worse, Samba, Abbas, Mohammed from Conakry and Seray tune in. They are just as bad; it's the Sahel Horror Show.

One day, Abbas comes back from town with Dave, who is seething from a gold deal that's turned sour. The dealer wants money before handing over the goods. Dave and his photograph with Prince Charles wants the gold before handing over the cash. 'Haven't you heard of recession? The white man has no more money my friends,' he keeps saying, calling Africans liars and scammers. Astou asks me to follow her to the kitchen when I narrow my eyes at Dave and get ready to let my temper loose. This silly man strikes a deal on wishful thinking instead of sense, Abbas offers him the refuge of our home and family, and he is calling us scammers and liars before he eats the chicken yassa Astou and I cook? Astou has seen flashes of my temper from a confrontation I had with Abbas when he walks in demanding instead of asking for food; reducing me to a servant that a man will never have in me. King's eyes glint with mischief, Jilly's lips curl into a smile and Abbas raises his eyebrows at her; everyone knows what's going to happen to Dave if I don't leave the room.

As the temperature rises, my legs and ankles become twice their increasingly fat size. I get bouts of nausea sparked by most things that touch my lips, mint tea being the chief instigator. As a result, I spend a lot of time with my head inside our toilet bowl, which always has a piece of crap floating in it. The heat also traps me at home.

The soundtrack at our house is one hundred per cent African, be it Tiken Jah Fakoly and Alpha Blondy on reggae, Ochestra Baobab and Bembeya Jazz National for our jazz sessions or up-and-coming stars like Vieux Farka Toure, Fode Baro and Titi. From Fodé Baro's 'Commissariat' I learn how to say tell me something in French: Dis moi quelque chose. To put up with my new-found obsession with 'Cameroon' by Alpha Blondy, Mbaye turns it into a French lesson. This is how I discover that the French word for heart is cœur and that swimming pool is piscine. By the time I leave Bamako for good, Samba complains that I'm a chatterbox and cab drivers moan that I drive a hard bargain.

We play Oumou Sangaré, Amadou & Mariam, Ali Farka Touré, Mory Kanté, Habib Koité and Salif Keita several times a day; going through almost all their discography and adding Bambara words to my vocabulary. One day while listening to Salif Keita's 'Africa', I ask my housemates to translate words I have been mumbling since I was a teenager. Astou says he's essentially singing out the joy we find in our countless dance forms and the variety of the food we have, like attiéké, ndole, fufu, alloko, thiéb, yassa and mafé.

Attiéké is fermented and granulated cassava popular in Ivory Coast and Mali, ndole is a Cameroonian dish made with peanuts, bitter leaves and beef or prawns. Fufu is soft, pounded cassava you swallow without chewing, alloko is fried plantain. It's called kelewele in Ghana. Thiéboudienne – or thiéb, as it is commonly known – is the national dish of Senegal. Yassa is an onion sauce served with fish or chicken. Mafé is the meat and peanut butter stew loved in Mali and Senegal, and cooked in different ways around the region.

'Any dish that's worth being a Salif Keita lyric is worth my time in the kitchen,' I announce to Astou.

I become her kitchen skivvy.

The way to gastronomic heaven is paved with about two kilograms of rice, a kilo or more of fish, six medium red onions, two green peppers, one packet of tomato paste, one small cabbage, three large sweet potatoes, a bunch of small carrots, celery leaves, tamarind paste and salt and pepper. This is thiéboudienne. It's the superstar of rice dishes. We buy our food from meal to meal, starting with a trip to the market. When we get back to the house, Astou washes and guts the fish while I tend to the fire, starting by shaking coal into place around the medium-sized brazier. I pour kerosene, light my fire and blow air into it using a square bamboo fan until the coals are orange. Astou takes over the fire with a silver pot she fills with a litre of cooking oil bought at the kiosk on our street, where the owner closes shop at prayer times.

While the oil heats up, Astou tears a handful of small celery leaves into the wooden mortar with black peppercorns, dried chilli and garlic cloves. I grind them into a paste she stuffs the fish with. Starting with the carrots, I scrub the vegetables until the dried mud they're always covered in melts in the water. I give them a final rinse in clean water. After deep frying the fish and removing it from the pot, Astou adds finely chopped tomatoes, a cube of chicken stock and a litre of water to the pot and lets it simmer into a sauce. Satisfied with the consistency, she adds peeled carrots, cabbage wedges and quartered sweet potatoes. She turns her energy to the rice while the sauce simmers. She spreads the rice on a flat bamboo sieve and tosses it in the air to remove the chaff before rinsing it on a metal dish with holes at the bottom, like a strainer, until the water is no longer milky white. The dish goes on top of the pot and the space between it and the pot sealed by wrapping a thin strip of cloth around it. She closes the dish with a lid and leaves the rice there until it's half cooked before transferring it to the sauce. She leaves it on the fire until the liquid has been absorbed. The dish cooked, the pot comes off the fire.

The smell brings everyone in the house to the balcony. Abbas is always the first person to start circling around us. Miriam, who is now his wife, keeps herself occupied by stringing beads into earrings and necklaces she'll sell in Madrid when she goes back home in a few weeks. Mohammed from Conakry, whom we call Papi Two, is helping her. Mbaye is on a chair under the tree outside the compound. Adama from Benin takes a seat next to Mohammed the herbalist.

Astou removes boiled cassava leaves from the fire and watches over me as I grind them in the mortar with chilli flakes before frying them with tomato paste. Lunch is ready, but first, Astou indulges in her favourite pastime. She walks over to Adama, who has already pulled out the small leather pouch that contains the cowrie shells he uses to read fortunes. It's always the same predictions – business is going to thrive, single people will get married to a good partner and those who are already in relationships will make healthy babies. We are all going to have a long life. A wide smile fills Astou's face when Adama tells her that she's going to give birth to twins. So will I, apparently, never mind that I have no interest in becoming a parent. Satisfied with her fortune, Astou walks back to the kitchenette to rinse the two dishes she'll serve lunch in. This afternoon's meal is prepared for Jilly, Mbaye, Samba, Astou, Oumou, King, Charles, Abbas, Miriam, Champion, the two Mohammeds, Doc, Oumou's son Omar, a new French visitor Emmanuel, Mustafa, Fana – who has gained weight – her son Ibrahima and myself.

On days when we cook yassa, Astou's favourite meal, she asks Abbas to read her fortunes before we go to the market; we're going to buy chickens, we might as well find out if ancestors want a sacrifice or not. For this meal, we take a ride in a sotrama to a market about six kilometres from Djicoroni Para, driving past sections of the road with stalls that sell clothes, pots, plates and other kitchen utensils. This market has a poultry section. Our chickens are not sacrificial. If they were, the ancestors would have specified what the colour of our protein needs to be. Astou 'weighs' a chicken in her hand before deciding whether it's going back to the cage or if it's headed for the butcher's machete. It's plucked and gutted here and brought back to us in pieces.

When we get home, Astou scrubs the chicken with a green Sunlight soap bar, before rinsing it in clean water that's mixed with bleach. I fall over with laughter when she asks me to pass her the 'javel', as she calls it. Everyone laughs when I tell them that we also call bleach javel. She gives the chicken a final rinse in water that's mixed with vinegar. I pound black peppercorns, dried chilli, garlic, deseeded green pepper and stock cubes before joining Fana and Oumou in turning the onions and carrots into squares that I rub with the spicy paste. Next, I start the fire on two braziers. One is for the yassa and another for the pot of rice. Fana rinses the rice and puts it on the fire. Astou heats two litres of oil and deep fries the chicken. When it's cooked, she transfers it to a bowl, and cooks the onion and carrot mix in the oil; stirring it constantly and adding a touch of mustard paste a minute or two before she removes it from the fire.

Now that we have a fridge, lunch is washed down with bissap, which I make by rinsing dried hibiscus flowers until there's no dust on them before soaking the leaves in boiling water for a few hours. When the liquid cools, I strain it and add a kilo or more of sugar and half a bottle of vanilla essence; refrigerate until it's ice cold, serve and revel in the compliments. To make nyamaku, we usually buy a kilo of fresh ginger and one bundle of mint and take them to the appliances market that's a five-minute walk from our market in Djicoroni Para, where one of the merchants charges a small fee to people who don't have blenders in their own kitchens to use the one he keeps for this purpose. We add water to the ginger and mint, strain it, add lots of sugar and vanilla essence and refrigerate before serving. Astou starts selling juices; we stop making bissap and nyamaku for our housemates' enjoyment. They have to pay like everyone else.

VIII

LOSING MYSELF

April 2009

WHEN I ANNOUNCE MY plans to start travelling, the question I'm asked more than others is, 'What are you going to eat?'

'On the up side,' a friend says, 'You'll be on a diet you can never abandon.' I do lose weight, but not from the enduring stereotype of Africa as the land of starvation. The region is obsessed with eating. There's food round the clock. I fill out on shawarmas in Senegal, gorge on fresh baguettes slathered in margarine in Mali, live on a diet of fried chicken and chips in Burkina Faso and promise to be careful in Ghana: Fat chance, not with the jollof and fried rice.

I also discover the only bean dish I like. Waakye is made with rice and black-eyed beans, and served with spaghetti, a piece of fried fish and tomato stew that has more oil than tomatoes. It comes with a dollop of a hot dark-brown condiment called shito. I eat like it's an ancestral instruction. In Abidjan, I stuff myself with fish, rice, grilled meat and stewed pork trotters; snacking on alloko and eating a breakfast of attiéké and fried fish. It's served with a mixture of raw chopped onions, tomatoes and habanero peppers. The plate is rounded off with a splash of oil. By the time I move to Djicoroni Para, you don't see me approaching, you hear the loud shuffle of my thunder thighs.

It's Sunday afternoon at number 227, and as always my right hand is the last in our communal dish. Abbas changes the music from Alpha Blondy's 'Jah Victory' to Tracy Chapman's 'She's Got Her Ticket'.

Miriam and I get up to dance, Samba takes a picture. I have four chins and my stomach looks like it's on its way to my knees. I have to lose weight. Adama the drummer introduces me to a traditional dancing teacher called Ibrahim. The boy's body is all muscle and no fat. 'Wait until I'm done with you,' he says at our first lesson.

Ibra turns the rooftop, previously my favourite place in Bamako for the cool, starry nights filled with Bob Marley, Morgan Heritage and Tikken Jah Facoly, into a painful experience. I fall and scrape my knees and bum. My chest is in flames. My joints feel like they're going to break into two from the squatting. I want to tell him off for not taking things easy as promised, but I can only huff out my words. Yet, my body has never felt this good.

We dance like this for five weeks; with me throwing tantrums that only make him push me harder. Now, in addition to the heat that traps me at home during the day, my body is too sore to go out at night. My torture becomes another display of social living. The kids on our street stop playing to watch me dance; cheering when I get my moves right, encouraging me to get up and try again when I fall. At first, the men at our house complain about being banned from the roof. A week later, they help me work out on weekends. Abbas and Mohammed from Conakry teach me boxing, King runs on the spot with me and Moussa tries to get me into jogging. The twins from the family that lives one floor below us, Awa and Bajuku, come over to play music, insisting that I get up and dance.

Walking down the street to get a sotrama to town, a teenage girl I've never seen before comes up to me to say she knows I'm trying to lose weight. She's a runner but offers to power walk with me. Oumou encourages me to keep going when I don't feel like dancing.

'Doni, doni,' she says. 'Little by little, that's how a bird builds its nest.'

Astou digs through her suitcases to find French editions of *Elle* and *Marie Claire* for dieting tips I never use. They keep me going until I feel confident enough in my commitment to travel to Conakry to continue learning traditional dances.

IX

AISHA

July 2009

'BORDER POST' IS NOT just a sign. It's also an announcement of impending combat. Out of all the battles raging on this war-torn continent, there's nothing quite like the stand-off between travellers and border control officials, or uniforms, as I call them. Provoke a uniform with so much as a hello and bombs will drop – invalid passport, expired visa, missing yellow fever vaccination and a litany of problems that only exist in the uniforms' heads. It's as if they're competing to be the Idi Amins of border posts. Like all such encounters, this one is brutal, as I discover in Kouremale, Mali, on my way to Conakry. Everyone inside the one-room office puts franc notes in their passports when handing them over. I stand my ground when the uniform says my visa has expired. 'You have to pay 5000 francs.' He waves me away while I presumably look for the money in my bag. His next victim is a woman who is also in my taxi to Conakry.

Her one-page travel document is accompanied by a 1000 franc

note. She pulls me outside, where she 'go beg' me to 'jus pei de man'. The thing is, I just don't feel like it. I've already paid too damn much to be here. Or, as I rattle off to my 'sistoh', 'In the fifteen years that I have been on my period, I have only ever used Lil-Lets; it's the most intimate relationship of my life, and my constant in a life that changes every few minutes. I now use OB, as if a period is a spelling bee. I haven't had privacy in a year and spent the last four months living in a house with ten men. I don't have a sex life and clean up 'number two' with water, soap and my left hand, and here's a further payment for you – I love it for being cleaner than the toilet-paper way I've known all my life. I have paid with my money, my comfort, my *everything*. Hell, I don't even look like the Lerato I've known all my life – excuse me if I'm not in the mood to bribe.'

The way my 'sistoh' looks at me storming back to the office, it's as if she knows a bigger fool is yet to be born. It doesn't matter. My visa is valid. The uniform persists. We go around in circles until it turns out that he's right. Technically. I sleep when others leave the bus to get their passports stamped at the border between Mali and Ivory Coast. I don't have a date of entry.

'You have to go back to Bamako,' he says.

'Other people are renewing their visas here. Why do I have to go back?' I fume.

'Because,' he smiles, 'I say so.'

'My sistoh why you de no listen?' the woman in the taxi to Conakry says when I offload my bags.

All the cars I approach are full, and it's too late in the day for a taxi. The uniform walks over to carry my bags to where he's sitting with three colleagues, brewing mint tea. We spend hours under the full moon and star-lit sky listening to Toumani Diabaté and Ballake Sissoko's *New Ancient Strings*.

He asks a trucker to give me a lift back to Bamako. My lost temper costs me 37 050 francs: 15 000 for a visa, 2 000 in passport pictures, 350 in taxi fares between Djicoroni Para and the immigration office in Hamdallaye, and another 20 000 on a ticket to Conakry – I really need to be locked away when I'm premenstrual.

I keep my mouth shut at the Bankan crossing in Guinea four days later when a uniform asks me to put money in my passport. My hand digs willingly into my bag at an immigration checkpoint a few kilometres later. This office has bamboo walls, a scratched table, pens with chewed lids, and a dog-eared notebook into which the two uniforms write our names and passport numbers. We hold travel papers in one hand and money in the other. The uniform demands 5000 francs to buy airtime to call me, to make sure I arrive safely in Conakry. The long, winding road to Conakry starts out on a smooth, tarred road before hitting the most potholed stretch in this infinitely potholed continent. At the second and third road blocks, only our driver, another Mohammed, steps out of the car. He pays with a smile that turns into a snarl the moment he's back in the taxi. 'Bandits,' he hisses.

Guinea is too beautiful for the six road blocks we go through to ruin the experience for me. The landscape looks something like a rain forest, with houses and people surrounded by a chain of hills and valleys and mountains that stretch on and on, some shrouded by mist, poking into grey skies that look like they're a squeeze away from pouring with rain. I know the fourth roadblock is trouble when two uniforms shine their flash lights into the taxi. Mohammed's bribe is just a start. They want us all to pay. The uniforms interrogate me with the usual questions about why I'm in Guinea. One uniform declares my visa invalid, and my passport expired. I have time and legitimate papers; I'm fighting this one out until I win. After an impasse is reached between me and the uniforms, they order Mohammed to follow them to the police station. My passport is checked as if I'm a suspected terrorist before a new problem emerges. My medical card is invalid. It's over four thousand rand spent on multiple vaccinations because, to quote *Lonely Planet* travel guide quoting the World Health Organization, I dare not travel around Africa without immunisation from diphtheria, tetanus, measles, mumps, rubella, polio, hepatitis B and a host of other diseases.

We wait until morning for the station commander. He starts by angling for a bribe, but after a fed-up guy in the taxi tells him that I'm a journalist, he relents and apologises for wasting my time. The town is wide awake when we leave the police station. I get to see the dense, green plateaus that make up the Fouta Djalon region. Mohammed stops to pick up a parcel of sacks bulging with raw plantain still attached to the stalks, to give to someone in Conakry. We are in a valley, misty with dense grey clouds tumbling over a mud house surrounded by tall bright-green maize plants.

Our next road block is in Coyan, a village so beautiful it has a brand of mineral water named after it. A group of young boys bathe in a stream flowing from a small waterfall. Mobile kitchens sell fat cakes, boiled eggs and bread.

We follow Mohammed and the uniform who's collecting our passports. I smile my way out of parting with more francs. An aggressive man wearing a luminous lime car-guard's top runs up to the taxi when it crawls through traffic at the last roadblock in Conakry. 'L'argent' he thunders, hands reach into the window to start collecting money while the car moves. Into my purse my hand goes again to get 5000 francs. I get off the taxi with my education in crossing African borders complete: You have to know when to shut up and pay.

My final destination is the island village of Soro. I get into the wrong boat and end up in Kassa. I sit at the pier while it empties out, waiting for a man who will inevitably show up to play my hero. Matthew sees me sitting here while surveying the pier from the barracks. He's in the army and wants to search my bags to make sure that I'm not breaking any laws. He carries my bags up a stony footpath to the barracks. He goes through them with another male officer and a female one. The Diallos are married and spend most of their nights at her place at the barracks.

He offers me his place. It's one of three rooms that the owner of the property, Monsieur Sylla, rents out to male soldiers. Monsieur

'One could not count the moons that shimmer on her roof, or the thousand splendid suns that hide behind her walls.' Saib-e-Tabrizi's ode to Kabul could be said of Mali as well. I found this Tuareg man at the Festival of the Desert in the Sahara; this sunset turned my three-day trek to Timbuktu into a magical moment. Sitting on the banks of Niger River in Segou is the highlight of attending the Festival of the Niger.

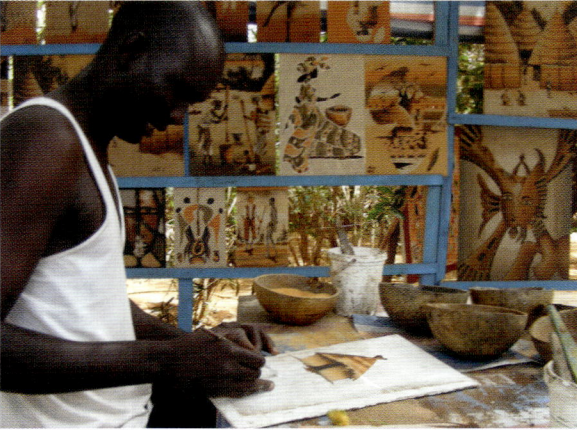

An artist turning sand into an object of beauty at Gorée Island in Senegal.

The first time being in Dakar felt authentic was when I attended a wedding with the female staff from Via Via guesthouse. The bride is decked out in gold.

Waiting for the infamously unpunctual train from Dakar to Bamako at Gare de Hann.

Bamako has been described as twice broken and thrice mended. It makes a shocking first impression, but the Malian capital city is one of the most soulful places I've been to.

The ancient trading city of Djenné, Mali was once the centre of Muslim scholarship in the region. Its mud buildings and rich history have turned it into a UNESCO World Heritage Site. The Grand Mosque is the largest mud building in the world, and the town's people plaster it with mud every year after the rain.

Monday is the main market day in Djenné.

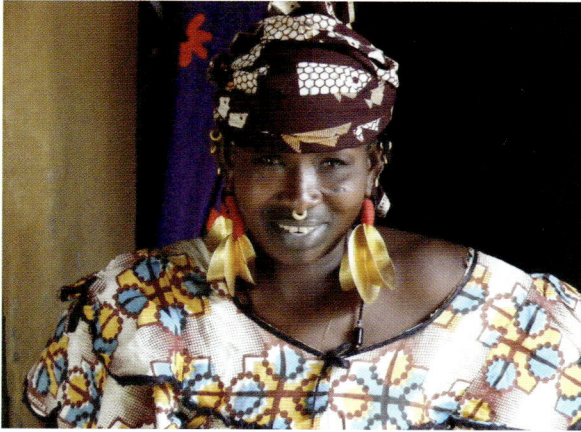

A photo taken on a day tour of Djenné. This Fulani woman, with rings in her septum and ears, is an unlikely style icon; while these are trends that come and go, to the Fulani women, this is the time-old standard of beauty.

We didn't spend more than an hour at Labadi Beach on a media trip to Accra in 2006 but it was enough to convince me to quit my life in Johannesburg to start living my dream of travelling around Africa.

If it moves, it qualifies to be used as public transport, never mind how old it is.

This is Africa, where frustrations like constant roadblocks are always outweighed by wonderful surprises, like the brief moment on my way to Conakry when we drive past this house in the Fouta Djalon region.

Thieboudienne is the national dish of Senegal.

Sunrise in Kokrobite.

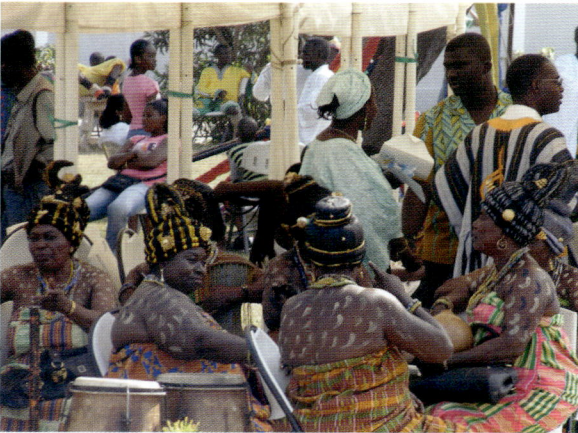

Ghana is the first country in Africa to be liberated from colonialism in 1957. Its first president, the great Kwame Nkrumah, is held in high regard, so the celebrations held to celebrate his centenary in 2009 were an occasion to end all others.

Barack Obama's election as America's first black president sent Africa into a frenzy of public declarations of admiration that were previously reserved for Nelson Mandela. This café in Lomé is one of many places named after Obama.

A funeral parade in Abomey, Benin.

Abomey was the capital of the kingdom of Dahomey. Their royal courts, at least what's left of them, are a UNESCO World Heritage Site. Photography is not allowed beyond this court where I imagine my heroes, the fearsome female army of King Ghezo, used to stomp.

The fetish section of Dantokpa market in Cotonou sells animal remains and other ingredients used in magic potions.

Every Thursday at dawn, a parking lot in Koforidua in Ghana turns into a bead market that has been held since 1928. It brings together traders and shoppers from around West Africa, but some wares are too valuable to sell. These brass bracelets are family heirlooms that have been passed down from generation to generation since the days of the Ashanti and Ghana empires.

Snails are a staple food on the Ivorian menu.

Sylla is a sour old man who regards me with suspicion when I go into their house to greet and introduce myself.

Matthew is at my door first thing in the morning to walk me to Soro. There are no boats between the two villages, no electricity except for four hours at night when a kiosk fires up a generator, and the villagers pay to charge their cellphones at the multi-adaptor. We walk through narrow spaces between houses to the wild side of the island where the branches of palm trees sway in the wind. Litter sticks to the vegetation. The clouds are dark grey and the ground wet from the rain. The rainy season is six months of incessant downpours. We go back to the only main street, walking along the shore, past houses with paint that's been washed out by water and time, jumping over the small furrows between some houses.

The ocean is grey and still. We get to a stretch of about six-hundred metres, bordered by mud houses, then walk past two big brown rocks on either side and keep walking until we get to Soro. The first houses in the village are on steep ground that slopes into verdant gardens; people work on the plants with machetes. A drummer called John walks us to his friend Mohammed's house. He's the best dancer in the village and agrees to work with me for 500 000 Guinea francs a week. 'Another thing,' he adds, 'I don't do private classes – you'll dance with the troupe. We dance at 10am and 3pm except on Sundays when we run to Kassa.' I refuse to run. 'Bien. I'll organise a few people to dance with you on Sundays, 9am.'

On the walk back to my place, the smaller village between Kassa and Soro vibrates with murmurs from a crowd of villagers sitting in the mosque; they're praying at a funeral. This is the moment that opens me to the grace of Islam – my spirit loves silence and solitude.

So begins my life for almost three weeks: I start the day with a cold bucket shower, armed as always with flip flops, the hope that I don't slip, a block of Lifebuoy soap and a burgundy mesh I use to scrub away the dirt that sticks to my skin. Back in my room, I get dressed and pack a bag with a sweater and the peach dancing pants given to me by Ibrahim. I then grab my umbrella and start my walk to Soro. Sometimes dolphins swim close to the shore. In Soro, Mory is the first person who sees me. He bites his tongue trying to pronounce Lerato and christens me Aisha. I have been teaching everyone how to say my name instead of settling on a local name. I put my foot down every day in Bamako when Charles tries to call me Aminata. But Mory refuses to consider calling me anything but Aisha.

'She is the wife of the Prophet,' he says, 'It's a very good name.'

He invites me to wait at his house and leaves me with his girlfriend, Mafodia, while he goes back to weeding their vegetable garden. Mafodia spends most of her time cooking, dancing or twisting her hair and applying white cream on her face to remove the melanin from it.

When the time comes for us to go the hall, what looks like the whole village follows us. People stop sweeping and cutting weeds, fires are put out and pots removed from braziers. The hall overflows with onlookers. Those who arrive late for the show put their heads through the windows.

'What's this?' Mohammed asks me, his long index finger drawing a line from my head to my toes. He calls Mafodia.

'Look around you. What do you see?' he shouts at us.

'Everyone is dressed appropriately,' she whispers, in spandex, leotards, harem pants and sports bras. My wide pants aren't acceptable.

'Fix it,' he shouts at Mafodia, who runs to her house to get a pair of harem pants.

My wardrobe faux pas sorted, he turns his back to face the troupe as they stand in a line against the wall, waiting for the drums to start beating. Mory, John and two other drummers take their places.

'Let's go,' Mohammed shouts at the drummers without looking at them. One beat, and he spins around like a provoked mamba.

'Do you call this drumming?' He doesn't wait for them to answer. 'This is a joke.' He leaps to the drummers, taking John's stick. He beats the drum until the room shakes.

He starts his classes with aerobics; another thing I hate. 'I don't care,' he hisses when I complain about not getting what I sign up for. I'm on the floor five minutes into it.

'Stop wasting time and get up. Now.'

His face shines with his smile again, but only for a split second. He gives us a five-minute break after the aerobic session so I can catch my breath. I lie on the floor sucking a plastic packet of water. Mofodia pours some water over my body to help me cool down.

Mohammed leans against the wall with a wide smile on his face. 'Getting what you're paying for?' he winks, clapping his hands to summon us to the dance floor.

The drums start beating and Mohammed shouts out his instructions again. 'Shoulders straight, hips loose, and a smile at all times, Lerato. People want happy dancers,' he says. 'Let's go,' he barks before stopping the drummers again. He pushes them to the side. 'Give me the sticks, hurry,' he says softly to Mory before beating the djembes until his body shakes. 'This is what I'm talking about.' He wants them to beat until sweat streams down their chests. Mory peels off his sweat-soaked clothes, leaving him in black swimming shorts. Mohammed doesn't want us to just dance. We must jump until it looks like we're flying and land en-pointe; he calls it ballet African. We move with vigour and land with grace.

I'm expected to keep up with everything except when they spin their bodies in the air. When the class ends, and some guys run into the sea, Mafodia holds my hand to support my exhausted body while we walk to the house. After a cold shower using Omo washing powder, I sleep in her bedroom. There's still the afternoon session to get through.

My routine stops on Tuesdays when I get a boat to Conakry, and walk around its litter-strewn streets to get money from Western Union, buy fresh fruit, and second-hand copies of *Time* and the *Economist*.

My weekly trek comes with hopping into a boat made for ten that's packed with thirty people, sacks of their shopping and live chickens.

The two boys who work on the boat each have a bucket which they use to fight the Atlantic as it seeps into our boat. 'We are going to die,' the woman next to me says as more people pile in. There are no life jackets. A young lady huddles with her two younger siblings and their plastic bags. A woman hops in and tip toes over the bags on the floor before squeezing her formidable curves between me and another person. She starts praying, softly at first, then fervently as we sail further away from Conakry's lights into the dark night.

The boat boys are still at it with their buckets. The boat rocks, and our prayer warrior goes wild. When she is not slapping my shoulder and thigh, she pinches my arm or raises hers to the heavens, praying in tongues. Or so I think. Guinea has forty languages; she could be making our dying prayer in her mother tongue. 'Amen,' we repeat after her when we reach Kassa. My amen is the loudest; I haven't got around to renewing my travel insurance. It expired ten months ago.

Monsieur Sylla's face always looks like he has just swallowed a bitter potion. I don't pay any attention to him on the Saturday morning I find him sitting in front of the gate, snarling as always, when I offer him my 'bon jour' on my way to the shower. He's still at the gate when I go back to my room, the cheekbones that usually cling to his bony face are puffed up with irritation. I'm getting dressed when fists bang on the wooden window. He screams at me to come out of the room. 'Knock on the damn door,' I say, my short temper on its way to getting lost. He continues yelling. 'I said come out. Now.' His wife and their four daughters are also at my door. 'I *said* I'm busy,' I yell when I open the door.

He jumps on me as soon as I leave my room. He thinks I'm lying when I say I'm travelling to write about Africa, and accuses me of being a spy. He wants to confiscate my laptop. I tell him that it will only happen over my dead body.

Word that his tenant is co-creating a scene reaches Mr Diallo. He sits at the head of the table while his landlord and I sit across from each other. Neighbours are in the yard for the show.

'You say you're not a spy but refuse to show me your laptop. You're a journalist but won't show me your work.' He wants us to go to the police station. He threatenes to kick me out; I yell that I don't have time to look for another place. We go on like this, with me telling him he's wasting my time, until he finally says what he has been thinking. 'Who's paying for you? Is it your husband or boyfriend?' I fling the table across the yard and lunge at him.

'Are you fucking kidding me, you little piece of male shit,' I scream, rattling in English before cobbling up a French translation. 'How dare you reduce me to my vagina? You piece of shit.'

I scream at him and everyone telling me to calm down. 'Swine,' I hiss.

End scene; storm to my room to get my bag and umbrella. Nothing irritates me as much as the assumption that I need a man to bankroll my life or make my dreams come true. It undermines my autonomy. The only thing I need from men is for them to step out of my way and spare me their patriarchal bullshit.

When I return from Soro, I stop at Joan's restaurant for my usual dinner of fried fish and a salad of avocado, lettuce, tomato and boiled sweet potato. She's from Ghana and calls me by my would-be Akan name. 'Efua, is that you? You know how to get angry, eh? Now the whole village is scared to death of you,' she quips.

'Good. People must mind their damn business.'

When I get home, I go to Monsieur Sylla's house with a kola nut for him to break for us bury the hatchet. Drama is the default language of West Africa and I'm fluent in it.

I move to Carrefour Cosa in Conakry after twenty-one days of dancing with Mohammed. My host is a friend from Bamako who invites me to stay with him and his cousins while house sitting for their aunt, who's in America. I get my second bout of malaria and spend my last days in Guinea in my bed. Looking at the mirror on the morning I leave for Bamako, I stare at my reflection for a long time trying to figure what's odd with the image staring back at me; I don't have a double chin anymore.

The only person who pays at the roadblocks on the way to Bamako is our driver. One of the passengers, the motherly Khadija, writes a prayer in my journal after wishing me many more trips around Africa. It says: 'La illaha illallah Muhammadur Rasulullah'. There is no God but Allah, and Mohammed is His messenger.

X

A Gift for My Soul

21 August 2009

RAMADAN IS HERE and life at number 227 Djicoroni Para is infused
with holiness. King and I are the only people who aren't observing
the most significant month of the Muslim calendar, when Allah
reveals the first chapters of the Quran to Prophet Mohammed. It's
the most important time of the year to Moussa, who spends all his
time reading the Quran and praying. The others start joining him at
prayer times. Around Bamako, pavements are covered with prayer
mats and the streets around the grand mosque spill over with
people. When the streets can no longer contain them, people stand
on balconies in buildings close to the mosque.

And yet, life continues as usual. Markets and kiosks are still
in business, the top floor of the Grand Marché whirs with Singer
sewing machines turning yards of cloth into boubous, sheep
carcasses still hang off nails at the open-air butcheries ready to be
sold off piece by piece, and the fetish market across the road is still
trading dead pythons and monkey skulls.

Before Mali, I only know Islam as one of many religions; and even worse, through my Christian socialisation, with some charismatic pastors often mocking prayer times as the law of an insecure and repressive God who doesn't allow His people the freedom Christianity provides. Ramadan becomes my teacher; my naturally restless spirit finds calm and the silence of the season quietens some of the storms in my head and heart.

I stop eating during fasting hours so that I too celebrate iftar with my housemates, when we break the fast. Dinner is usually a bean stew and baguette. It becomes a feast during Ramadan, with kebabs, grilled fish, fried chicken, couscous, green salad and alloko.

It's the rainy reason. Astou invites me to sleep in her bedroom, making me part of her morning prayers, even if it's only by observation. I have never seen prayers as dignified as hers, when her lips move quietly as tears stream down her face – this is the grace that draws me to Islam.

I'm usually happy to move to my next destination but the thought of leaving Bamako for good fills me with profound sadness. I will no longer zoot across town to see Habib Koité and his band Bamada on stage nor will I be a few minutes away from his house, where we spend a long afternoon, drinking tea while he translates some of the songs for me. I will no longer cook with Astou or brew bissap and nyamaku for Moussa and Mbaye; there will be no rooftop bonding sessions with Jilly at dawn, when we drink café touba – coffee that's flavoured with cloves and Selim pepper – while I crochet his locks. I will no longer storm into Astou's tailor's shop with yards of pagne and bazin to turn into boubous. Ousman and his son will no longer wave hands blackened by the coal they sell at the market. I will no longer hear nteri, friend, when I walk around Djicoroni Para.

On my last night, Astou digs through her suitcases for my farewell present: A photograph of a much younger Habib Koité taken in a private moment. I give her a necklace from Timbuktu. We hug and cry and sit in an awkward silence for some time until I feel brave enough to ask her a question I've had since we met.

'What's it like to not have a clitoris? Because honey, mine is begging for attention and it's a problem.' I haven't had sex in months and, frankly, I need a shag. But instead of looking for flings and one-night stands, I think about how problematic my clitoris is now. Female genital mutilation is still rife in Mali.

Astou laughs, confessing that she's been dying to find out what sex feels like with a clitoris.

She tells me that her friends have started breaking with tradition, refusing to mutilate their daughters. I guess not all revolutions are loud; it doesn't make them any less powerful.

Astou's not the only one with tears falling down her face when she makes her first prayer of the day, Fajr. It's the morning of my last day in Mali. Sitting at the back of a cab on my way to the bus station, Djicoroni Para is no longer the scrapyard I label it on my first day here. It's home, where I learn French and lose my morbid obesity. It's where I find my sense of belonging.

One of the things I used to feel and think about a lot when I lived in Mali is that all I have known about it, besides Timbuktu and Bamako being the capital city where most of my favourite artists reside, was that Mali is a poor country. Everything I read about Mali, from travelogues to news features, always finds space in the word count to mention that Mali is one of the poorest places in the world. Yet, where others only see misery and despair, I find family, unconditional love and belonging. In Mali, I'm not 'moody' or 'difficult' and I don't have 'an attitude'. I'm understood as someone who needs her solitude and time alone to replenish daily. Just as Adama the drummer was introduced to others with the declaration that he is a joker, I am accepted as someone who loves to withdraw into her own world and that I should not be disturbed when I'm in this space.

Malians love differently, with tenderness and the utmost care of the other person's heart. To be held with love, as Malians do, is a gift for the soul.

XI

Leaving West Africa

September 2009

THE TRIP FROM BAMAKO TO Accra is drama free at all borders.
In Koloko, between Mali and Burkina Faso, a Burkinabe uniform
buys me a sweet cup of mint tea while he searches my bags. In
Paga, between Burkina Faso and Ghana, the chief uniform gives
me a multiple-entry visa at the cost of a single-entry visa after I
put on a Nollywood-worthy performance to beg for a discount. My
return coincides with a series of events celebrating the centenary of
Kwame Nkrumah's birth. Rita Marley, who has a home in Ghana,
is a speaker at one of them. The main celebration is held at the
Kwame Nkrumah Memorial Park. It's also attended by diplomats
and royalty. The royals are dressed in volumes of kente togas. Their
necks, wrists and heads are weighed down by gold and beads; their
umbrella handlers are on hand to keep the harsh sun from touching
them.

I'm in Ghana for a short stop before going to Togo and Benin.
I leave for Cotonou on my birthday, using the occasion to get

taxi drivers to pool their money together as a present. I flirt with a uniform at the Aflao border in Togo to get out of paying for a transit visa. I walk into the immigration office cleavage-first with a shiny red pout and a hand that never leaves my chest when the uniform talks to me; after all, I'm a woman travelling alone in a region manned by some of the most lascivious men in Africa. South Africans don't need a visa to be in Benin. Still, the two female uniforms at the revolving gate we walk through want some francs in their hands; I pay.

Cotonou announces itself with smoke that tears through my lungs when I take a breath. The fumes sting my eyes until they well with tears. The revving of thousands of public motorcycles called zémidjan fills the air. Streets whir with tailors turning yards of bazin and pagne into boubous and fanciful ensembles. From my window on the fourth floor of my hotel, the city looks like it's rotting. A cloud of smog hovers over it.

I celebrate my day with a tequila-soaked party at a club called Soweto. I'm with Diana, who I meet at my hotel. We're banging shot glasses on the counter when she recalls a conversation from earlier about men, and how she keeps several of them.

'What I mean is that, for the right price, I will leave a club with any man who asks; and it's not always with a condom.' Her frankness forces me to own up to sex with Kevin and his sneaky removal of the condom. It's time for the HIV test I've been too scared to take.

I take it a week later, and wait two days for the results. I call my uncle's wife, mmaMalome Matheko. I want to tell her how stupid I've been and how disappointed in myself I am. Instead, I tell her about the empty pool at El Dorado Beach Club and the fishermen mending their nets and boats at the beach. I spend the afternoon fighting tears and chain-smoking.

I sweep my anxiety to the back of my mind again and almost feel like myself when I get in trouble with a spirit I photograph when I walk into a parade of masked spirits. The spirit runs after me with a whip in his hand. I get on a zémidjan and tell the driver to take me to the hotel. He refuses, saying the spirit will catch us and beat him as well. I raise my hands to show surrender while deleting the pictures of the parade. The spirit grabs my camera to go through my pictures. He wields the whip in front of my face before rejoining the parade.

I almost run after them to ask him to whip me; maybe physical pain will take my attention away from the torment of my guilt.

Monday, 12 October 2009 will not be the day I discover that I'm HIV positive; it will be the day I go to the biggest fetish market in Africa. I collect the envelope with my test results and get a zémidjan to Dantokpa market. My curiosity and inability to wait make me open the envelope, and while the zémidjan rattles over potholes, I let out a beastly grunt. My tears soak the driver's back.

My test is negative, but there's still a lot of reckoning to be done. Love and lust in the time of HIV call for more than merely using a condom. I failed myself in the worst possible way. My actions did not match my words. I'm so obsessed with keeping my life in order, no unwanted pregnancies or sacrificing myself at the altar of patriarchy, only to make a mistake that reduces me to just another girl with a disastrous relationship with her reproductive health.

Dantokpa squeezes vendors, thousands of shoppers, hawkers and stalls and kiosks with just about every item under the sun into twenty-thousand square metres. The fetish section is the most interesting. There's a section with herbs, tree barks and plants used to make medicine; and a section that sells talismans and animal remains. The scene is the same in all the shops I visit or peek into: The skulls of many species in the animal kingdom, dried vultures, owls, vipers, cobras and pythons. The snakes are bound with rubber bands.

At a shop called Doctor Séïbou and Son's pharmacy, Séïbou tries to sell me a love potion. For 30 000 francs, he'll mix herbs that I must rub onto my hands, then whisper my date's name three times to make him fall in love with me. There's no problem that he can't fix. With the right potion and animal parts, bad luck turns into good fortune, dead-end relationships make it down the aisle, struggling businesses prosper and wombs become fertile. He charges me 5 000 francs to browse.

From Cotonou, I trek for three hours in a minibus to Abomey. Red dust covers every building and surface, and the reception at my hotel. I find the proprietor half naked but for the large towel wrapped under his big stomach. His tongue sticks out of his mouth as he reads the contents of a blue file.

'My children call me Da – that's what you'll call me, my daughter.' The reception is made of a random collection of items. There are yellow ceramic lemons, a polished silver flask next to a crunched up, used bottle of mineral water, a dusty vase and a dessert baking tray. A dislodged door leans against the wall on one side of the room. The space across the room has a hammock hanging on a steel frame and a torn brown leather chair, three drums and life-sized puppets in floppy hats. He charges me what I can afford, and wiggles his bum around the chair to get up and lead me to my room. It's as dim as the reception.

On my way to Houndjroto market to look for tomatoes, cucumber, avocado and boiled eggs – my daily diet – I walk into a funeral procession of mostly women humming and twisting their bodies as they walk in front of a coffin. Four of them hold framed photos of an old man.

Abomey is dotted with small huts where I find dry milky liquid and blood, feathers and egg shells left as offerings to the effigies of voodoo gods; another reminder of the beauty of places that can be modern without losing their roots, in this case the prominence of voodoo as the national religion and way of life.

We turn the reception at Da's hotel into a dance studio for my class. Da becomes the drummer while the teacher he finds for me shows me how to wind my body in a voodoo dance. For our next routine, I march on the spot three times with a knobkerrie in my right hand. I move forward three paces and back, and repeat.

The dance of the Mino, 'my mother' in Fon, is the only connection I can have with the female army whose ruthlessness earned them a reputation as the most powerful army in the Kingdom of Dahomey. When Benin was the Kingdom of Dahomey, it was ruled by a succession of twelve kings who live up to their father's principle that 'the kingdom shall always be made greater'. Wars were waged and enemies conquered and sold as slaves. Every conquest was followed by sacrificing forty captives whose blood would be mixed with palm oil and alcohol for libations at the palace.

Of all the kings, Gezo is the most fearsome. His power comes from surrounding himself with the army of women known to amputate their breasts if they stood in the way of their speed and aim on the battlefield. Their war-cry, my guide says, was 'let the men raise the kids'.

The royal palace is all that remains of this world. Only the wings that belonged to Gezo and his son Glele are still there. Sometimes, when a sign says 'no cameras', it means none are allowed unless you want to talk about a fee. At the royal palace, there are no exceptions to the rule; not even for a fee. I can only take pictures of the compound.

Canons gifted by a European slave-trade partner are mounted in front of one of the buildings. The walls that fence the compound and the outsides of the palace have sculpted figurines of lions painted in gold, a green chameleon holding a machete, a sculpted bronze dog and other important symbols. There's no knobkerrie in my hand when I get to Gezo's throne. Still, I march on the spot and walk back and forth in three paces until I reach it. The throne sits on the skulls of four of his greatest enemies – delivered to the king by the Mino. Today being Monday, and traditionally still a market day, women are not allowed at the royal tombs.

From Abomey, I travel just over one hundred and nineteen kilometres to Ouidah on a road lined with people taking cover from the sun under stalls with brittle palm-leaf roofs to sell green pineapples and mangoes arranged neatly in metal dishes, with bamboo baskets next to them on the ground. Some stalls and tables have bottles with petrol. I love Benin because voodoo is as public as the minarets of a mosque or church clock towers. And just like people of other religions have mass celebrations, so too do Mahu's children. The biggest of these gatherings is the Voodoo Festival, held in Ouidah in January, when the devout parade around town in ceremonial dresses, offering animal sacrifices to Mahu, who is a feminine spirit. God is a woman in Voodoo.

Ouidah is subdued in November and its main attraction is the Temple of Pythons, set across the road from the grey Basilica of Ouidah.

My plan is precise: Tick through the list of things to do and head to Lomé.

I leave my bags in the hut at the temple's entrance, my skin already recoiling just looking at the red-painted letters that read Temple des Pythons, with a snake under the words. My guide plays on my fear of snakes, saying they let the pythons roam around town. My eyes flit around the yard.

A statue of a woman with a bare chest stands in the compound. There are huts, some with bare walls and red ceramic roofs, while others have paintings of people with tribal marks on their faces. In one of the paintings, a man in a white boubou stands in a blue frame. His round skull cap matches the indigo toga with yellow flowers wrapped over his boubou.

The pillars at the entrance of the building have paintings of pythons. In another hut, four snakes are carved into the door, two of them almost touching their tongues as they look at each other.

'Are you ready?' my guide asks, standing outside one of the huts. I make travelling decisions around the probability of seeing snakes. Rumours of snake sightings stop me from going to mythical places I want to visit, like Lake Fundudzi in Venda.

I have been mulling over visiting Ouidah, petrified by the thought of coming face to face with pythons, for more than a year. Standing outside the hut, sweat pours down my face while the guide cajoles me to be brave. I follow him inside. Long and short pythons with bodies that are as thick as wrists padded with fat coil around each other and stretch out side by side next to the wall. Others lie on the steps. A particularly long one is wrapped around the neck of a cement bust of a man. He asks me to pick the one I want to put on my shoulders. Forget getting over an emotion I find irrational, I'm not putting a reptile known to swallow animals twice my size on my shoulders unless I've had gallons of vodka first – to hell with getting over my biggest fear.

A short zémidjan ride later, I'm outside a black and white building with the words Kpasse's Sacred Forest written in red. I pick my guide Remi based on his perfect English and his authorship of a slim, black and white book about the forest. The path leading up to the throne has a statue of a panther on one side and a figure with the backside of a frog and the front legs and face of a baboon on the other. There are statues of some of the gods who act as intermediaries between Mahu and her people. The horned human figure sitting on a stool is Legba, the gatekeeper of towns. The huge erect penis between his legs symbolises fertility. Shango, the god of rains, thunder and justice, has metal stick legs and a round body, and a red rod in one hand.

And so goes my afternoon, surrounded by trees and deities that fight chicken pox; a king's messenger with two faces, one at the back of his head; and a new bare-chested female Voodoo initiate in a white wrap. The forest stretches out over hectares of land, but to go beyond the pink building, you have to be initiated. Aidohwedo, the horned god of continuity, bites his tail with a mouth of sharp teeth next to the entrance. King Kpasse is the founder of Ouidah. Legend has it that instead of dying, the king turned into an Iroko tree. The king's court is the ruins of a house with walls that are covered in algae. King Kpasse is covered with rough bark and a string of dry palm leaves around the trunk. Next to him is a mouldy substance with the dry remains of a chalky offering.

'If you make a wish it will come true,' Remi says. I wrap my arms around him and wish for Africa.

We move on to metal figurines of more gods. One is a flattened-out zinc basin that looks like a dress. It's Ogou, the god of iron. The man with two heads sticking out of his regular one is the god of children born with deformities, Tohossou. There's also Tchacatou, a Voodoo doll, with nails on his body. From here, I go to the beach front to look for a hotel, past a swamp that has derelict grey houses on dry land, and thin palm trees behind them. The street has life-sized statues of more Voodoo gods.

The next morning on my way out of town, I walk on the soft sand that looks golden in the sun, amid whitewashed huts with thatched roofs, palm trees around them and along the beach, to a cement arrow engraved with the words 'Visit the Door of No Return'. I'm the only person at the peach-coloured monument with white pillars. The part at the top has four rows of slaves with chains on their backs. Some pillars are detailed with symbols: A mermaid, Aidohwedo, the god of continuity and wealth, a vase, a palm tree, what looks like a crab and a dog and a man dancing in a ceremonial skirt with a skull and crossbones etched on his bare chest. Cowrie shells are cemented on the others. Without emotional historians to recount the horrors of the Transatlantic slave trade, I can reflect on one of the greatest crimes against Africans' humanity without feeling like a sham. I struggle to mourn slavery because, to paraphrase Lucky Dube in 'Victims', we're still licking wounds from brutality and humiliation. Africans are still in ball and chains; enslaved by racism, sexism, poverty, violence and bad politics. I will not cry about the past, no matter how gruesome, when the present is just as ghastly. I will not put on a performance of sorrow and despair.

Later that evening in downtown Lomé, I club hop until I end up at a packed nightclub with a playlist that features the standard favourites of P-Square, D'Banj, Flavour N'abania and other Nigerian hiplife stars setting fire to dance floors across the region. I spend a day in Togo's easygoing capital; going to the main market and fetish market, the museum and the beach. As far as destinations go, Lomé is like Ouagadougou. It's great but it doesn't excite me.

When I return to Ghana, I take the long way from Accra to Kumasi, down the coast through Busua and Dixcove, before getting a bus to visit Kristle, my friend from my Abidjan days. I mark the end of my stay in the region of my obsession and the city that inspires me to travel Africa with a visit to Koforidua on a Wednesday, so that when the town rises the next morning, I too join the people who meet to trade beads in a weekly market that's been around since 1928.

In West Africa, beads are as ornamental as they are ceremonial; given as heirlooms, presents to mark the coming of age and for special and regular occasions. The bead market brings together merchants from around Ghana and other parts of West Africa. The sheer variety of wares at the market in Koforidua is astounding; some look like spikes, others like discs and shells. There are oval and rectangular beads and wooden beads carved like traditional masks. The variety of textures, shapes and colours is endless; some are from Ghana, others from Mauritania, Mali and Nigeria. Maasai beads from East Africa have also found their way here. At one stall, when I ask about how much large brass bangles cost, the seller says I could never afford them. They date back to the days of the Songhai and Ghana empires, and have been in his family for just as long; passed down from generation to generation. He's here to exhibit them. Ultimately, this is what I love about West Africa: The region upholds its traditions, and the old and sacred don't die so the contemporary can live.

I leave Accra for Johannesburg on 20 November 2009. In *Afrika My Music*, Es'kia Mphahlele writes that Ghana and Nigeria gave him Africa. I used to wonder what he meant but now I understand. Being here has given me a relationship with my blackness, the continent and myself that I still don't have in South Africa. In West Africa, who I am as a black African is not questioned. It doesn't shrink to fit into whiteness and Western ideals, and it never has to fight to be legitimate. My skin colour and heritage don't make me lesser until I prove myself worthy.

I don't know when I will come back, only that it will not be soon. To keep the most important year and five months of my life alive, I'll wear ankara and keep a collection of pagne. When an occasion calls for my best dress, I will swoop into a room in a grand boubou with yards of cloth layered over my head. To my traditional plate of ting, samp and ledombolo, I will add attieke and jollof rice, and when the hibiscus flowers in a supersize blue plastic bag I buy at Makola market run out and I can no longer make bissap juice, I will turn fresh ginger, mint sprigs, a touch of lemon juice, sugar and a hint of vanilla essence into nyamaku. I'll pepper conversations with 'Inshallah' and express bewilderment by saying 'wallahi'. I'll say 'Alhamdulillah' – all praise be to God – instead of 'bless you' when someone sneezes. This way, my experiences in the region of my childhood obsession and adulthood affirmation will never fade with time.

XII

VAGABOND

May 2010

I TRAVEL BECAUSE IT'S ONLY when I'm on the road that I get to recreate myself in every moment of my existence. Take the morning of 1 May 2010. I'm at the mall with my mom, aunt and sister when I decide that there has got be a better way to spend R1 200 than on a winter coat. Two days later, I'm in a Greyhound to Maputo for R220. I arrive just after midnight and go on a joyride in a cab looking for a place to stay. Fatima's is fully booked. The Base has a bed in a dormitory I share with young European travellers who all walk in from a night out giggling at their clumsy dance moves and futile attempts at remembering the Marrabenta hits they're now hooked on.

I hit the dirty streets of central Maputo in the morning, walking aimlessly until I find a street with shops that sell African-print cloth and tailors that sit on the pavement across the shop sewing curtains. I enjoy Maputo for its colonial buildings still dominating a city that has cranes that hang permanently in the sky. The

Saturday morning crowd of shoppers and hawkers hustle for space with battered chapas and tuk tuks. Boys walk the city streets selling coconuts. Like West Africa's streets, Maputo's turn into a full shopping spree that happens at red traffic lights, parrots included. I used to think travelling is expensive. The time I spend in Namibia, Zimbabwe and Malawi in the beginning of 2010 proves me wrong. I've blown more money on clothes I never wear and wild parties that only end with massive hangovers. I could afford to travel all along. I just didn't prioritise it.

The senselessness of never travelling before backpacking in West Africa deepens at the pungent fish market. Walking from stall to stall looking for lunch, I'm awed by the variety of options: Crabs, prawns, squid, tuna, yellow fish, lobsters with claws that are still moving. It's all kept fresh in buckets filled with water and blocks of ice. And, unlike back home, where eating well is not a human right, the fish here is dirt cheap. It's cooked and served a few metres from where it's caught. I'm in Maputo with one mission – pick a random place on the map as long as it's coastal and off the beaten track. My pencil lands on Quelimane, one thousand five hundred and sixty-five kilometres away.

Like other trips out of Maputo, mine starts at Junta bus station, which connects the city to other provinces in Mozambique. Touts run over, shouting destinations around the country: Xai Xai, Tete, Napumla, Vilankulo, Beira and many other places that Junta connects Maputo to. I arrive at 4.30am and find the bus empty. I move from one hard, stained seat to the next until I find a two-seater with even cushioning. The bus becomes chaotic as it fills up: A man plays Marrabenta from a boom box, a mom and her toddler scream at the top of their voices. The volume is louder than a shebeen on New Years' Eve. It's 5am; this is going to be a long trip.

The man who sits next to me proves my fear founded when he opens his mouth. Paulo's teeth are covered in thick, yellowish goo. He smells like morning breath and spits when he talks. It lands on my face. I hang my head outside the window. This makes him think I'm uncomfortable, so he gets up to find the pagne he rolls into a pillow for me. His armpits smell like a pit toilet. 'Much better,' he says. His spit lands in my eye. He doesn't stop talking and, at times, he wakes me up so I don't miss seeing the places and people we drive past. I'm happy to see him leave the bus in Xai Xai.

I arrive in Quilemane expecting a town with air that smells like the sea and avenues lined with palm tress. I find dusty streets with potholes. The street the bus station is on smells like used cooking oil and fried eggs. It's already dark, and the dust that hangs in the air shines through the street lights. I check into a pensao run by two old, grumpy Portuguese men who refuse to give a discount.

Mornings in Quilemane are dreamy. The air is cool, and the vibe chilled. I treat myself to a cappuccino in one of the restaurants and watch life on the streets go by, with boys following people around to beg for money. The traffic on this side for now is the occasional Land Cruiser. In the afternoon, I jump on a bicycle to the market, where I walk between old women selling tomatoes and okra on plastic plates. I'm looking for a chapa to take me to Zalala beach. I get into a roofless chapa, take a seat on a bench welded to the floor at the back, and make room for yet more people and their shopping until there is no space to move my feet when I get cramps.

'Excuse me, does anyone speak English?' I ask. I guess not, going by the blank stares.

'I do, but it's just a little,' the man on the bench across from me says. Mr Samson is a retired pilot, trained in Russia, and a staunch Jehovah's Witness. He's also going to Zalala beach.

Every day around 3pm, fishermen come back to shore with boats tilting with the weight of their catch. Most of it arrives already packed into fifty kilogram sacks. Bidding starts before the catch reaches the beach, when Mr Samson and other buyers walk to the boats. Fish that's not in sacks is put on the ground for people who want to shop for dinner. There are many different kinds of fish I've never seen before, as well as lobster, prawns, crab and squid.

I buy three lobsters and a kilo of prawns. Boats are turned upside down, some to get repaired.

As always on a beach in Africa, a soccer game starts. People who aren't swimming or playing soccer repaint their boats. On the way back to Quilemane, the long road that goes through all the village we passed on the way to Zalala turns into a market of sorts, with tables piled with raw and fried fish. When we reach my stop, Mr Samson asks where I'm going to cook my seafood. I was hoping his house before finding out he lives out of town. He writes a note in my journal and tells me to go to the restaurant at the back of the bus station. His friend owns it. It reads: 'Ao senhor Quinbane. Ou Paulo, ajudára preparare comida. She is a South African journalist. Henrique A. Samson. Nicoadala.' Mr Samson puts two handfuls of squid in my bag before I jump out of the chapa.

Senhor Quinbane's restaurant is hidden behind buses parked for overnight trips that start at 5am. He's not at the restaurant when I arrive and, considering that this is a place where people buy their food, the manager cannot let me cook in their kitchen. He suggests getting a bicycle to his employer's house. I look for a person who speaks English at the ticketing office next to the entrance, who tells the cyclist where to drop me off.

It's a slow, bumpy trip to a three-storey building where we find two women chatting outside. One of them is Senhora Quinbane. Her husband isn't home. Her English is only as good as my Portuguese – which is limited to pao, bom dia and obrigado; bread, good morning and thank you.

Senhora walks up two flights of stairs to their place. Her three children watch DStv in a lounge where most of the space is taken over by a lounge suite and a lazy-boy chair, a room divider with several collections of dinner sets, family pictures, certificates, vases, jugs and glass sets. She leaves me in the kitchen. The family cat walks around the plastic bag with my seafood. Senhora returns with her son, car keys and a note that never makes it to my hands, telling the manager that it's okay to let me use the kitchen.

'Now, tell me, what is it that you need?' the manager asks me.

'I want to cook rice and seafood stew,' I declare, showing him my plastic bag.

He waves me to a plastic chair in the yard. He returns from the kitchen with Angelina. She takes the black plastic bag and motions me to sit down. She gets two knives and two basins, which she fills with cold water. Angelina doesn't speak English. She shows me her ring finger. She's married with two kids – I already know she's a cook. My empty ring finger says I'm single. I type on an air keyboard to say I'm a journalist. We stand next to each other, knives in hand. She works slowly so I can mimic her cleaning of the fish.

She puts the squid on the table, slicing it open to remove its eyes and membrane. My turn, but the squid keeps slipping and Angelina takes over. By now there are six people hanging out with us. I may not know how to devein prawns or open a lobster, but I do know how to get a brazier going. I let my coals settle, with room for the flame to move after I start it with just a bit of paraffin and fan it until every coal is orange. Then the cooking can start.

Angelina boils the seafood for about ten minutes. She goes inside to get another pot, which goes on the fire. She adds oil, thin onion slices, one diced green pepper and two cloves of garlic pounded in a wooden mortar and pestle. She adds very finely chopped tomatoes into the pot that I keep stirring as she commands me to – by rotating her fist.

We speak in oohs and aahs and nods, using phrases and hand gestures. When the tomato sauce is cooked, Angelina adds the seafood to the pot, followed by a pinch of salt, a cube of stock, a touch of black pepper and some Rajah curry powder. She stirs the stew for the last time, taps the spoon on her hand, licks it and gives it two thumbs up. She disappears inside to get containers.

'Angelina, the food is for all of us,' I tell her, my hands pointing at all of the group now assembled.

After we finish eating, two of the men help Angelina clean up, then we hug goodbye.

They go home, and I'm off to get my bags from the hotel. I must be on the bus to Nampula at 4.30am; I might as well sleep in it.

I'm not the only passenger. While some sleep on the seats, I sleep on the pavement. It's better than spending the night on a soft surface that comes with snores and endless farts.

I'm going to Nampula to honour two favours Mr Samson asked of me – that I take the time to listen to a Jehovah's Witness, and go further north to Ilha de Mozambique.

We arrive at night when the island is mostly dark, with only a few lights switched on. I don't have a place to stay, but the driver knows about a hostel. He drives up a street with weeping willows, dropping me off where rows of houses start and cars can't drive through. The hostel is on the second or third street up the alley.

When the front door opens, a sleepy woman in a worn-out cotton nightdress with long, silky hair appears. She takes me to the kitchen through a lounge that reminds me of apartheid-style four-room houses for its close space.

In the kitchen, she gives me a seat at the table with her two children and feeds me a lightly spiced potato soup with pao that's crispy on the outside and dense on the inside. It's not buried under flour, like they bake Portuguese rolls in Johannesburg.

'Please forgive me. We were not expecting anyone, so I made a simple meal,' she says. Honestly, the only thing she needs to apologise for is giving me a normal portion. Were this my mother's kitchen, I'd join my thumb and index finger and wipe the dish clean.

It's low season for travellers and I have the dormitory to myself. My itinerary on the island: Check out markets, shops and a museum, then go to Pemba. A few people who I reveal this plan to agree that it will work. There are minibuses throughout the day from the island to Nampula, where getting a bus to Pemba is as easy as standing on the side of the road.

In the morning, I walk to the beach for sunrise.

This side of the island smells like a pit toilet, so I don't stick around. The beach has pieces of driftwood and brown plants spewed out by the ocean. At three kilometres long and five hundred metres wide, the island is made for wandering by foot, even with the bicycles carrying two people and mopeds parked on some corners. When the Portuguese built the island as their capital they wanted to evoke Europe, with square limestone houses that have small, square windows made with wood. The colour palette features corals, peach, yellow and the bright, dark red of the island's museum, where a display of various types of boats is the main feature of the collection. The historic buildings have long lost the sparkle on their white walls to water and black, mouldy stains. I feel transported to an older, more romantic era, when signs were carved in wood and hung on buildings. Here, even the traffic signs hang off houses, and even though the Farmacia sign of the pharmacy is written on white glass, stepping inside still feels like walking into a postcard from an old world – where pills and potions are stored in glasses and their labels handwritten.

There is a park lined with trees that are painted white around the base of the trunk, like others around the island; and pockets of green spaces with grass patches in geometric patterns. Perhaps as a nod to the weather, and to the practicality of walking being how most people get around, there are green benches around town so you can sit and watch life go by: Young girls in bright hijabs that have rhinestones, fishermen with their catch, people cruising on mopeds, and school children running back home or going to the mosque in groups.

Most of the town's people are Bantu. Some, like my landlady, look like more diverse versions of Ilha's heritage, which includes Arabic sultans who counted the island among their conquests along the Swahili coast – from the island through Tanzania and Kenya, to Somalia. The island is still Muslim.

I'm in an unlikely tropical paradise. Even if it's one that smells like crap, with grandiose houses that time has turned into crumbling ruins; it's one of the most beautiful places I've been to.

The houses in Macuti Town are built with mud and palm roofs. There are kiosks that pack groceries, baby clothes, toys, drinks, plumbing pipes and more into little dim rooms, and street corners where people sell bread. I take my place in the line for bread.

A man sits outside a house with coral pink walls that have brown dirt stains at the foundation. He sells hot rolls from a bamboo basket with a wide mouth. While we wait our turn in line, a woman in a white doek and yellow wrap stands next to him to put her bread in a sack. By now, the town is fully awake. The market is in full swing. Piles of second-hand clothing have been laid on the ground. People who sell vegetables, mostly shiny tomatoes and okra, sit across from them, their produce arranged in pyramids. Some people sell fish and rice. I'm minding my business along the waterfront when I notice a girl undoing her braids in the middle of the road.

'Excuse me. Shouldn't you sit on the pavement?' She's younger than me, so I can play big sister.

'It's not like a car is going to drive by,' she laughs.

I help her undo her hair for a while and then, after promising to meet outside the hospital for lunch before I leave for Nampula, I continue my walking tour.

In Nampula, I stand at a T-junction unbothered that the sun is setting on the horizon with no sign of any bus. I sit and eat fried prawn kebabs. Later, after the area starts to empty out, Alberto from the house across the street comes over to ask me about my plans. He says there are no buses for long distances other than at 5am. He offers me a place to sleep.

For most of the night, we sit outside, under the skies, with his grandmother and cousins, listening to Marrabenta songs. At dinner, we eat rice and a watery fish stew from one large enamel dish. When bedtime comes, and the cousins roll out their sleeping mats on the porch to escape the hot bedrooms, I lay my kanga on the floor and fold a pair of jeans into a pillow.

Alberto wakes me up 4am and offers me a glass of water, toothpaste and a bowl of water to wash my body. I'd rather miss the bus and spend another day in Nampula than wake up.

He wakes me up again at 6.30am. His friend Mohammed is thirty minutes away. He's a truck driver on his way from Maputo to pick up goods on a route that passes through Nampula and Pemba. The truck is empty and Alberto needs to transport industrial plastic drums and copper wires. Our lift is called Phoenix – a big, sleek chrome machine fitted with a three-quarter bed behind the front seat. There's a side table and a small basin. I sleep most of the way to Pemba, getting up when Mohammed and Alberto stop for breakfast. Mine is tea and hot bread.

It only occurs to me when I'm fully awake that I'm in a truck with strange men, in a place I don't know. It's too late to think this plan through. I lie back on the bed and read while the guys converse in Portuguese.

The trip features what are becoming usual snapshots of tropical villages – people running after cars when they slow down, selling baskets full of mangoes, bananas and cashews. In Pemba, Alberto walks me to the minibuses parked along the road to find one to the beach front. He refuses payment for the lift and gives the driver money for my trip.

A brief hug, and we become a memory.

The driver drops me off at a junction with a casino, telling me that there are no chapas to Russel's campsite, less than a kilometre from here.

Walking through thick sand with a head that's becoming dizzy from the sun, and people who drive past when I flag their empty bakkies, I feel like I'm trekking across the Sahara. The result is a heat rash that covers my whole face and body, making me look like a rough-cast wall.

Pemba has three faces. The city centre with three ATMs, one each for First National Bank, Barclay's and Standard Bank, an internet café, one big supermarket and streets lined by hawkers; there's the village of mud huts, and the shoreline that's not made for play, where fishermen and villagers hang out.

Tourists and expats live it up at Wimbi beach; the playground of my favourite side of Pemba, with waterfront mansions, five-star hotels and less expensive ones across the road from the beach. The sea is clear and light blue close to the beach, with light turquoise pools, and gets darker as it stretches on. Kids bathe and play in the water. Seagulls swoop, a topless sunbather lies on his stomach. He is wearing a black fedora and reading a book. A beach boy with jet-black dreadlocks and strings of beads on his wrists sells necklaces with cowrie-shell pendants and bracelets made with red, blue and green plastic beads. Kayaks are drying on poles suspended across palm trees.

Further up the beach, where the surface juts with sharp, jagged rocks, groups of women pick shells they put in plastic basins. Some of them work in pairs to pull green nets across the water. All feet are in flip flops, and pagnes are gathered and tied at the knees so they don't get wet. A man is waist deep in the water with his net. Kids pick at a bed of rocks. Towards sunset, Wimbi beach is no longer the exclusive turf of swimmers, sunbathers and beach boys – a group of boys take off their T-shirts and plant sticks in the sand to mark out a makeshift soccer pitch. A long game of soccer ensues, where goals are celebrated with back flips and dips in the sea.

Couples stroll hand in hand, the water fills up with black bodies, and girls walk around selling peanuts and other snacks.

Walking around the beach, I see a growing crowd at the parking lot. I follow it to find a circle surrounding a guitarist who scrunches his face as he plays and sings. While everyone in the crowd of tourists and locals smile, a young boy watches with folded arms, looking bored.

I start feeling restless after a few days in Pemba, and find my next adventure by putting my pencil on the map and going where it lands.

The tougher the trip, the greater the satisfaction of being at my destination. Take Ibo, in the Quirimbas Islands. My trip starts at 5am in Pemba at the back of an open chapa that drives around town several times until there isn't any room left for more people and the bags and the sacks of rice, bananas and peanuts they jump in with. One man has five live chickens.

When we finally get going, it's mostly on roads that leave us covered in thick layers of dust.

The eight-hour trip ends at the village of Tandanhangue, where we wait until 4pm when one of two boats that connect Ibo and the mainland arrives. The only restaurant sells cold tea, hard homemade biscuits and hot Fanta Orange. The only drinking water is muddy, with bits floating in it. I hang out with Joia, who I meet in the chapa. The male nurse breaks my heart when he reveals that there are no ATMs in Ibo, and that the only budget hotel, Miti Miwiri – after the two trees in the yard – only works with cash. He mends it by offering me a room at his house.

When the boat arrives, we wade in the water to get to it. There are four other people with us. An old man in a newsboy cap grins at me the entire journey.

There's a woman caught between her crying toddler and restless chicken, and the boat's captain. We're surrounded by swamps of mangrove forests that you can walk to from Ibo when the tide is low.

We dock at a pier that's really just a small concrete slab, with plastic tables and five chairs, and an extension cord connected to an unseen source of electricity.

The path to Joia's house is overrun with weeds. Ibo has white-washed coral-themed five-star beachfront hotels with walls that are covered in bright pink bougainvillea, where you can drink US$15 cocktails while looking out at the sea.

Ibo is stuck in an exotic time warp of buildings that crumble, some with tree trunks in the walls. The beachfront hotels are the only places that have power round the clock. The rest of the island is powered by generators that start running at 4.30pm.

Home is a commune Joia shares with two teachers. Meals are rice and crab curry or fish stew. Entertainment is hanging out at Miti Miwiri at night to charge our phones and dance with aid workers who are here for a conference.

Kids take turns to go to school in the mornings and afternoons. When they're not in class, their heads are buried in their books on their patios at home.

The younger ones run after me asking to pose for pictures. I relent. Their friends ask for pictures as well – rinse and repeat, replete with kung fu poses. Ibo, for the monied, offers nature walks, dolphin safaris, birding, scuba diving and island hopping; I can only afford to walk and visit the Fort of São João Baptista, which housed slaves, the Cowrie house which is named after the beads that cover it and the Igreja de Nossa Senhora do Rosário Catholic church.

The island feels small after two days.

Joia asks his Maputo-bound boss to give me a lift to Pemba. We leave on a speed boat and drive to Pemba in a Land Cruiser.

My twenty-first and last day in Moz starts in a daze. I stumble out of Brazuca bar at 5am after a wild night with a South African whose parents are turning a barren island into a paradise getaway. I walk to the ATM to get cash, and quit my place in the line when a policeman offers me a lift on his moped. The bus has already passed my stop. It has my bags; spending another day in Pemba is not an option. He makes several calls before finding the driver's number. When we catch up with the bus, my seat is already taken. An old woman offers me a seat on her sack in the aisle. I move to a free seat when it becomes available and sleep my way to Mocimboa da Praia. The driver doesn't understand a word of English. He leaves me at a drinking hole where he finds someone who speaks enough English to tell me how to reach the Tanzanian border.

The fellows take a break from their beers to take me to the junction where I catch the chapa to Namoto border. My ass, dressed in granny panties, sticks out in the air when I hop in. There's no place to sit in the chairs and the floor. I squat over some legs and hold on to parcels for support. Rami offers me his seat. Another passenger gives me her kanga, which I use as a cover when the dust starts rising.

Mozambican uniforms are notorious for demanding bribes. The only time this happens to me is at the Namoto office. They don't even examine our passports and travel documents. A uniform walks people to an office; no doubt to demand more money than what they put on the table. When my turn comes, I show them my stories and threaten to complain to their Minister of Tourism through an open letter. They believe me, and I become a legend for being the only person who doesn't pay to leave the country.

We get back on the road, to the banks of Ruvuma River and wait for the boat with scores of people and goods that include storage boxes and a mini fridge. The boat drops us off at a sand bank where the Tanzanian leg of the trip starts. Today's sunset casts a purple hue over a horizon dotted with acacia trees; hippo and crocodile snouts break the surface of the water. The effects of last night's tequila shots are out of my body, and I remember that I didn't withdraw money for the trip. Rami pays for my boat rides and the dala dala to the Kilambo border post. The office is closed and the only uniforms on duty are the security guards at the boom gate. One of them offers to call the man who runs the immigration office so we don't spend the night at Kilambo.

The uniform arrives in a crisp yellow shirt and brown pants with a freshly ironed pleat. He's polite and efficient and never asks anyone for a bribe. I keep moving to the back of the line until I'm the last person left in the office. A Tanzanian visa is US$50. Rami looks uncomfortable when I ask for a loan I will repay when we get to an ATM.

'Kaka, hakuna pesa,' I say in broken Swahili, calling him brother in the hopes that this and using his mother tongue will make him more open to my suggestion. I want to leave my passport and continue to the nearest ATM in Mtwara. 'I will return in the morning to pay for my visa, tafadhali,' I explain, using the Swahili word for please. He says I have to retrace my steps by more than one hundred kilometres to Mocimboa da Praia. It's too late to find transport to Mozambique, and in any case, there's no way I'm going back. We run around in circles until he starts walking to the door.

'I guess you're sleeping here, then,' he says.

'I don't have money for a hotel,' I retort. 'Maybe I can leave my passport and laptop?' I try again.

'That's not how it works,' he says. He pages through my passport and laughs that I have many visa stamps yet lack the common sense to never arrive at border crossings without cash. 'Fine,' I say, suddenly nonchalant about my predicament. 'I guess I'm sleeping at your house tonight, but tell me something, what are you going to say to your wife when you show up with this?' I unwrap my kanga to show the little black dress that shows my thighs and cleavage.

'You don't have to leave your laptop here but the passport is staying. Make sure you are back here by 10am,' he says.

'Asante sana. Thank you,' I say, my voice sweet as honey again.

In Mtwara, Rami and I hop from bank to bank looking for an ATM that works. The cheapest hotel he finds is a run-down place owned by a Senegalese man. I backtrack to Kilambo in the morning and then back to Mtwara to catch the bus to Dar es Salaam.

June 2010

The loud, crowded Ubongo bus terminal in Dar es Salaam packs hundreds of buses that cough out plumes of black smoke into its small space. A tout snatches my bags and trots to the exit without waiting for me or finding out where I want to go. He minds my bags while I look for a dala dala to Posta; the landmark I use to get to the Young Women's Christian Association.

Unlike the YWCA in Accra, and the permanent scar it leaves in my memory, this house of God doesn't have suffocating rules. They allow male and female borders but no couples. The nuns who run it don't judge our revealing clothes or police our movements. The walls between the rooms are made with boards, making me privy to my neighbour's phone conversation about how gratifying it is to 'spread joy in Africa', he says with a heavy American twang.

'The project didn't work but, you know, we went there with sweets and stuff, and seeing those poor African kids smiling because we gave them lollipops made a difference, like wow, dude.'

I remind myself to keep staying away from Westerners and their condescending attitudes.

Wandering around the city centre, I see people jumping in and out of overcrowded dala dalas with windscreens proclaiming Allah's greatness and blessings. Most women wear burkas and school girls sweep the ground with their skirts. Vendors sell boiled eggs from plastic buckets, peanuts and sweets from boxes and water from wheeled cooler boxes. Men and boys walk around selling strong black coffee from metal kettles that are fitted with round zinc contraptions filled with hot coals. The coffee is served in a small oval ceramic cup.

There's wonder in walking around Dar. Markets explode with colour from fruit and cloth, the sound of car horns mingles with the Swahili that rolls off tongues like a melody, and streets are lined with people selling papaya, pineapples, mangoes, black-skinned avocados and coffee, always. No one gawks at me and the touts I meet at tourist landmarks don't make me repeat myself when I tell them I'm not interested in what they're selling or in the mood to party with them in the evening. One of the many things I love about travelling alone is that I can withdraw and stay in my head for as long as I want to. I'm not in a talkative mood in Dar.

At the forex bureau I go to to change the Zambian kwachas and meticals to Tanzanian shillings, the only people in the multiracial room who don't speak Swahili are myself and a Malawian man. I'm not used to people who aren't black speaking local languages as a rule instead of an exception. In this regard, Dar es Salaam thrills me.

Waiting in line at an ATM, we're joined by a Maasai man wrapped in a shuka; a dagger dangles from the leather pouch on his waist. More than turning what used to be blots on the map into places I know with all my senses, my travels are also an affirmation of my blackness. They give me the opportunity to experience being black and African without disguising or denying myself to fit in. If this were South Africa, the Masaai man would have to wait until Heritage Day in September to dress like this in public, or be on his way to a traditional event.

Kigamboni Ferry Terminal comes with a reputation for pick-pocketers and fast-talking touts who steal money by claiming to be ticketing agents. My cabby drives slowly into the parking lot and rolls up the window to block out touts who are already running next to us.

'Remember to be careful,' he says when he leaves me at the ticket office. A man I have not seen until now grunts at me and puts my bag on his shoulder, making me shove my way through the large crowd waiting to walk into the ferry. When he finally talks to me, it's to say pesa – money – with his palm turned upwards. He leaves me in the dim, sweltering lounge with red seats. It smells like samosas and popcorn and sounds like a crèche from the kids playing in the aisles.

I walk to the deck to watch Dar fading into specks of low-rise buildings. Men lean on the rails to smoke. I jump around people sitting on the floor to find my place among them. One of the corners is packed with boxes of live chicks. I wedge myself next to a mother and her two kids. They make room for me on their plastic mat. Like every woman who is not a tourist, she is dressed in a burka. Hers is plain; others have sequinned collars. The scarves they use to cover their faces have been removed. Their daughters are also dressed religiously.

All faces around me offer a history of Zanzibar at a glance, their African and mixed heritage that comes from Persians and the Portuguese conquerors who stopped over to trade ivory, slaves and spices, and stuck around to rule the Indian Ocean coast from northern Mozambique to Somalia.

Stonetown comes into view with white clouds tumbling over two church towers and the round minaret of a mosque. Dhows carrying sacks of goods sail past yachts. Boats that are not in use have been left in the water sans sails. There are cargo ships, and a dock packed with office-sized containers.

The women gather their bags and children, and fix their burkas.

Meet Africa's most relentless touts – the papasi. It's the Swahili word for ticks. Like the pests, they hang on to me from when I walk out of the port, rushing over to offer organising taxis, accommodation, sunset cruises and a trip to Prison Island. Taxi drivers join the swarm around me. I walk over to an old man leaning against his bicycle. He charges me 100 shillings to carry my bags to the hotel.

I walk behind him as he pushes my bags through alleys with weird angles that make walking around them feel like being in a maze. I catch glimpses of women in long burkas that sweep the ground behind them, school boys in white tunics and skull caps, and thin cats scavenging for food.

Old mamas flatten balls of dough into chapatis they fry on iron-cast pans. Curio shops hang Maasai necklaces and Tingatinga paintings of stick people and sunsets on their doors. Kiosks sell rice and beans from buckets left on stoeps. A chorus of 'karibu sana' follows me.

Stonetown still evokes its grand old days with wide mahogany and teak doors decorated with engraved patterns and brass spikes. After checking into Pearl Guest House and using a shared shower, I hit the streets to look for food and an internet café, and get lost in its maze until I end up at the beach.

It's almost sunset, and the town's people are making their way to Forodhani Gardens. The setting sun is dark orange and sits low on the horizon. The sea and buildings behind us radiate with its colour. Families, couples and groups of friends walk around the gardens; some stop to get a drink or ice cream at the kiosks or to watch the daily sunset show put on by boys who perform acrobatics to jump into the ocean; the boys in Zanzibar are fish in water.

Further down, people set up tables for the daily food market. I walk over to a man with a juicer. It's a coral blue steel contraption with two rollers he presses by spinning the attached wheel. He presses the sugar cane until all its cloudy juice flows through a silver furrow to a red bucket with a block of ice. He pours it into a jug, adds fresh lime juice and some ginger. My drink in hand, I roam around the tables considering my meal options. There's king fish and lobster. Juicy beef kebabs are piled next to tandoori chicken pieces that are pink from the spice used to cook them. The fat mussels entice me as much as the prawns, tuna steaks and octopus. Mountains of sweet potatoes and stumpy chips compete for a place on my plate with stacks of chapati and fluffy coconut bread with sesame seeds.

I walk to a table that only deals in the local speciality: The Zanzibar pizza. The vendor flattens a ball of dough into a paper-thin base. His deft hands get another ball he layers into the base. He spoons mince meat that's mixed with chopped onions and green peppers on the base and adds a spoonful of soft, processed cheese before cracking an egg into the mixture. He adds a dab of mayonnaise before mixing the fillings and folding the base into a square. He tops it with another layer of dough and cooks it until it's brown. It's also served as dessert with Nutella and bananas.

I walk back to the tables with the seafood, making small talk with the vendors in Afrikaans, for a plate of coconut bread, chips, shark kebabs and king fish. I sit with other diners on smooth, concrete benches and think about how lucky I am that I get to have moments like these, when I can eat like the Motsepes in South Africa on a shoestring budget. I really pity black life in South Africa. We think we are better than the rest of the continent, yet our life lacks flavour and creativity. The only thing we do with sugar cane is eat it, and until your money moves you from working to middle class, the only fish on your plate is hake, canned pilchards, canned tuna, and river fish if you're lucky.

I get lost again on my way back to the hotel. The alleys lead to dead ends or into homes where I walk in on families getting on with their evening rituals. I follow one of my favourite smells, that of bread that's still baking in the oven, until I end up in Darajani Street. It's almost 11pm, and the few tables that are still serving chapati and tea are being packed up. The vendor offers to walk me to my hotel, which turns out to be nearby. I order sweet, milky spice tea – masala chai – and make conversation in my growing Swahili vocabulary; the music changes from Bongo Flava to a Lucky Dube compilation when I mention my nationality.

I wake up to the sound of the muezzin calling the town's mostly Muslim population to Fajr. I open the wooden window to look at the square; men dressed in white, cream and dark grey tunics walk slowly on their way to the mosque. I go back to bed. My sleep ends when I hear the faint sounds of someone beating on a piece of metal. Back to the window I go, and discover that the sound comes from boys who jiggle coins while selling loose cigarettes and peanuts. Shops are opening for business, men pull boxes of water and other goods on makeshift wheelbarrows. An old man sits on a stoep at the square with a flask and small porcelain cups. Kahawa, as coffee is called in Swahili, is the island's favourite drink.

This is my second trip to Zanzibar. The first is a weekend media trip by Metro FM as part of their travels to broadcast some shows from around Africa. I spend the weekend hungry and frustrated by the oh-so-slow pace of life. Things only get done eventually here. Walk at a quick pace and people urge you to walk 'pole pole', or 'slowly slowly'. Ask when things will be done and the Zanzibari will tell you Inshallah. If you want things to happen right now, like I do, you'll hear, 'haraka haraka haina baraka', which loosely translates into doing things in haste will make you miss your blessings. I'm back to appease the guilt: I cannot accept that I hate one of the most beautiful places I have been to.

I start my day by retracing the steps I took in 2006. From the hotel, I turn right into a passage so narrow that our bodies touch when we walk past each other. The shops sell perfume, soccer shirts, burkas and kofia. Old men sit behind small tables fixing watches or drinking coffee. Darajani market is a long white building and spills over into the streets around it as well. It's teeming with tables selling fresh produce, packets of spices, soaps and oils made with turmeric, rose water, ylang-ylang, aloe, clove, coconut and lemon grass. The aroma of spices like nutmeg, vanilla and cinnamon mixes with the smell of incense. The sound of people haggling over prices is muffled by clucking chickens and hooters.

Vendors display different types of rice, beans and lentils from baskets, their names written on cardboard in Swahili. The produce section displays pyramids of shiny red tomatoes, red onions, potatoes and brinjals, a selection of apples, pineapples, papaya, green-skinned oranges and mangoes. The dark avocados are bigger than my hands, granadillas have yellow skin and bananas come in three sizes: Sweet ones that look like giant thumbs on their stalks, long and thick ones that are green or yellow, and the ones with red skins that are said to do the same job as viagra.

There are a lot of things I've never seen before, like soursop, jackfruit, dried octopus and fresh ones that end up in a coconut curry served on basmati or jasmine rice, and on street corners sold in deep-fried bite-sized pieces called bitings. The fish market is in a long room with wet floors covered with scales, splashes of blood and bits of fish gut. Fish mongers slap their catch against the ceramic or concrete work stations. Some cut whole fish into pieces. Cats hover around, as usual. Large groups of men gather around the newspaper stands to read front-page news. Most of the newspapers are in Swahili.

There are tables with dates packed into airtight plastic bags or see-through containers. Men who sell coconuts sit on the floor, hacking and shaving them with machetes; they serve these with a straw. I drink my coconut water next to a vendor and give the fruit to him when I'm done so he can scrape the flesh for me. There are shops and vendors selling kitenge and kangas, the colourful pieces of cloth that are bought for their patterns and the messages written on their hemline. I buy several, including a yellow one with Barack Obama's face on it and the words 'Hongera Barack Obama'; congratulations Barack Obama. I cool down with homemade tamarind juice from a man who sells it by the glass from a bucket near a dala dala station.

The market is the only part of my morning that works out. The rest of my plans fall apart when I get lost along the way to the Slave Market. I give up on asking for directions and follow different groups of tourists to eavesdrop on walking tours that show them the town's 'famous historical doors' that date back from the time of sultans. Some of them are as old as Stonetown. The group I join at

St Joseph's Cathedral speaks Italian. I wander off, dodging papasi trying to sell me tours, then packets of spices when I say no to their trips. I stumble into a square called Jaws Corner. The walls of the buildings are painted with a shark or plastered with posters of politicians campaigning for votes in upcoming elections. There's a wall with a TV stand. Groups of men sit on the stoeps or lean against their bicycles drinking coffee and ginger tea, or playing bao, a traditional game that involves moving seeds around eight holes. Other than the old woman who sells the tea, I'm the only woman, and this bothers some men.

The old man I buy my coffee from scolds them, and tells me to sit next to him. They're angry that I'm invading their space; even worse, I'm dressed to reveal my legs and thighs in a short dress. Women here still cover themselves from head to toe in public.

I walk back to Darajani street to get a dala dala to Nungwi, where the island's strict dress code is reinforced by a hand-painted board of a woman in a bikini. A red cross covers her body.

Zanzibar lives up to every cliché of a paradise island, with soft beach sand and sea water that comes in various shades of turquoise. The women's kangas flutter in the warm breeze. On the way back to town, we pick up an old man lying on a stretcher made with a bamboo mat pinned to bamboo poles. His body twists with pain, his pink lips frothing with saliva whenever he howls, which happens every time we hit a speed bump.

Day three, morning two and I still get lost around Stonetown, so I make my way to the beach by following cars instead of walking around the alleys. I end up at Tembo Hotel, where the barman lets me lounge on the beach furniture even though it's reserved for guests. He gives me ice for the drinking water I arrive with and lets me buy cool drinks at a kiosk instead of paying tourist prices at their hotel. He looks after my bag while I splash in the ocean and sometimes buys me cool drink from the bar. He always says 'karibu tena' when he serves. It means 'welcome again'. Tonight's dinner is a discovery that will keep me coming back to Zanzibar. Urojo is a yellow soup I've seen around Stonetown's alleys, food markets and on stalls along the main roads. It's on lone tables set under trees on random streets during the day and outside people's houses at night. Tangy with a hint of heat, it's made with flour, grated raw mango, garlic paste, chilli powder, fresh chillies, boiled potatoes cut into bite-sized cubes, turmeric and coconut milk. It's topped with kebabs, lentil fritters, crunchy potato shavings and a splash of coconut chutney made by adding grated mango, chillies and lime juice. I eat urojo several times a day during my stay.

My search for a room to rent starts outside the post office in Shangani, which should also be known as Papasi Central. When I refuse their offers to organise jaunts, they try to sell me Tingatinga paintings and packets of spices. I stand quietly, listening to a guy singing a tune from a compilation of folk songs he's selling. His crusty lips and ashen face make him look like a crack junkie.

'Jambo, jambo bwana, habari gani? Muzuri sana. Wageni, Wakaribishwa. Zanzibar yetu hakuna matata,' he croaks. It translates into something along the lines of 'welcome, welcome sir. How are you? Very well. Welcome to our Zanzibar, where there are no problems.'

He tells me to go to the big tree close to Mercury Bar; the men there will know what to do with my request. One of them gives me a phone number with the repeated instruction to only call it at night. I call Star minutes later. He agrees to meet me at Babu Chai's stall that evening.

'Do you know why they call me Star?' he says when we meet.

'I only come out at night; never call me during the day again.'

We find a place on Aisha's property. Her family lives on the first floor. I can live with them, which is cheaper but comes with having to abide by family rules, or I can rent the apartment on the ground floor. My kitchen is more of a micro kitchen, with only room for a sink, a cupboard and floating shelves with pots, a pan, plates, cups and glasses, and a two-plate gas stove. I have hot water, a lounge with a hard three-seater couch and an even harder armchair. The dining room has a rectangular table with six chairs, everything in mahogany, and a shelf with a German-Swahili dictionary. I put my books next to it. The bedrooms are my favourite for their traditional four-poster beds with stained glass on the head board.

Nyumba yangu. My house, in Hurumzi, where I can invite people over for tea so that when they're at the door, they can say 'hodi' to ask if they can come in, and I can reply with 'karibuni' to let them know they're welcome; just as I pictured it in my head when I learnt about greetings in Swahili in my guidebook.

With a new life comes new touches to old habits. Now when I go to the fish market, it's to get three tuna steaks, which I can buy for R15. I can also make my own masala chai by boiling tea and milk with a premixed chai spice made by blending ginger, cinnamon, cardamom, cloves, nutmeg and black pepper.

The only problem I have with my house comes from my hopeless sense of direction. I always get lost on my way home, meaning all trips back start at the post office to find a papasi willing to walk with me until we find my landmark – the soccer goal post painted on the wall opposite the property's main entrance.

One of them is a boy who regales me with wild tales of trekking to South Africa on trucks when he can find a lift, and on his feet when no one stops for him. His eyes glisten when he gets to the part where he jumps over a fence at night, his heart beating with the excitement of making it to South Africa and the anxiety of walking into wild animals. He spends a few months in Joburg working as a street barber to raise money to go to Cape Town, where he sneaks onto a cargo ship on its way to Europe. He's discovered in the broiler and sent to jail, then back to Dar es Salaam. He ekes out a living selling Tingatinga paintings that no one buys.

One afternoon at Africa House while treating myself to my favourite cocktail, the dawa, made by muddling vodka with honey and fresh lime juice, a white woman walks in with a pet monkey that runs around the bar before settling next to the barman. It's my cue to leave.

I walk across the road to hang out with a group of dudes sitting under and on a tree. A road sign reminds drivers to drive slowly. 'Endesha pole pole', it reads, repeating the island's favourite word, pole pole. The house next to us is falling apart, and the only thing to see are the boys getting high on heroin or the one who always sits alone on the stoep to read his Quran.

This is where I meet Ali, who tells me from the branch he's sitting on that he has seen me swim. He offers to turn me into a fish in water. We start our lessons at the beach next to the old house, where he misses the afternoon soccer games to help me. The game pauses for prayer time.

Ali and I meet every morning for two or more hours before going our separate ways. Occasionally, we hang out at the café where he introduces me to avocado juice. It's another thing I don't know until I visit Zanzibar. We also hang out at Stereya, a local joint with beach boys dressed in tropical shirts, their locks tucked into wool hats with Rasta colours. I love Stereya for the yard with coral blue walls, cheap Kilimanjaro beers and Maasai men in full traditional clothes with starry-eyed holiday squeezes on their arms. When I'm not here for the cheap and delicious plates of basmati rice served with fried cabbage and red bean stew cooked with coconut cream, I'm at the jukebox lining up a playlist with 'Thank You Mr DJ', 'Weekend

Special', 'Do Me', 'Yori Yori' and 'Falling in Love': Ghana and Nigeria meeting South Africa in East Africa. Hakuna matata indeed.

It's the morning of 11 June 2010. The World Cup fever that infects every place I've been to finally catches up with me. I go to Dennis's curio shop next to the Gallery Bookshop. I wait for him to finish sweeping so he can help me find a vuvuzela and my national flag. We walk to the old town across from Darajani Market, going into every shop that sells Euro soccer jerseys and soccer balls, and always leave empty-handed. One shop owner ends my search by telling me that it's foolish to leave the home of the vuvuzela empty-handed hoping to find it thousands of kilometres away.

It still doesn't kill my buzz, though: My friend Violet is arriving today to start her new life in Zanzibar, while her husband, Tshepo, takes up a post in Dar es Salaam. They've also been bitten by the African travel bug, and used to live at Nkatha Bay on the shores of Lake Malawi. She fell in love with Zanzibar while attending Sauti za Busara, a music festival that celebrates African music in all its diversity and being trapped here after a power failure that lasted weeks, making it impossible to access money.

We meet at Mercury Bar, where we catch up on what's happened in our lives in the two years since we've seen each other. Violet walks outside to buy smokes, and runs back to the table giddy. 'You won't believe who I found outside.' Her voice is filled with wonder. An old woman whose woolly, white hair is covered by a loose pink chiffon scarf catches up with Violet. It's Bi Kidude. I've been looking for her for weeks; walking around Stonetown, going around the island asking people if they've seen her. The answer has always been no, followed by 'you'll know when she's around'.

Other than the Amazons of Dahomey, the nineteenth-century female army who would sooner cut off their breasts than lose a battle, the three women I admire more than others are Winnie Madikizela-Mandela for bringing apartheid to its knees, Miriam Makeba for her politics, activism and treating husbands like property she can acquire and discard at will when society says marriage is the be all and end all of a woman's life, and Bi Kidude. No one knows for sure when Bi was born, only that it was when the island still used rupees as currency. Bi has always wanted to be a singer like her hero, Siti binti Saadi. Against the odds set by her conservative society where women needed a man's permission to even leave the house, the legend around her life goes, Bi disguised herself as a man to get on a boat to Dar es Salaam. She became a global star in the 1980s, when her hair was already grey. She still performs around the world and she's known for long walks in Stonetown. She slouches on a chair at our table, pulls out a box of cigarettes and orders a hot Kilimanjaro beer. We order pizza and watch South Africa play against Mexico.

Violet's Swahili is enough to keep the conversation flowing. It's the only language Bi speaks, and she is genuinely shocked that I'm black and not fluent in Swahili. She's back in town for a few weeks of rehearsals and I'm welcome to drop in provided I keep my mouth shut, seeing as I don't speak Swahili.

Violet stays with me, and I move in with her at her friends Abbas and Sophia's place a week later when my lease at Aisha's ends. Before Violet, life is great but it doesn't have female friends. When I try to befriend a woman I meet at an internet café, hoping that her recent arrival from Harare will bond us, she's polite but refuses to meet me for tea.

'It's as if I have a scarlet sign on my forehead that tells women to stay away from me,' I complain to Violet and Sophia.

'Haven't you noticed that all local women are conservative and you are not?' Violet says. 'The way you dress is as good as having a scarlet sign.'

This explains why some males, including boys, snarl at me. The daring ones, like a man who confronts me at the market and a boy who tries to fix the kaftan, yell at me to my face. I kick the man in his stomach, and pull the boy by his ear until it turns red.

'My name is Lerato, not Fatma,' I hiss after putting the fear of God and ancestors in their hearts.

I leave Zanzibar at the beginning of July to catch the rest of the World Cup in South Africa. Violet has turned Southern Africa into her stomping ground. She suggests going to Zambia aboard the Tazara, and uses her Swahili to buy my ferry ticket back to Dar at a Tanzanian price instead of a tourist one.

I sail away knowing that my return is not a question of if; it's a matter of when. And I do visit again in 2012 to attend Sauti za Busara, where I'm enthralled by the eclectic line up of artists from around the region and Africa. This edition is headlined by Nneka and Tumi and The Volume. Even at the after party held in Kendwa a day after the festival ends, the music is strictly African and just as varied as the shows at the main events. I return to Zanzibar again in 2016 to attend Busara with my partner and tick swimming with dolphins off my bucket list. More than anything, I keep coming back for urojo.

July 2010

The Tazara is a train that runs between Dar es Salaam and Kapiri Mphosi, two hundred and eight kilometres north of Lusaka. It's the slowest way to travel between Tanzania and Zambia, but what it lacks in speed it makes up for by going through the Selous Game Reserve, where, Violet promises me, I'm bound to spot some game. I overlook its reputation for breakdowns.

I catch the train on a good day, when it leaves Dar es Salaam on time. The crew comes into our cabin to deliver blankets, sheets, pillow cases, soap bars and a roll of toilet paper. My cabin mates are a demure Amina and Mama Anna. The only time Mama Anna is not talking is when she is sleeping. I go to the toilets to assess my dietary options. There's an overpowering stench of industrial bleach and the toilet bowl is clean. The bucket next to it is filled with water: It's safe to eat solid meals.

I split my waking hours between the restaurant and the cabin. On the first night, I go to the restaurant to look for backpackers to swop stories with. I hide out there on my second day when Amina disembarks in Mbeya; the south-eastern town that connects Tanzania to Mozambique and Malawi. Amina's departure gives Mama Anna more room to put the sacks of rice, dried fish, bundles of green bananas and other stuff she buys whenever we stop. It also turns me into the only audience for her never-ending stories. The only time we have a serious breakdown is at the Tanzanian side of the Tunduma border crossing. We wait for more than an hour for repairs.

Everything about the trip, from the scenery and the food at the restaurant to the exit and entry between the two countries, is pleasant. We arrive in Kapiri Mposhi on Sunday night; only a few hours later than the expected time of arrival.

I continue to the Intercity bus terminal in Lusaka by minibus. The terminal becomes a real hive in the morning. Two women set up stalls selling ankara cloth. Some people have already taken their places on benches outside a café next to the police station and others who spent the night at the terminal form a line outside the bathroom; waiting our turn to use the showers.

Intercity connects Lusaka to capital cities and towns in East, Central and Southern Africa. It makes selling tickets a fierce competition. Destinations are written in bold letters or beamed on screens. Bookers Express's tagline says they're 'Recognized for putting customers first.' CR Holdings Time Buses catches attention with a board that has departure times next to each destination. The right side of the board has vertical letters that spell 'DAILY' in white letters with black stripes. The bus for Johannesburg leaves at midday.

I'm going home to feel the fever of the World Cup. Just like I do in the first half of 2010, I'm based in Pretoria and travel to neighbouring countries when I miss the road. When I go to Harare to visit Johannes, whom I meet on the flight from Accra to Johannesburg, I find a city that's trapped in a 1990s time warp; *Waiting to Exhale* is on at the cinema. Harare is a pretty city, with jacarandas in full bloom and sparkling swimming pools. It's not the Harare of the first years of independence, when Zimbabwe is called the bread basket of Southern Africa, but it's also not a city where only misery lives, as the *Sunday Times* newspaper has been saying for many years. The shelves at Spar are piled high with goods, the cooked food section has a long line of people waiting to buy sadza and stew with muriwo, as kale is called, the streets around the taxi rank and bus station are lined with vendors who sell piles of bananas, oranges and apples. At the Harare gardens, families and couples picnic on the manicured lawns, and children lick trails of melting ice cream from their forearms.

On Sunday afternoon, Johannes and his friends take me partying to a downtown bar that's packed with patrons; there is no sense of doom or the gloom South African media says are the only things to experience in Zimbabwe. We clink our bottles of Heineken, toast to Harare's comeback and dance to 1980s R&B. The only time I feel the city's financial problems is on Monday morning when I walk from ATM to ATM in the business district until I find one that hasn't run out of the American dollars that have long replaced Zimbabwean currency.

From Harare, I travel by bus to Blantyre in Malawi, to catch a bus to Nkatha Bay. Violet and Tshepo lived here before relocating to Stonetown and Dar es Salaam. She insists that without visiting Malawi my travels will lack a dash of magic that can only be found along the shores of Lake Malawi.

My stay at Butterfly Lodge is the most romantic time of my life. I arrive at dawn and wait a while for a taxi to take me up the hill to Butterfly Lodge. Here, ecotourism and leaving a positive mark on the community are a philosophy. There's a heap of compost that we take fruit and vegetable peels to. There are toilets with running water but, unlike the pit toilet, they don't have a view of the scuba divers playing in the crystal clear Lake Malawi as it flows to the horizon.

I get a discount rate on my chalet when I volunteer to work at Gulugufe crèche. It's one of several community programmes initiated by the proprietors of the lodge. I'm 'Madamu' Lerato in the mornings at Gulugufe, where I sometimes run out of my class after the roll call for giggles that turn into loud laughs; the kids in the village have names that come from the Bible, and mostly the Old Testament. I cannot believe that, in 2010, there are still people in Africa whose lives are just starting with names like Abraham, Daniel, Ruth, Esther, Isaac and Solomon. I'm Sister Lerato in the afternoons when the artists who run curio shops along the stony road discover that I'm friends with Tshepo and Violet. I look forward to laundry day, when I wash my clothes at the lodge and give them a final rinse in the lake. I swim after items that float away. I'm a regular tea guest to parents who want to show their appreciation to people who work at the preschool and people with family members in South Africa. I've always had wanderlust but could not think of anything more boring to do with my time than to spend it in Southern Africa. Malawi – the warm heart of Africa as its people call the country – makes me fall in love with the region.

Wherever I am in Southern Africa, I always make my way back to South Africa by taking a bus to Mozambique, where I spend a night or two in places like Tete and Xai Xai before continuing to Maputo to get a bus to Pretoria. Mozambique is one of the most beautiful places in Africa, and now that I know how cheap it is for a Southern African to experience, I can't get enough of it and the early morning walks on the beaches and hot evenings dancing with strangers who treat me like a lifelong friend.

XIII

GOING TO UGANDA

November 2010

I'M AT HOME IN Mabopane watching CNN when Giles comes on screen. The young man sits cross-legged at a hotel patio, calmly telling the reporter why he stands by his words. His tabloid, *Rolling Stone*, ran a series of stories calling for gay Ugandans to be killed. 'Hang them,' one headline instructs.

I'm on a bus to Kampala a few days later to interview Giles. I hope I don't kill him first. I start my trek in Gaborone, so I can get Botswana into my passport. 'The bus leaves at 8pm sharp,' the lady at the office says when I buy my ticket to Lusaka.

The afternoon moves in slow motion at the Gaborone-Lusaka Express bus company. The only passengers around for about three hours are me and Mme Gloria, already settled with legs stretched out on her straw mat. Her luggage includes two mink blankets in see-through bags and a large suitcase that's empty for now. When she returns to Gaborone in a week's time, it will be filled with the African print cloth she trades in. Her arm is swallowed by a handbag that's big enough to fit a newborn, and comes out with a container of Ntsu snuff. Next out is a roll of two-ply toilet paper. My mother Dikeledi and the women I spent every day of my first four years on earth with – my two aunts Mapula and Mangaka, their mother mmaMalebane, grandmother mmaMandla and great grandmother mmaMabote – sniff Ntsu. I stretch my legs, rummage around my bag to find my container of Ntsu – I sniff it on days when missing my grandmother becomes unbearable.

The courtyard fills up at around 6.30pm. 'The bus leaves at 8pm sharp' turns into 9pm and 'we don't know where it is'. Two men who work at the company set up a table with peanut butter and jam sandwiches we wash down with watery orange juice and lukewarm Ricoffy and Joko. When the bus shows up at 10pm we're hustled out of the yard like we're the ones who are late.

The trip starts with a prayer. The pastor marches up and down the aisle in his shiny grey suit, casting out demons and binding evil spirits from coming into our lives. 'We beg you father God to remove evil spirits that cause road accidents in the name of Jesus. We pray for wisdom for the driver, oh God. We bind the spirit of tiredness and cover the road with the blood of Jesus as we ask you to be with all the drivers on the road tonight.' His prayers become personal. 'Father, in the name of Jesus Christ, our mighty Saviour, we pray that you help the barren to fall pregnant, and that you grant patience and understanding to the married. Father, don't forget single people oh God. I pray that you send them divinely chosen life partners. And last but not least, Almighty God, we pray for peace and prosperity in the continent and around the world. In the mighty name of your beloved son, our Lord and Saviour, Jesus Christ of Nazareth. Amen.' He forgets to bind the spirit of drama.

The bus breaks down twice before we arrive at Kazungula border, where we crawl through customs when it turns out that one of the passengers in our bus is travelling with a dozen boxes of flat screen TVs. Our waiting game continues while we wait for the ferry to take us across the Zambezi River, where we have to use a different bus to Lusaka. It has peeling white paint and windows that won't close. The driver hits the road gently, as if he's petrified that the bus will breakdown, and it does. The first and second breakdowns are from flat tyres that take more than an hour each to repair. The driver blames the last break down on the engine. We drive into the Intercity bus terminal just after midnight.

I rent a plastic mat and find a spot to sleep on the terminal. I'm excited to be one very long trip away from Kampala; even the cockroaches that run around us seem like a necessary detail to this snapshot, you know, something along the lines of 'determined to confront a homophobe, the Vagabond sleeps among roaches when she discovers that there's no place to pitch her tent'. This is what I tell myself, otherwise I'm merely losing all standards of hygiene and not even questioning it. The platform goes back to normal at dawn. I return my mat and pay to use the showers.

Buses to East Africa have bodies painted in multiple bright colours. Their windscreens have declarations like Inshallah, Allahu Akbar, Mashallah, Allah Kareem – Arabic for if God wills, God is great, God has willed and God is generous – and mirrors decked with faux fur. Other than short stops in villages and small towns, the only long breaks we get are in large towns like Mbeya in south-western Tanzania. My diet for this trip is oxygen, and drops of water when I can no longer stand a mouth that feels like sandpaper. It's bad enough that I'll only shower when we get to Kampala; there's absolutely no need for me to put myself through a bush toilet break for number two. The Ugandan man I'm sitting with, Johnson, is slightly wounded that I refuse to share his biscuits, grilled mealie, cool drinks and full meals when we stop for food. I have a handful of cashew nuts to appease him.

A cool breeze blows over Dar es Salaam, where I discover that the direct bus to Kampala is actually a drop off in some alley in Dar that has ticketing offices that double as storerooms. One of the men who works here offers me a plastic chair among the group of colleagues he's sitting with. A boy walks over with a flask to sell strong, black coffee flavoured with a hint of ginger. I pass on the offer to join them as they work their way through piles of bitter green leaves called qat, that they chew with gum until the leaves form a large ball in their mouths. They spit it on the ground and start again.

We sing along and dance to Mafikizolo's 'Ndihamba Nawe', Brenda Fassie's 'Weekend Special' and Lucky Dube's 'Back to My Roots'. We sit through Yvonne Chaka Chaka's 'Umqombothi' when the fellows ask me to teach them how to pronounce the name of their favourite song. We get back on our feet to jam to 'No One Like You' by P Square, 'Fall in Love' by D'Banj and 'Yori Yori' by Bracket. My body is in Dar, but my mind is back in Osu in Accra and Stonetown.

Our lift to Ubungo bus station is the Falcon bus that arrives just before sunrise. The station goes from calm to chaos with masses of people bumping into each; their luggage on their heads or on wheelbarrows pushed by touts. As engines cough to life with white and black smoke, hawkers walk around selling fruit, boiled eggs, cold samosas and chapati. The driver who gives us the lift to Ubungo is shocked to discover that we're still in the bus because we're waiting for it to fill up and begin the journey to Kampala. 'Do something,' I tell Johnson who has been sitting next to me since the beginning of the trip. We're in his home region, after all. He says I mustn't worry and goes back to watching other buses leave the station.

The bus driver says he knows nothing about a trip to Kampala. I follow him around, my voice moving between gentle pleas and loud demands for him to make a plan until he finds us seats in a Kampala Coach. Stepping into the bus, I start thinking that the reason it takes an hour and a tantrum before we get seats is due to the embarrassing state of the 'luxury' coach. The leather seats are hard. Some of them are unhinged from the floor and move when the bus driver flies over speed bumps or makes a sudden stop, which is often. When I'm not banging my head against the overhead compartment, I'm picking myself up from the aisle after being tossed off my seat. Apparently, the aim is to arrive in Kampala maimed – if we actually make it there. We break down just outside Dar and wait an hour for the mechanic to come to our rescue. Another breakdown keeps us off the road for two hours. The tedious trip gets worse after dark, when the driver pulls out a plastic bag full of qat.

However, this is Africa. The bad is always outweighed by the good. Tanzania is big and beautiful. We drive past pineapple fields and Mount Kilimanjaro. In Moshi, mountain tops peek out of grey clouds, while villages are set in lush plains that stretch as far as the eye can see. At one of our stops in Moshi, three Maasai men lean against the wall at the Kampala Coach office. Their thin, long bodies are wrapped with shukas held together by leather belts overlaid with beads. The leather pouches at their waists have daggers; one of them has a knobkerrie in one hand and a cellphone in the other.

The only time uniforms cause minor trouble is at Busia border between Kenya and Uganda. Two of them want to search our bags, which I don't mind. What I do take exception to is hands poking into ziplock bags that contain the lifetime supply of Lil-Lets tampons I now travel with. Even worse, they want to know what they are, and disbelieve me when I tell them what I use them for. They walk me to an office, collecting a female uniform along the way. She's never seen tampons before either.

'Why don't you just use pads?' she asks, pressing a tampon.

XIV

HANG THEM

November 2010

THERE ARE PLACES I feel before I get to know; when I step on the ground for the first time and I just know that my life is about to change. Uganda is one of them. At the border, I stand at the door for a few minutes taking in the country's first impression. Touts stand outside the door waving SIM cards and airtime vouchers. Forex traders brandish wads of cash. 'Shilling sister. Tanzania, Uganda, Kenya – we change everything.' I get money to pay for my visa from the ATM.

The uniforms here are polite, smiling at everyone, demanding none of our money or poking their heads into our property.

'Welcome to Uganda,' a uniform says when his stamp lands on my passport.

Kampala is one hundred and forty-five kilometres from the border. We pass many trucks and bakkies filled to capacity with bundles of dark green bananas called matoke – the country's beloved, tasteless staple. Road trip food in Uganda is like a mobile feast: chunks of fresh fruit, meat and poultry on skewers and fat chips. I can eat again now that I'm almost at my final destination.

Kampala announces itself with a bang, literally, when the security guard slams the heavy steel gate at the entrance to the Kampala Coach against the wall. We park next to the only bus in the yard. People on their way to Kigali continue to the lounging area that's a flight of stairs from the ticketing office and the store room. I leave my bags here to walk the city for a while; my previously weary body energised by the bumper-to-bumper traffic and the get-up-and-go energy I pick up from the bus seat. It makes my feet light as I press between stagnant cars, buses and matatus. Only mopeds, called boda boda in East Africa, can move. The foot traffic is just as crammed. Our bodies touch and we almost step on each other. I walk into a one-storey building, where I spot Sudanese and Congolese restaurants.

The fast-moving crowd shuffles me back to the street. The crowd swallows me, and spews me onto a street laid out with rows of tables and customers eating pilau or kikomando, the bean and shredded chapati dish that's named after the giant lizards.

I go back to Kampala Coach offices to get my bags and hop on a boda boda to the Old Taxi Park for a matatu to Lunguja. The park and the section of the city it's in heave with masses of people. We're four weeks away from Christmas and the season's shopping is in full swing. Pavements have turned into mini markets that sell produce, clothes, books and entertainment systems. The taxi park can't contain the matatus and people waiting for their turn to board. I have to pull my stomach in to walk between the matatus. A young boy hawks fruit salad in five hundred millilitre containers while we stand in queues that snake out of the park. For the equivalent of R3, I enjoy cubes of firm mango, pineapples, papaya, watermelon and jackfruit. The quality of my life in Uganda remains unmatched.

Backpackers' Hostel is on Natete Road. It's ideal for my new rule of stretching my shillings as far as possible by only using matatus and camping. My ankles are still swollen and my back still strained from sitting in a bus from Monday morning to Thursday afternoon. I walk off the exhaustion by going up Natete Road. I turn around less than five minutes later armed with a copy of *The Onion* and *Red Pepper* tabloids; seduced by the sex they use to sell.

Almost all content has to do with sex – who is getting it on with someone who isn't their partner, who needs to get it pronto and who they can possibly get it on with. The most hilarious thing about the stories is how they don't use the words vagina and penis. Instead, they're yoyo and khandaha and gologo and anaconda. No one's sex life is off bounds, dead or alive. The former dictator Idi Amin leads a two-part series in a list of Uganda's most sex-crazed citizens. The list has one hundred names.

I start my search for someone to help me understand Uganda's relationship with its LGBTI citizens at the Nando's restaurant on Jinja Road in the business district. I meet Bob online via his blog, and in person a day later. Bob is not his real name. He used to tell journalists his real one but they'd betray his confidence and use it instead of his moniker. He has stopped speaking to journalists on record and tells me to call Pepe Julian Onziema. 'He won't mind talking,' he says. He also introduces me to French photographer Bénédicte Desrus. She has an interview with David Bahati and invites me to tag along. David is the member of parliament who is championing an anti-gay bill that proposes the death penalty or life imprisonment for LGBTI Ugandans. He says gay people must die because that's what God says. 'The Bible says those caught in sin should suffer death. The Quran says hang them and throw them over a cliff – I'm only obeying God's words.'

He speaks softly and patiently when we challenge him. 'God chooses people He uses to deliver humanity from calamity. In your country, South Africa, He used Nelson Mandela to deliver your people from apartheid, He used Martin Luther King Jr to speak about the racial evil in America, and just like He used Mother Teresa to help the poor in Calcutta, God is using me to deliver Uganda from the evil of homosexuality.'

Uganda is crazy about God. There are as many posters announcing festive partying as there are those advertising spiritual revivals. Young boys walk the city hawking posters with Jesus' face and Bible verses, and the city's skyline features the domes of its many mosques.

So when David says he's God's chosen one, he means it. It's impossible to miss the framed picture on his desk, where he kneels in the middle of church pastors and elders laying their hands on his head. If David gets his way – and he's working day and night to make it happen – the bill will be a law by 2011. Then the country will be free from people he accuses of sodomy and of being rapists. He claims young people are lured with booze and money to become 'homosexuals'. He doesn't have any evidence of his accusations and won't answer our questions. Instead, he goes on about God and culture.

I'm calm until I decide to screw objectivity. This bigot wants to incite Ugandans into hating and killing each other.

'Do you know how absurd you sound?' I yell. 'You want to dictate who consenting people can love and have sex with? What does it matter to you if I sleep with women?'

We stare at each other while I gather my camera and notebook from the floor. According to the bill, anyone who is even suspected of being gay is guilty, and those who don't report the suspects are also guilty of aiding and abetting. 'I said, what's it to you if I sleep with women? Shouldn't you arrest me, and aren't you guilty of not arresting me?'

My antagonism only makes him more determined to explain that he is on a divine mission. 'God help us deliver Uganda from evil,' he says. God deliver Uganda from this bigot, I think. We can't keep writing Africa's history with blood. People like David, who use their power and influence to incite violence, are the ones who should be locked away.

Bénédicte and I meet again the next day at a café a stone's throw from Makerere University. It's packed with people who are out for sundowners. Bottles of Nile Special, Tusker and Bells beers and a local gin called Waragi, also know as 'the spirit of Uganda', cannot come to the tables fast enough. I order a Nile Special and wonder if I will be able to stop myself from throwing it at Giles's face. David frustrates me; Giles angers me and breaks my heart. At twenty-two, he's a young man on a continent that's still trying to wipe the blood stains left by its brutal past. The best way to use his influence as the managing editor of a popular newspaper cannot be to call for war on fellow citizens.

Even more annoying is the fact that he's just a boy who is looking for attention, more than anything else. He has been revelling in it for weeks now, and smiles when he recalls his interviews on global news networks. He peppers the conversation with words like evil, sodomy and vile. He says *Rolling Stone* is meeting its obligation to God and citizens when he steals pictures of 'known and suspected homosexuals' off Facebook pages, publishing them with home addresses in some cases. 'Homosexuality is a creeping evil and affliction spreading through Uganda like wildfire,' he complains. 'My paper is strengthening the war against the rampage that threatens our society because, as you know, homosexuality is a sin, and it is unAfrican.'

At first, it would seem as if I'm turning a molehill into a mountain but a closer look at the facts proves me right – Ugandans are out to get me. They don't just want me dead. They're determined to make sure that I return to South Africa a mangled corpse. I first come to this realisation on the day I move across town from Lunguja to Bugulubi. Red Chilli Hideaway is walking distance from the main road but I have a backpack and camping gear, so I get a boda boda. I still haven't figured out how to sit on one without shifting my weight to one side. The boda rider keeps telling me to sit in the middle, whatever this means. He puts my stuff between the headlights and revs his motorcycle. Instead of moving forward, it leans upwards and topples me to the ground. I've been avoiding boda bodas because they're known as coffins on wheels, but they're the only way to move around the city without having a traffic-jam-induced psychotic episode.

Other than being East Africa's party capital, Kampala also has some of the worst traffic jams in the world. The boda boda nearly falls again when the rider drops me off at Red Chilli. The establishment has hostels with shared kitchens and chalets, a swimming pool, restaurant and gardens where I rent a spot for my tent. Guests are tanned road hogs with bundles of bracelets on their wrists, and groups of young overland travellers who sound, dress and act the same. They move like a flock and keep to themselves.

I pitch my tent between the dormitory and the swimming pool and stay away from other residents in keeping with my rule to avoid Americans and Europeans. The only resident I hang out with is a young man I will call Peter, who is visiting from Mbarara in Western Uganda. I get a boda to Kabalagala one afternoon to lunch at Ethiopian Hut restaurant. It's one of several in the area. I visit it in particular because it was bombed by terrorists months before my arrival. The blast put Uganda on the travel advisory list. I visit the restaurant to defy the advisory.

Going to Ethiopian Hut is my way of letting Kampala know that I'm not afraid of its other recent headlines. Besides, Ugandan food is bland. The only local food I eat is a rolex, made with an egg fried with chopped onions and tomatoes and rolled into a chapati. Ethiopian food is fragrant and spicy. My initial anxiety about going to Ethiopian Hut is a waste of energy. I find beefed up security that includes body scanners.

I keep going back to Kabalagala for the grills that come out onto the pavement and get fired up to cook fish at sunset, the fresh bundles of qat on sale, and the zouk music blasting from Congolese restaurants.

Pepe Julian Onziema stands in the middle of the road with a cellphone in one hand, and another waving at me. I'm interviewing the human rights activist at the offices of Sexual Minorities Uganda (SMUG). To be gay in Uganda is to blend in, disguise and hide yourself. People have aliases for interviews and the offices from where they do the mammoth task of fighting for universal human rights, and their right to be, don't have signboards or anything that makes them stand out from the suburban homes they hide among. Growing up a girl, Pepe feels misplaced, like she doesn't belong in her body. She's a boy. We meet at the beginning of his transition. His mother dies knowing this about Pepe and his family offer love and support when he comes out. The problem with his sexuality is that, like his colleagues at SMUG and other LGBTI Ugandans, he has been attacked for being himself. It's not that all Ugandans are hateful, it's that given the leeway by people like David Bahati and Giles, some Ugandans feel free to show their homophobia with fists and machetes.

Pepe has been attacked several times in the CBD, and is currently avoiding it. This morning, he looks like someone who is still settling into his body in oversized jeans and a blue tartan shirt. Anyone with a TV knows Pepe from the media interviews and court appearances he makes with others in the community to fight David Bahati's hate bill.

'Bahati is not going to stop us, he is certainly not going to stop me. They can intimidate us and arrest us – we are still not going anywhere.'

I confess that David scares me. 'He's determined.'

'I'll be honest, we live in fear,' Pepe says. 'But I know I'm going to fight that bill with everything in me.'

Pepe's lucky. His family has always on been on his side. For many of his comrades, coming out or even being suspected of being gay comes with rapes and attacks, losing families and jobs. Pepe, who is openly gay and regularly appears on local TV, is self-assured in his mission to change the story from hate to acceptance and freedom.

'Why do you keep living here when you can be free elsewhere in the world?' I ask.

'Do I want to live freely in a free country? Yes, of course. But my ideal of freedom is Ugandan. This is my home. I want to be free here.'

He stands up, straightens his jeans and leads me inside the office, where colleagues, including Frank Mugisha, are behind their desks. Unlike the LGBTI people in one of Bénédicte pictures, where a group of lesbians with blurred out faces burn twigs praying against the passing of the hate bill, the mood at SMUG is confident. Everyone here is public about their sexuality and not backing down from their position on the battlefield.

'I'll only stop fighting when we are free. When I'm no longer a criminal,' he says. He's willing to face whatever the law throws at him. 'Like Nelson Mandela, I'm prepared to die for my freedom. Obviously, I don't want to be killed. But it's all the same anyway. We are attacked, and shamed. We are denied access to health care and fight every day just to be who we are. We are not going to back down.'

Our interview turns into the beginning of a friendship and, on my part, admiration that keeps growing with time.

'This talk has been heavy,' he sighs, 'Meet me at Sappho tomorrow night to see a different side of me,' he says when I leave.

'What happens there?' I ask.

'That's when I get to smile from ear to ear,' he says, flashing his smile.

Sappho is a bar in the same suburb as SMUG's offices. 'You'll know you've arrived when the boda boda drops you off at Jakobo's pork joint,' he says by way of directions. Pork joints are to Uganda what chisa nyama joints are to South Africa. Unless you know what the small rainbow flag at the door means, the bar passes for a regular one, where couples and groups of friends meet on Fridays to drink and dance the night away. Pepe is still on his way but his people – made up of colleagues and friends – offer me a seat at their table when I tell them who I'm here to meet.

Sappho is Uganda's first and only exclusively gay bar. Its owner is the feisty radical feminist Kasha Jacqueline Nabagesera, founder of Freedom and Roam Uganda. FARUG is the first organisation established to fight for the freedom and human right to not be heterosexual.

I'm at the table with Kasha, Sandra – whose moniker is Crazy – two Peace Corps workers, an American student, and Gerald, who is also an activist. The mood is positively jovial. Everyone in the bar is gay or here with a gay friend and hanging out as an act of defiance against the hysterical national homophobia.

The soundtrack is set on Nigerian hiplife and Tanzanian bongo flava music and the throats watered with waragi, Ugandan beers and Italian wine. By the time Pepe arrives, I've made friends with almost everyone in the club; meeting Angela, Didi and his date, Long Jones and several activists and other LGBTI people who work in corporate Uganda. As always on a night out in Kampala, I crawl out of the club at dawn. Sandra invites me to party with her on Sunday night in Makerere. It's a regular club but one area of it has turned into the gay corner. We are here to gather information for Sandra's research project between drinking, flirting, dancing and unwinding with students, nurses, admin workers and teachers. David Bahati is high on goodness knows what if he thinks his bill will succeed.

Away from David's hysteria and the religious freaks there are many Ugandans who are simply not interested in being part of the narrative of homophobia. I meet some of them again on Wednesday night at a club in the CBD and make it a point to ask people I meet whenever I'm out and about what they think of the bill. The consensus is the same – other than religious fanatics and political nuts using culture to incite hate, people are mostly not interested in policing who can love whom and what consenting adults do behind closed doors. But it doesn't mean that everyone is accepting, as I discover on World Aids Day.

After a public event attended by healthcare workers, where the LGBTI community and activists also have a tent, we go to a hotel for a more intimate recognition of the day. There are seminars on safer sex and leaders from different NGOs talking about their experiences and challenges with accessing healthcare while gay. As a moral stand, two doctors have set up a consulting room to offer health checks and HIV tests. Where their peers take the option of turning away patients because of their sexuality, these doctors are allies and adamant that they will not be caught on the wrong side of history.

While waiting for my HIV test results, the nurse makes small talk with me and pleads with me to tell everyone at the event that 'what they are doing is wrong'. Her husband is one of the two doctors. She's not here because she believes in universal human rights, she is tending to her marriage while looking for sneaky ways to assert her homophobia.

'I'm leaving tomorrow morning' becomes the story of my life in Kampala. I'm a slave to the intoxicating night life and besotted with the city's people. I love its overcrowded streets, afternoons of chewing qat, the café culture in Kabalagala and evenings on friends' balconies, when the city's seven hills twinkle with lights.

Although Peter and I hang out together at Red Chilli, he still keeps to himself most of the time and is always guarded when talking about his private life. One Friday when I tell him I'm leaving 'tomorrow morning', he says I should stay the weekend to attend a party with him in Entebbe on Sunday. A friend with a beachfront mansion has a party. 'You have to meet him,' Sammy says. He's Dr _____, a businessman, father and husband in his fifties. When we arrive at the house, we find our host at the beach with three couples who are around his age. This is Dr _____ the husband.

We greet them and join his sons at the house, where he's setting up the music system and serving drinks to a group of his friends.

When the sun goes down, our host strides into the lounge with a gin and tonic in one hand, and the other one flinging in the air. He's still in his khaki shorts and his tropical print shirt has made way for a flowing kaftan. 'Finally,' he says, 'the boring people are gone. It's time to enjoy myself.' He plonks himself on the couch and raises his glass for a toast. 'Here's to being gay or straight, depending on what I feel,' he laughs. He's bisexual and belongs to a generation of gay people who didn't dare explore their sexuality beyond acknowledging it to a few trusted friends, like Peter.

'The wife lives in a different country and the kids don't really care,' he says, explaining his rather interesting double life, where he is 'gay at my beach house and straight elsewhere'. We clink our glasses and join the kids at the party outside. There's no more than ten people, yet the set up, with a full sound system and two long tables with beers and spirits, is high gear. Ugandans party as hard as they work and worship.

When I finally leave Kampala, it's to play in Jinja. It's Uganda's adrenalin and adventure capital. Jinja is subdued compared to Kampala. There are no potholes in sight and the wide boulevards scarcely have people. It's still a friendly town and the Luganda word for friend, mukwano, follows me around on multiple invitations for tea, lunch and beer. I stop putting myself through the hell of camping and move back to hostel rooms. My fun comes from a loud sunset booze cruise with mostly European travellers. They're either on their way to track mountain gorillas or just back from there so all talk is about their wildlife encounters instead of an analysis of Africa's problems and straight-faced declarations that, bad as colonisation was, it did bring development and education to Africa. Still, I spend most of our time sailing past the tranquil villages with the crew or on the dance floor. After sailing the White Nile, my inability to listen to wild stories without wanting my own encounter gets the better of me, and I book a rafting trip with Nile River Explorers.

I line up with five others to sign an indemnity form. I'm the only one who is excited by the thought of playing in grade five rapids with rocks that snap bones on contact. I strike up a conversation with a United Nations worker based in Khartoum and tell the three women who are silenced by their anxiety to take it easy. I love experiences that come with a hint of danger, and by the sound of the roars that we hear before we see the rapids, rafting the Nile is going to be my kind of fun.

The twelve rapids have threatening names like Rib Cage, Big Brother, Hair of the Dog, Madness, Silver Back and Overtime. Our adventure starts with a safety drill. Our guide, Yo, gives us life jackets, helmets and paddles and shows us how to row. We jump into the raft for a trial run of what to do when it inevitably flips over. 'Firstly, the raft will capsize,' Yo says. 'That's just a fact. Your safety depends on how you act in the water. Always paddle hard towards the raft and if you can't, you must float instead of trying to swim. No matter how strong you think you are, the rapid will carry you if you swim.' The paddles are another worry. The sticks are hard with handles that dislocate jaws and the bottoms can crack skulls on impact. I jump into the water laughing when he tells us to practise getting back in the raft.

Everything goes downhill, taking my bravado with it, when I try getting back into the raft. It's as easy as holding the rope around the raft and flinging my left leg into it first then pulling my body in. Everyone passes the test, while it takes Mr UN and Yo to pull my limbs to drag my body back in.

The Nile River, at our launching point, is calm and flows gently. Action starts at Rib Cage. It's mild and makes our boat swirl like a cool version of a merry-go-round. Next up is Bujagali

Falls, between rocks covered in bird poo. Thousands of bats flap in circles above us. Yo says we're about to capsize and those of us sitting in the middle are definitely going to fall into the river. He tells me to hold on tight to the rope; my hands act like sand in the water. I fall into the water and get pulled into the rapid. My waist feels like it's wrapped by two very strong legs that refuse to let go. I forget to float and try to swim before Yo paddles towards me. He and Mr UN haul me back in – something they do every time I fall into the river, which happens whenever we are at a rapid. I heave while water gushes out of my mouth and nose. The only faces that aren't red are mine and Yo's. 'This is ah-may-zing,' I finally scream.

Madness lives up to its name and sets me off on a pattern of capsizing into the water while the others hold tightly to the rope. This time, I'm rescued by Hassan, the champion kayaker who works as part of the company's safety crew. All rafts are accompanied by an extra raft and kayak with safety crew. They enter rapids ahead of us. I heave and spew out more water from the orifices on my face. My head is spinning and I can feel the blood coursing through my body.

We finally hit a stretch of the river without rapids. Here it flows through green fields and past villagers bathing or washing their laundry; some of it is left to dry on the grass. Birds swoop above or glide on the water. The crew gathers around us to hand out chunks of pineapples and biscuits. We jump into the water to swim or float until Yo tells us to preserve our energy: 'You are going to need it.'

The next sets of rapids are a lot like the previous ones. The raft gets toppled, we go underwater, I'm pulled back into the raft and let water run out of my mouth and nose and start laughing at how great rafting is. We paddle over twenty kilometres in almost four hours, until I complain about being bored.

'Wait and see,' Yo promises.

'To think you made me sign an indemnity form for this,' I say, rolling my eyes. He laughs with me. We get to a stretch of the river where even Hassan and the safety crew get back on land. At the end of the footpath, Yo offers us the option of staying on land. We are at the Bad Place; the most violent of all rapids. Three people in our group sit under a shade, Mr UN thinks twice about jumping back in the water while I, cool as ever, coo 'this is what I signed up for'.

I'm a firm believer that if it doesn't kill you, it makes a damn good story; and if it kills me, well, then it's better to go out with a bang. Still, my feet refuse to move when I try getting into the raft. I freak the hell out of my mind looking at the Bad Place and its vortex but my curiosity will always win over my anxiety. What happens next is an event that lasts seconds but feels like a lifetime.

The Bad Place tosses me into the river, pulling me into its violent current. The strap on my helmet snaps open, and it floats away from me. My life jacket moves up to my chin, then my lips, before touching my nose.

'Indemnity. In-dem-ni-tee, Lerato Mogoatlhe, as in security or protection against a loss or financial burden; noun, not joke,' I say to myself whenever I open my eyes and see the sharp rocks that keep getting closer. I can't see Yo or Hassan.

The Nile gushes into my mouth and nostrils until breathing becomes my latest problem. I struggle to keep my head above the water and my life jacket keeps moving up from my body. I'm screwed and there'll be no orgasm at the end of it. I hear Hassan's voice telling me to jump in but I can't move. My feet keep sliding off the kayak and my arms are completely paralysed.

'JUMP IN, LERATO,' he screams. His voice is tinged with desperation. Yo and another safety crew member paddle over to help Hassan pull me into the kayak. My head is hot. My heart wants to jump out of my chest. I'm dizzy. There's a bonfire in my lungs. I cough violently and regurgitate the Nile. Everyone is as bewildered as I am. Hassan keeps asking if I'm fine. It takes a long time before I can talk, and when I do, all I can do is shout: 'I feel fantastic.' It's the best fun I've had in water so far.

XV

JOHARI

December 2010

A CREATURE OF HABIT, I leave Jinja for Nairobi aboard a Kampala
Coach bus to once again bounce off my seat and hit the overhead
compartment while our driver fuels himself on bags of qat; I take a
handful of his leaves when we stop for food in Kitale. We share the
road on both sides of the border with trucks, matatu, boda boda,
flocks of sheep and goats and herds of cattle. Pavements are mini
markets that sell anything from everyday stuff like coals, produce
and washing soaps, to full lounge sets, door frames, sheets of zinc
and other building materials.

When we get to Kisumu, and we leave the bus to stretch our legs
or buy snacks and drinks, our driver gets two more bags of fresh
qat to keep him high for the rest of the trip to Nairobi, through
parts of the Rift Valley in Naivasha, Ngong and Nakuru and the tea
regions of Kericho.

I sleepwalk through my first moments in Nairobi in one of
the streets downtown crammed with buses and taxis, and sleep

through my cab ride to my backpackers in Kileleshwa and its lavish mansions and bungalows with parking lots that are occupied by Mercs, Beemers and Range Rovers. The garages here have a wide selection of Belgian chocolates, and Italian and Argentinian wines. I'm a firm believer in naming buildings, roads and other public spaces after heroes and freedom fighters, and in languages that didn't come to Africa on boats. Affluent places with African names are an anomaly in South Africa; it makes Kileleshwa and Nairobi all the more amazing to me. This city fills me with an overflowing sense of black pride. It takes hold of me within two hours of arrival, after I've checked in, showered and taken a bus to town. Lately, I arrive in new places dressed to impress conservatives.

It finally hits me that the reason Nairobians seem so different is that everyone dresses how they want to, from women who are fully covered in burkas to those in micro minis and tight jeans. I'm dressed for Kampala in a little black dress I dial down with tights and a kanga on my chest. I remove my ballet pumps and unwrap my kanga to spread it out over my thighs, then get rid of my tights. I make my lips shimmer with a red lip gloss and put the kanga in my bag so my cleavage can breathe. My ears dangle with Rwandan handwoven sisal statement earrings with swirls of red for the blood that unites us, the gold of the minerals that are still lining the pockets of an elite few, the green of Africa our beautiful land, and the blackness of our skins, which I buy in Kampala for my visit to Makerere University.

I jump off the bus downtown to a street that's crammed with buses and cars, kiosks with neon lights. Women in long ponytails, pencil skirts and killer heels walk side by side with those in full Islamic robes; their kohl-lined eyes making them even more mysterious. There's a sense of belonging no matter who you are. The crowd's light on their feet and people walk like they're late for a meeting with the president. The sense of purpose is tangible and exciting. This is the only city I know besides Johannesburg that's charged with zeal. Nairobi gets under my skin in a way I know I'll never recover from. It's in how cosmopolitan I find it, and how Pan-African it is.

Looking up to see the name of the street I'm on, written in black over a white narrow wood panel, the name is Tom Mboya. The trade unionist and anti-colonisation activist is considered to be one of the founding fathers of Kenya. This moment is the reason I believe in streets and public spaces named after our liberators and black heroes; because these are the names we encounter whether we are interested in history or not. They make us ask 'who are you and what did you do to be here?' I want being out and about to be a celebration of Africa's liberation.

I keep walking with my eyes glued on street names. From Tom Mboya, I turn into Luthuli, as in Chief Albert Luthuli and Africa's first Nobel Peace laureate for his contribution to the fight against apartheid. My smile turns into a wide grin that plasters my face whenever I'm in the city centre. By the time I get the bus back to the backpackers, I've been on Nkrumah Lane, and Gaborone and Accra roads. I've strolled around Monrovia Road, named after the Liberian capital city and home of freed slaves who returned to Africa. There's also Harambee and Taifa streets. Taifa is Swahili for nation and Harambee is the concept of pulling together to get the job done. Banda Road is a nod to the first president of Malawi, Hastings Banda. Whether it's named after Ghana's second largest city or not, Kumasi Road reminds me of shopping for kente cloth in the Ashanti Region.

On Kaunda Street, I'm not just reminded of President Kenneth Kaunda of Zambia and his country's support in the fight for my liberation, my mind flashes with a picture of me buying an orange in front of a bright red building next to Intercity bus terminal in Lusaka. Down Kigali Street trailing a hawker with red roses and white lilies, my heart beats wildly with anticipation – Rwanda's capital city is my next destination after Kenya. Mama Ngina is the wife of liberated Kenya's first president, Jomo Kenyatta. The street named after her has banks, electronic shops, kiosks with airtime vouchers in low shilling values so that a voucher for 500 bob comes as six 50-shilling vouchers, and Prestige bookshop, where the selection of *New York Times* best-sellers is anorexic and the collection of literature about Africa by Africans and from the diaspora is thick.

Along the street is a dreadlocked statue of the leader of the Mau Mau uprising against the British rule, Dedan Kimathi. In my capital city and hometown Pretoria, the statues that loom the largest in public are of Afrikaner leaders whose ideal of freedom didn't extend to black people.

Being on Mama Ngina street is bittersweet: it's rare to see women honoured in public.

At the corner of Tom Mboya Street and Haile Selassie Avenue, my mind recalls the Emperor's 1963 speech to the United Nations General Assembly. It says: 'On the question of racial discrimination, the Addis Ababa Conference taught, to those who will learn, this further lesson: That until the philosophy which holds one race superior and another inferior is finally and permanently discredited and abandoned; that until there are no longer first class and second class citizens of any nation; that until the colour of a man's skin is of no more significance than the colour of his eyes; that until the basic human rights are equally guaranteed to all without regard to race; that until that day, the dream of lasting peace and world citizenship and the rule of international morality will remain but a fleeting illusion, to be pursued but never attained. And until the ignoble and unhappy regimes that hold our brothers in Angola, in Mozambique and in South Africa in subhuman bondage have been toppled and destroyed; until bigotry and prejudice and malicious and inhuman self-interest have been replaced by understanding and tolerance and good-will; until all Africans stand and speak as free beings, equal in the eyes of all men, as they are in the eyes of Heaven; until that day, the African continent will not know peace. We Africans will fight, if necessary, and we know that we shall win, as we are confident in the victory of good over evil.'

My right hand shoots up in the air with all the power and pride in me. 'Amandla,' I shout. Nairobi, capital city number fifteen in my travels around Africa, is the one. I hum Miriam Makeba's 'Aluta Continua'; Nairobi's Pan-Africanism is my affirmation. This is why I call Nairobi johari – my jewel.

Other cities have zoos. Nairobi has a national park with lions, rhinos, leopards and buffaloes. I don't have money to pay tourist prices that are significantly more expensive than what locals pay, so I visit the David Sheldrick Wildlife Trust instead for my wild life encounter with rescued elephants. They splash water at each other and nuzzle visitors with their trunks. It's in the national park anyway and even though the lone black rhino is caged, it's still a close enough encounter with it.

I'm in a matatu from the trust back to the city centre when the most beautiful person I have ever seen walks in. I have never looked at people and thought 'this is what I would look like if I moulded myself'. Her tall and lean body is in fitted black pants, her crisp white shirt decked out with a thin cotton scarf layered around her neck and her long nails shine with a purple lacquer. Her thick, jet-black hair is bundled into a top knot. She has a radiant dimpled smile and kohl-lined almond eyes. She meets my gaze and holds it with her smile.

'Excuse me, are you from South Africa?' Don't ask me why, but I love pretending that I'm from Ghana and have a weak accent to prove it.

'You are from South Africa; you look like it and sound like it. Anyway, the conductor isn't scamming you, fares go up during peak traffic,' she says, answering the question I pose to the conductor when my change comes back with 20 bob less than I pay from town to the trust. The matatu engine has been off for more than fifteen minutes and the only movement in the road is from hawkers and monkeys chasing each other on nearby bushes.

Her name is Arrot. She's obsessed with South Africa, I'm besotted with my Pan-African dream city, Nairobi. When we arrive in town and I ask the conductor where I can find matatus to the Somali neighbourhood of Eastleigh, she suggests hanging out in town instead and planning the trip to Eastleigh for a day when she can take me there. She has a meeting she can't get out of this afternoon. We have lunch at a Somalian restaurant. We don't see each other until two and a half weeks later when I ask her for a favour.

My introduction to Nairobi at downtime is from my friend of many years, Heidi Uys, who spends most of her time working on TV productions in Lagos and Nairobi, where she has just wrapped up filming a reality singing competition.

She takes me to Blankets and Wine on Sunday afternoon. If Nairobi is my deal, Blankets and Wine seals it for me. The monthly gig is held at a school's sporting grounds for live music performed to a picnicking audience that makes me fall hard for Nairobians. The vibe is hip and urban and the dress code Afropolitan. Maasai shukas double as picnic blankets and wraps, some have been turned into dashikis. Kitenges, kangas and kikoyis have been turned into shorts, playsuits and jumpsuits and mini and maxi dresses. Everything that the world is wearing at the moment has been given a trendy, African twist. Dreadlocks have crowns of cowrie shells, earrings are shaped like Africa, belts are decked with Maasai beads that are also on necks, wrists and ankles, including on the men. Several people have poodles in their arms.

A hipster boy band called Sauti Sol is on stage when the power goes off. The music dies but the party goes on while we wait for a generator to be set up. When that plan fails, Sauti Sol performs acapella on the field, surrounded by a crowd. The moment turns up tempo when someone starts playing drums. The sky is becoming darker and a full moon hangs behind the abandoned stage. The party moves to a bar in Westlands, where, in keeping up with Nairobians, I drink like it's the night before prohibition. Joburgers drink and party like it's a national sport; Nairobians do it like it's for Olympic glory.

My next stop after Nairobi is the Swahili coast, but not before I meet my Facebook friend David Odhiambo, who calls himself Kenyan Zulu on social media. He loves South Africa and adores all things Zulu. He feeds his interest by reading *City Press* newspaper online. This is where he encounters my travels, joining me in them digitally from my time in West Africa.

We meet at a nyama choma joint close to the post office in the city centre, where the love for grilled goat meat that West Africa puts in me is reignited. Here it's served with ugali and I once again remember my love for kachumburi, as the combination of raw tomatoes, onion and fresh coriander is called.

David is soft-spoken and one of the sweetest people I know; the reason he insists on meeting me before Christmas is so he can give me a Christmas card. 'In case you miss your family and get lonely, know you are not alone,' he says. We are still friends.

A few days before I get the bus to Mombasa, a Kampala Coach bus becomes the target of a bomb blast that kills three people. I call my mom in case she hears about the attacks on the news to tell her that I'm going to avoid the area and show up two days later at the said River Road area for my trip to the coast. Security is always on high alert after an attack. It's the safest time to travel, I think; when every passenger and their baggage is scanned with a metal detector.

It takes just over eight hours to get to Mombasa, which, as expected, announces itself with the Mombasa Tusks, the aluminium moulds put on Moi Avenue for Princess Margaret's visit in 1956. After securing my seat on a Tawakal bus, I pass time by getting a tuk tuk ride around town. Mombasa has everything I've come to love about the Swahili coast; language that rolls off the tongue like a melody, boubous that flutter in the wind, the fresh coconut water I drink with a plastic straw from the fruit before eating the soft, white flesh. In Mombasa town, the rambling aged buildings add a tinge of fading splendour that's messed up by the piles of human crap I keep side stepping. The Mombasa of white beaches and crystal waters is a ferry ride away.

The eight-hour trip to Lamu goes through other enchanting coastal towns and villages that only come alive when the bus drives by, when people sell mangoes and grilled mealies before going back to their comatose state. Our final stop, Mokowe Jetty, is in a yard with sandy ground and an area with empty, ramshackle cafés. The pier is a slab of crumbling concrete that leads to the dhows, where boatmen hold our hands to help us jump in. Other than the two boatmen, I'm with a young European couple on a backpacking adventure in East Africa, and a burka-clad mother whose toddler's eyes are lined with kohl. The mother's hands and feet are completely covered in red henna designs. For the first time since dhows and pirogues have become my mode of transport, we are given life jackets.

All arrival to Lamu is by dhow, even for people who fly to the coast. Getting out of the boat takes two boatmen holding my hands while I hop in and out of other boats to get to the jetty. I walk over to a man sitting next to enamel kettles he's put over a fire to boil bitter Arabic coffee. Small ceramic cup in hand, I plonk myself among other people sitting on the pavement and look out to the sea and around me. Other than the half-empty restaurants with menus written with chalk on black boards left at the entrance, there are also tables with Maasai jewellery. After several cups of kahawa, I find a donkey to carry my bags from the waterfront to look for a hotel. December is high season, and sometimes, I play the hotel version of musical chairs, going from Stopover, to Pole Pole and Yumbe, which I can't afford anyway, until I find a hotel that isn't brimming with white travellers. I find myself opposite Ali's kanga and tailor shop. Other residents are Mombasa families who are holidaying in Lamu; the oldest town on the Swahili coast and its most magical destination to me, where we dine under a starlit sky while a taraab orchestra plays softly on their string instruments.

'Allaaaaaaaaaaaaaaaaaaaaaaaaaahu akbaaaaaaaaaaar,
Allaaaaaaaaaaaaaaaaaaaaaaaaahu akbaaaaaaaaaaar,
Allaaaaaaaaaaaaaaaaaaaaaaaaahu akbaaaaaaaaaaaaaaaaaaaaaaar.'

The adhan echoes around the Old Town, each declaration of Allah's greatness chanted in long notes that sound like a prayer relay, with notes carried across town from one mosque to another. The first call to prayer is my favourite morning sound, and the reason I gravitate towards Muslim countries and Christian ones that don't tolerate Islam on condition that the muezzin muffles his voice at prayer times. The laid-back atmosphere from last night has made way for streams of people on their morning shopping trips and chores; boubous and kanzus fluttering in the breeze.

The main square is dominated by a large tree. People – mostly men – sit on the concrete benches around the street, reading news-papers, cooling down with glasses of concentrated and home-made juice. A spirited game of bao is in session on the concrete platform where slaves were displayed for sale. Along the street, another of many that are also called Harambee, heavily perfumed women huddle at counters in kanga and beauty shops. The men gather around newspaper stands that hang the daily reads on makeshift shelves and we all peek at the table of Nollywood movies without stopping to buy.

We constantly press our bodies against the walls of the narrow streets to make room for donkeys – there are no cars other than the ambulance that stands on bricks instead of wheels and the commissioner's car. Everything we use and eat that's not from the earth or sea is brought from the mainland and carried around the town on wheelbarrows and donkeys. There are six thousand of them. They have names and a hospital at the water front. They get taken for walks and coddled lovingly while being bathed in the sea. In a mural with Scooby Doo, he's depicted as a donkey instead of a dog. Even with its varying states of ageing faster than it gets renovated or spruced with fresh coats of paint, Lamu Old Town is a wonder to experience.

There is a house between the Old Town and Shela that acts like a border between these two different sides of the same coin. It doesn't shock me later when I discover that it belongs to Princess Caroline of Monaco, although I'm surprised to discover that Lamu is the playground of people who holiday in St Barts and yacht around the Mediterranean coast, people Naomi Campbell and Kate Moss. This year's celebrity-in-town is Jude Law. Rumour of his presence spreads around Shela beach and follows me to the floating bar at night; I never see him. Shela is also the coastal paradise of well-off Europeans who have bought prime property from locals, making them move further into the island while they turn the waterfront and houses around it into villas.

It creates an almost rarified atmosphere in Shela. Everyone is lean and sun kissed. Their kikoyis and kangas aren't worn; they are styled to look perfectly laid-back without losing their wearer's sense of vanity. Here, the Maasai beadwork is perfectly put together instead of having some of the haphazard final touches of pieces on sale at the Maasai market between Shela and Old Town. Sisal coffee tables have thick collections of photographic series set in Africa, the clientele don't utter a word of Swahili and treat everyone, close friends included, with a detached coolness. They're not here to be one with the people or break free from their European lifestyle. If anything, Rafiki complains, they are here to turn Shela into mini versions of cities they still keep homes in, where everything is in perfect order and the sound of the muezzin is silenced at prayer times. So, while Shela is beautiful and always gleams with newness that only money can add to a place, it's only good to look at. Its warm African soul is making way for Western sterility. 'Perfect', I overhear a bronzed woman whose taut face doesn't match her significantly wrinkled neck say. For people whose bank accounts aren't always on the edge of broke, there's windsurfing, deep sea fishing, sunset cruises and camel rides, which I can afford but pass on because I'm almost as scared of camels as I am of snakes.

It's a few hours before 2010 ends and I still don't have anything special to do. Moonrise restaurant in Old Town has a three-course dinner and cocktail evening planned and other than being a waste of money I'll definitely regret spending on tuna steaks and dawas, the crowd isn't the type that share their space and emotions. I'll get a smile, at most, not the joie de vivre that has come to define my life on the road, when groups of friends invite solo diners to join tables and replace silence with laughter.

I'm friends with three tour guides-slash-beach boys from Nairobi. They're at Petley's with the European girls they're trying to romance for visas and one-way tickets out of Kenya. Their meal-tickets are girls who are barely out of their teens, who firmly believe in peppering all conversations with how fulfilling it is to visit Africa and how heartbreaking it is that the education and development given to Africa by colonialists have been neglected in liberated Africa.

'You have to admit that colonialism wasn't all bad,' as one of them argues with me. I stay away so my boys can work them without me turning into Teacher Lerato who admonishes bullshit;

besides, I'm not here to free Europeans from their mental slavery.

One of the Maasai guys I'm friends with, Joseph, invites me to hang out with him and his crew at a shebeen between Old Town and Shela. He's into me, and refuses to believe that not every single female traveller dreams of falling in love with a Maasai warrior. Or as I tell him, 'I don't fetishise African men.'

I don't want to spend my evening rebutting his attempts at seducing me with admittedly fascinating stories of his village life or the time he and other morans circled a lion before killing it as a show of manhood and bravery.

I hang around at the waterfront in Old Town and maintain my sanity by hanging out with a group of middle-aged friends who spend hours at a dhow shop chewing mirar, as qat is called in Kenya, then walk the shore before joining a small crowd of people gathered around a tarzab ochestra putting on a free show outside the museum.

One of the mates who are romancing their way out of Kenya has ditched his potential girlfriend after she falls for another holiday fling. He's going to party at Diamond Beach and I'm invited. I cram into the dhow with a big crowd of local boys and a few backpackers who also stay away from their kind's false sense of superiority; this time, there are no life jackets.

I love travelling in Africa for the predictable clichés that infuse mundane moments with magic. On our way to the party, it happens when someone starts singing 'Malaika', the Swahili love song I first know as a Miriam Makeba song. We all sing along, clapping our hands to create a beat. And as I look up to the dark, starry sky, I realise once again that our beauty as a people comes from our hearts and spirits. More than anything, it's these simple moments that keep me on the road and in Africa.

The club is already packed when we arrive, and the deejay is blasting ragga, zouk and bongo flavour hits. I never make it to the bar to buy a beer. Instead I join the bodies grinding against each other in rhythm with the beats; this is my scene, when the dance floor becomes playful and we run our hands on each other's bodies to add more fire to the lust-soaked atmosphere.

When the deejay plays RDX's 'Bend Over', we lurch onto each other and dance the dutty wine like we're in the Caribbean, dry humping and frisking each other. When the song chants 'now let me push in' we prop our bodies doggy-style and simulate the lyrics. We're dripping sex appeal but we know it's just fun. Our laughter rises above the song. My ragga high wears off and I leave the club to wander around the beach.

Groups of people sit around bonfires passing bottles of vodka and tequila and spliffs; some people dance to the beat of the drummers in the mix. I'm sleepy but the only boats leaving for Old Town are private ones. I ask someone to wake me up when a public boat leaves.

I've spent two years across three regions in Africa, sleeping at taxi ranks and border crossings, napping in strangers' houses while waiting for transport to my next destination. My safety has never been on the line, even when I pass out at the most remote spot on the beach. When people do come over, it's to check that I'm still fine and, finally, to let me know that the public boat is leaving. This is why I return to Lamu two years later after its reputation is tainted by pirates who kidnap a European. The Lamu I know and love is not hateful or unsafe.

1 January 2011

Surprise, surprise – the town that believes that life must unfold pole pole, slowly without any urgency in how we move, is hyperactive this morning. It's just gone past 8.30am and the air is already thick with the smell of samosas, chapati and thick coconut pancakes called vitumubua. The slow shuffles around the square on the Kenyatta road have been replaced with quick steps. There are no people huddled around news stands or squeezed into shops. Donkeys aren't shaking with the weight of goods that have just been offloaded from the main land. We greet each other in passing and keep moving. It's the day of the dhow race – one of three times in the year when the island puts on a massive party. The others are to celebrate Prophet Mohammed's birthday and the Lamu cultural festival, when the island explodes with music and dancing that culminates in a donkey race.

On the first day of every year, the best boatmen in a town where half the population spend their time in the water leave their fishing nets at home and sail to Shela Beach. I walk there and for the first time since my arrival, the three old men I drink coffee and chew mirar with are not in the shop, the Maasai market is also closed and the morans walk around empty-handed instead of waving trinkets they sell to beach bummers.

In Shela, people have already taken their places at the beach and along the walls that separate hotels from the beach crowd. Rooftops and patios are filled with hotel guests in bikinis and beach shorts, beers and cocktails in hand. The usual beach crowd in swim wear is joined by women and children with boubous; their ice lollies melting in the sun. There are no windsurfers in the water, only boys frolicking between boats that are lined up for the race. They have names like *Upendo*, *Beyonce*, *Subira* and declarations like *Nakupenda* and *Friends Forever* and are decked with national flags from different countries. One dhow has the flags of Kenya and Sweden, another has the flag of South Africa. Many flags feature Bob Marley's face. A dhow with a sound system and Aladdin's Genie as a mascot sails behind them to set the party mood.

When the race gets going, anyone who isn't a fish in water screams and blows whistles from the sidelines while more than twenty boats race across the sea and back. They tilt and sway from the weight of several boatmen hanging on the poles.

Team Peponi wins the race, and the beach turns into a party with small groups of people jamming to whatever floats their boat;

like a series of parties that are happening at the same time instead of one massive jam session.

I leave for Nairobi the following morning and call Arrot for the second time in three weeks to ask for a favour. I'm running out of money again and need a free place to stay until a pay cheque shows up in my bank account.

She meets me in town a few hours later to take me to the house she shares with her friend Nick in Ongatha Rongai on the outskirts of the city. The name means small wilderness or plains in the Maasai language. Rongai of 2011 is chaos, with rows of low-rise apartment buildings that haven't been painted, leaving them looking like their construction is still in progress with large concrete bricks and splatters of dry cement. The open drains have rusted zinc and nailed planks used as walk ways over them. The shacked kiosks are squeezed between business centres with dental and medical offices, internet cafés and kinyozis that sell their haircutting services on hand-painted boards that show clippers and different haircuts. Beauty salons use old-style hairdryers, and the verandas in front of shops are occupied by gas cylinders.

There are as many kiosks of M-pesa mobile money agents that move cash around the country to places where banks don't go, as there are other types of businesses. The stretches of dusty pavements have been taken over by vegetable stalls, wheeled carts with slices of watermelon and pineapple, hardware shops and welders melting metal into gates.

Hawkers walk slowly between them with buckets of boiled eggs they serve with a teaspoon of kachumbari. Women sit on stools fanning braziers to grill mealies or cook githeri, the hearty Kikuyu dish made with boiled maize and beans. Butchers hack fatty goat carcasses that hang on hooks nailed in front of their counters with machetes. The air is dusty and black from the smoky, loud, colourful matatus that stop abruptly. This makes cars honk furiously at them while bicycles and human traffic weave seamlessly in between. At the market area, vendors pile bundles of kale, called sukumawiki, which translates into stretch the week, as a nod to its affordability and popularity, on the ground. It smells like the bountiful fresh coriander that's always on sale.

It's love at first impression. On the walks I go on to explore my new home, herds of cattle and goats vie for space with residents, who include women tottering over mud puddles in high heels. I always smile when I run into the chic woman who walks the white Pomeranian poodle she keeps at hand with a studded red leather leash. Gravel roads give way to footpaths between grazing fields and open skies where birds swoop freely. Here, there are no apartment buildings or walled gates. Houses have yards with fruit trees, and my solitude gets broken by herders walking their flocks back home at sunset, when the sky becomes dark blue and the full moon rises behind flat zinc roofs. This side of Rongai smells like soil after the rain.

The Maasai market travels around different parts of the city to sell art, crafts, cloth, jewellery, shukas, kitenges, kangas and kikoyis. It's at Prestige Plaza on Tuesday, Capital Centre in South B on Wednesday, Junction Mall in Dagoretti on Thurday, the Village Market in Gigiri on Friday, the High Court parking lot downtown on Saturday and the Yaya Centre in Hurlingham on Sunday.

It makes economic sense for me to shop on Saturday, when Arrot's status as a resident gets me better prices. Even though they sell a variety of goods, including beautifully coloured calabashes for home decor and carved masks from the DRC, I'm only interested in Maasai trinkets. Arrot and I walk around the section with old women who sit on kangas on the ground; their goodies laid out in front of them while they turn beads into necklaces, crowns, earrings, bracelets and anklets. I point at what I want and let Arrot do my haggling in case my accent gives away my mzungu status.

My first buy is a necklace with seventeen colour-blocked triangles in green, red, white, orange and blue between the white beads and loose, green strings with cowrie shells at the end, a blue and white choker with chains that have small metal disks, two bracelets and anklets and a crown I buy after the old woman says it brings out my eyes with the red beaded strings that frame my cheekbones. The effect makes a car full of fellows in Westlands call me 'Maasai mrembo' – beautiful Maasai. It's not unusual for me to catch a glimpse of myself in the mirror during the day and recoil at how I look. I hate mornings, and dress to cover instead of adorn my body. I wear little black dresses to be practical instead of being chic and often, the only thing I like when I catch these glimpses is the kanga or kintenge I drape across my neck as my only accessory. I don't stop traffic. People don't use the fractions of seconds when they see me in passing to holler that I'm beautiful. This moment is the beginning of a new relationship with clothes; one where I'm a traffic-stopping beauty without looking like a product of a mass marketing fashion campaign. Besides being my home, the source of my Pan-African politics and the scope of my work, Africa becomes my standard of beauty.

I'm in the affluent side of Nairobi to apply for permission to visit Kakuma refugee camp at the offices of the Refugee Affairs Secretariat. After decades of fighting to become their own nation, South Sudan is voting for secession from North Sudan. I want to write the historic moment from the perspective of the largest community of Sudanese refugees in the world, in Kakuma.

XVI

A New Sudan

February 2011

BUSES TO KAKUMA ARE in Kitale, where my pick of coaches have names like Western Emirates, Palm Dam, Happy Safari and Climax Coaches. The usual cacophony of travellers and hawkers with boxes of snacks, posters of Jesus and Christian books that comes with my wait for the bus is broken by a woman who keeps whacking her toddler's head whenever the baby cries. My heart is in my hands for more than sixteen hours, including overnight, on roads that get smaller and sandier as we put more distance between us and the hills of Kitale.

This is the worst bus I've been on. Some cushions have fallen off the seats, windscreens have cracks and broken windows have been covered up with plastic and cardboard boxes. Those that still have glass are covered in layers of grime and dust blanks out the landscape unless we force them open with twigs. The dust that rises when we drive comes back into the bus, and settles on us.

The Turkana region is rural semi-desert. The spare and desolate villages we pass are populated by men and women who hang out in separate groups; the men sitting on stools they walk around with and the women leaning against mud houses and shacks. Layers of beads cascade down their necks, and their hair is styled into mohawks with shaved sides.

Without the hills that look indigo in the fading darkness, the trip to Kakuma wouldn't be worth the trek. We arrive just after sunrise, when the light proves that the town lives up to its name. Kakuma means nothing in Swahili. It's a one-road town with some shops, a bus office, a dilapidated hotel with grime-stained walls and a Somali restaurant that only sells rice, boiled goat stew and chips. There's a police station and an office complex where newly arrived refugees go to register their presence. The path to the camp has signboards for campaigns that promote safe sex and ending gender-based violence. Signboards without campaigns have logos of the United Nations and aid agencies that work here.

When the boda boda drops me off at the camp, the thing that stands out the most is how inhospitable it looks. People live in UN-branded tents and mud houses that don't all have windows or doors and yards are marked with enclosures made with shrubs.

I arrive at the polling station covered with dust and sweat, and the nasty whiff I catch in the air is from my armpits. The only people around are Augostino Loro, the head of the polling station, and a voting officer called Joseph. Most of the voters made their mark in the first two days of the voting process, and while the polls are still open, everyone is meeting at the Southern Sudanese section of the camp for a celebratory lunch; I'm invited. 'It hasn't started yet, maybe you should go to your hotel to freshen up,' Joseph suggests. I don't even have enough money to buy my ticket back to Nairobi; ditto a hotel room. 'I want to start working. Do you mind if I go with you to the camp? Besides, waiting for the party to start will give me time to just hang out and get to know people,' I tell him.

A tall, upright woman with bushy white hair strides into the compound with a gun in one hand and a cross on her back. Moving between the gathering crowd and the mud huts, she crouches behind a wall of dry shrubs to shoot at her enemies. 'Free Sudan,' screams a woman in the crowd, her fist punching the air. 'Free Sudan,' everyone roars back. Dripping with sweat, the old woman returns from her war and stands in the middle of the crowd. She points her gun at the sky and pulls the trigger. Her body shakes when she fires her gun. 'New Sudan,' the crowd yells before falling into a lull the old woman breaks again when she jumps away from the crowd to start running around the yard.

She hides behind a hut, then creeps between trees to get to another hut, like a soldier on the battlefield. She stands in the middle of the crowd again when she returns from war, and holds her gun with both hands before pulling the trigger for the last time. Her weapon is a cracked plank with a rusty nail in the place of a trigger and her war gear is the cropped camouflage jacket she is wearing over a pastel pink two-piece.

15 January 2011 has lived in the prayers of Southern Sudanese people for more than three blood-soaked decades. To the thousands of Southern Sudanese refugees who call Kakuma refugee camp home, today is a balm on the wound that festers every time they go to the town's main road, where a sign reminds them that they're only five hundred and sixty-two kilometres away from Juba; their capital city and a home that's become too volatile and poor for them to follow the road for one hundred kilometres to the Lokichoggio border.

We are gathered here on this sweltering afternoon to celebrate what everyone tells me is inevitable: Africa is getting a new country. Speakers keep their words short, recalling the heartbreak of fleeing their villages and the farms and livestock they lost to war. Several decry that while some forty-four per cent of their land is rich with gold, diamonds and ore, among other minerals, they live in desperate poverty. More than the hunger and fear they feel trekking to Kakuma, some on their feet, they remember the countless loved ones who paid with their lives on and off the battlefield for South Sudan's independence.

The tears and chants of a new and free Sudan are followed by lunch. Meals are usually a flat bread called gorrassa served with beans or boiled corn kernels. Money is scarce, and almost everything people in the camp live on is from the World Food Programme. They have pooled their few shillings together to feast on gorrassa with beef cooked in water and fried in its fat, cabbage that's been fried brown, and an okra and spinach dish that slides off my fingers. I only eat what I like when I want to, but I feel rude for letting myself be disgusted by the okra, so I tuck in. We toast to freedom with warm Fanta Orange and Coke.

I hang around Joseph when the crowds start getting thin, waiting patiently when people ask him when they can go back to the station.

'It's not as if we need the votes, mind you, we know that South Sudan is going to be free after today, but people want to vote because we have all waited our whole lives, so we want to be able to say "I voted for our freedom", he tells me.

And then that awkward question again: 'Are you going to your hotel? Things are going to be quiet until the evening.' The only plan I have for now is waiting until the hotel closes at night, so I can steal a place to sleep on the porch, or get the bus that's leaving for Nairobi in the morning if I can sell my phone. I tell him I just need a place to shower instead. He passes me off to a teen girl called Elizabeth.

She shares four mud huts with her grandmother, aunt and several siblings and cousins. Elizabeth loves beauty and order, and her bedroom matches her taste. They are among the better off families here with huts that have doors and windows and floors made of cow dung. Elizabeth's hut has a double bed, three white plastic chairs, a dressing table, and a square mirror that only shows her face. Her ceiling is an orange and green kitenge covering a grass roof.

Act two of the celebrations is a parade that grows in numbers on the way back to the polling station. It starts with a group of women who form a dancing circle while waiting for their friends. The old woman who had a gun at lunch is centre stage again, and her weapon replaced by jazz fingers she waves in the air. A group of drummers turn the station into a party zone, and as a small group of voters make their mark, the large audience dance and sing some more. People cry, holding onto each other in long embraces. Augostino addresses the crowd before final votes are cast. 'It's obvious that most of us voted against unity. Like everyone, I have lost family members. My uncle was killed when the plane he was travelling in on his way to Khartoum was shot down. This is why I grew up wanting freedom,' he says, to cheers and chants of 'new Sudan.' He adds: 'Some are questioning if a free South Sudan will be a success. Well, I believe it's better to be a free dog than a caged lion.' The crowd cheers. 'We are not talking about "if we get freedom". We know we will separate from the North, so we're talking about the future. It will be bright for us but there's a lot of work to do. Infrastructure is poor, hospitals and schools are in a poor state and there is a lot of rehabilitation to be done but we're optimistic that everything will go well.'

I follow the voters inside the station and stick around for the count. The office has two tables. One has boxes with all the ballots and another is empty other than folded papers with the words 'Yes', 'Unity', 'Unmarked' and 'Invalid'. To count, one officer opens the ballots like an envelope at an awards show and holds it up for everyone to see before passing it to the officer who puts each vote under its marked section on the table. All ballots go to 'Yes'.

'It's unanimous,' the officer says when he opens the last ballot.

The results will fly to Juba, where they'll be counted again with other ballots from around the world.

Act three: We leave a trail of dust clouds behind us, hurrying to the sports ground in Zone Three of the camp. I'm with Elizabeth and her friend Kirr, who is 'visiting home from Adelaide to witness the birth of my country and celebrate our freedom with my family'. He's an engineering student who has found his way out of the camp.

The crowd is the biggest I've been around all day. We form a wide circle that grows to the edge of the field. Even with the screaming and singing, you can still hear the loud banging from the drums. From opposite sides of the circles, a single, straight line with about seven people moves to the middle of the circle in perfectly synched shuffles, their right hands waving long thin sticks as they leap like antelope into the air. There is more crying and laughing, someone faints and everyone has the time of their life. My cheeks are wet with tears.

I walk to a young girl who has been keeping to herself since I first laid eyes on her at the polling station. 'This is so emotional,' I say, breaking the ice. She turns her face to look at me. Her soaked blouse is all the answer I need. 'I don't remember my father,' she says at last. 'He was killed in the war when I was young and my three siblings don't know him at all.' The camp is the only home they know. 'When I remember my mother's struggle to raise us, and the days when we had nothing at all to eat, I know our suffering was not in vain.' Somewhere in the crowd, the old woman is still going strong with her gun and cross back in her hands.

Elizabeth and I go back home so I can collect my bags. She offers me a place on her bed when she finds out that I don't have money for a hotel. We visit Kirr and his family on Sunday morning, and I get a snapshot of what childhood is like when you're born into war. It reaches his village in Atar in the Upper Nile region when he's three years old. He flees to a military camp in Dima in central Ethiopia when he's nine.

'Think of it as being like any child who goes to school, but instead of playing games when we go on break, we'd learn songs of the revolution and how to use guns.'

In the years between Ethiopia and moving to Kakuma, Kirr sees people drowning and dying from diseases and animal attacks. About growing up a child soldier, he says: 'There is a saying that "a child of a snake is also a snake". The career of your father becomes yours as well. My father and uncle were also in the struggle; I learned about freedom from them and, like them, I fought for it.'

I show him photographs from the celebratory lunch and ask if he knows the old woman with the toy gun and the cross. We find Adhiu Dau-Duot at her house in a dress that has been turned into a rag from being worn many times through the years. Her energy from the previous day is gone, as if her body suddenly remembered that it's eighty years old. Kirr leaves me at the house while he visits his girlfriend. She's Kenyan and they met when he lived in Nairobi. Alone with Mama Adhiu, one of her grandchildren becomes our translator as she takes me through her life. She talks with many gaps in her story to avoid the most painful parts of her life. She doesn't remember what exactly in her violent political times made her become a guerrilla, only that she was around twenty-eight. Her husband was also in the struggle. 'The toughest part about fighting in a war is holding on to life and protecting it. We used to eat anything to feed the belly. I ate sand and leaves; we did everything to support life, even if it meant drinking urine so we don't die from thirst.'

The pain of losing her home and husband is nothing compared to losing five children to the war. She put her gun down in 1992, after the arrival of her last-born child. Starting over in Kakuma in 1994, she lived in a tent, slowly building her hut with her hands. She shoots up from the chair, pouncing to her gun before aiming it at the sky. Her grandchildren laugh. She doesn't want to go back to South Sudan.

'This is my home and there is no one to take care of me in Sudan; but now that my country is free, I can start enjoying my old age.' She's been holding her breath, waiting for freedom for fifty-two years. 'My biggest fear was dying before Sudan becomes free.'

Later in the afternoon, I walk around the camp, meeting residents from DRC, Darfur, Ethiopia and Somalia on my way to the town. The river is dry from the drought that's killing livestock and plants before they grow. I hang out with Turkana teens between trying to hustle money for my ticket. I only have 80 bob on me. Everyone I approach is too broke to buy my phone.

'And even if I had money,' a Congolese guy says to me at the camp, 'No one uses a Nokia 3310 in 2011.'

That evening, Elizabeth and I sit under a jet-black night sky with a crescent moon, eating a stew of mushy corn kernels seasoned with salt and gorrassa. Liz plays a song on her phone. She and her cousins sing along at the top of their voices. I don't get up to join them when they dance, even when they pull me off my chair.

Before Kakuma, refugee camps are a place I know in name and through news reports of humanitarian crises; a halfway house for people looking for a place to stay a while between war and peace. I don't say this to anyone, but even with the thousands if not millions of shacks and mud houses I've seen, even after living on grilled plantain and peanuts for two weeks in Accra to fend off hunger while waiting for pay day, I don't silence the voice in my head whenever it whispers 'what a sad, pitiful life'. I see myself not as a woman at home but an observer to tragedy. I relate to the camp as someone who is conditioned to only see hopelessness and suffering.

Watching Elizabeth and her cousins dance, I'm ashamed of myself for belittling their home and sniggering at the crumbling buildings and shaking my head in despair at the woman sitting outside her doorless hut with her son; too conditioned to recognise that what I first think of as a place that's not fit for habitation is actually a home, and that the people I insult with my attitude are rebuilding their lives from rock bottom, one mud brick at a time. The school I pitied gives Kirr and many others wings to get scholarships and education at universities around the world – something that my okay final school report wouldn't qualify me for.

Elizabeth sits next to me and plays the song again. 'Listen carefully,' she instructs.

Emmanuel Jal is her favourite musician, and 'Stronger' is her theme song.

Emmanuel sings about growing up in the village of Tonj and the effects the war had on his childhood. He talks about how he comes from people who overcome pain without losing their humanity. The chorus echoes the universal belief that what doesn't kill us makes us stronger. Emmanuel is counted among the forty thousand child soldiers known as the Lost Boys of Sudan, who walked from South Sudan to Ethiopia and Kenya, where Kakuma refugee camp was set up in 1992 to house them.

Emmanuel has never lived in Kakuma; still, his story inspires Elizabeth. It affirms her humanity and legitimises her dreams. She's not just some displaced person who relies on aid for food, education, health, sanitation and jobs. As if she's reading my mind, Elizabeth says, 'Sure, it's tough being a refugee and our life is hard but you know what? Kakuma is our home.'

I ask her to play 'Stronger' again, and I'm the first to get up and dance. For the first time since my arrival, I stop thinking of Kakuma as a refugee camp: It's home, and mine too after Elizabeth takes me in.

I want to rewrite narratives about refugee camps because of this moment.

I retrace my steps to town just before midday on Monday to keep looking for someone who'll buy my phone. This time, I can see clearly. My heart swells with pride at the kids who are in school, I marvel at the yards that are being swept clean and smile at the mud pile that's being mixed with water and twigs to build new homes. The market becomes a bustling business centre with shops that sell coal, food, produce and household goods. There are kangas and kitenges, black and colourful burkas, other types of clothes, utensils, coals and kerosene; shoes, a hair salon, DVD rental, a TV to keep up with soccer games and life beyond Kakuma. There is a butchery and an Ethiopian restaurant next to a building advertising itself as a 'hotel', where a group of men lounge over coffee and bags of mirar.

I never get around to finding a buyer. Instead, a Turkana man called James takes me to the police station where he asks police officers to pool money for my ticket. They pay for my ticket to Kitale and give me 2000 shillings to cover my bus fare to Nairobi, padkos and my matatu from downtown to Rongai. I feel like the luckiest person in the world; loved unconditionally and so cherished that the weight of travelling around Africa is also carried by people who sacrifice the little they have to help me live through another day.

I leave Nairobi for Rwanda a week later on a Kampala Coach bus, retracing my steps to Kampala, where I transfer to a bus to Kigali. David and Arrot are no longer my friends. They are my family.

I have an insatiable wanderlust and know no other thrill as addictive as turning places that I only knew by name into the story of my life. More than everything that makes me roam Africa, I'm most intrigued by ancient places. The Djinguereber Mosque in Timbuktu still stands as tall and proud as it has been since 1324 when it was built on the instruction of Mansa Musa. This is my favourite picture of myself.

A collection of one of the thousands of manuscripts that remain from days when Timbuktu was the centre of scholarship. They are still passed from one generation to the next by families, making them some of the most precious heirlooms anyone can inherit.

Tuareg men put on a sword 'fight' at the Festival of the Desert.

This photo was taken on the afternoon of my first visit to Djicoroni Para in Bamako, where I end up moving in a group of more than ten vagabonds. Djicoroni Para is easily one of the most downtrodden places I know, yet it is also my treasure for the unconditional love and sense of belonging I find here.

The Malian hot season brought me to house number 227 Djicoroni Para. The four months I spent here helped me find my feet as a vagabond. My purpose of rewriting African narratives was crystallised here. The white woman is Miriam, next to her are Abbas and Mohammed from Conakry. Mohammed the snake charmer enjoyed regaling us with stories of his trips to the Gambia more than beading. The woman at the other end of the balcony is Oumou and the boy next to her is Champion at his tea station.

If yassa is good enough for Salif Keita to sing about in 'Africa' then it's worth me learning how to cook it. I become the kitchen skivvy to sisters Astou, who is sitting on my left, and Oumou.

Every day at around 3pm, fishermen bring in large hauls of fish to Zalala Beach in Quilemane.

Pemba has three faces. My favourite is the beachfront one with its crystal blue waters and live music wafting from a parking lot behind the beach café.

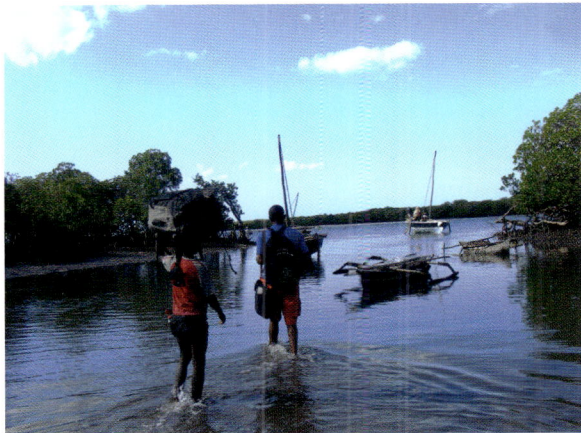

Destinations that are the hardest to reach, I find, are often the most rewarding. Ibo in the Quirimbas Archipelago in Northern Mozambique is one such destination.

The famous Zanzibar sunset.

Stone Town, where time seems to have stood still since the days of its Omani rulers and Swahili rolls off the tongue like a melody.

The Swahili word for paradise is peponi. It's an apt description of Zanzibar.
© Mahlatsi Maredi

Lake Tanganyika at sunset during the rainy season turns indigo, adding an air of mysticism to Bujumbura. The lake flows in Tanzania, DRC, and Zambia as well.

Sixteen drummers wrapped in green, white and red cloth file onto the stage, an open field in front of a school, with drums on their heads. They move in sync. An elder dressed in a raffia robe leads the troupe.

Lamu has narrow streets that are ruled by donkeys. The oldest town on the Swahili coast is full of little surprises that make it one of the most wonderful places to experience.

Adhiu Dau-Duot waited fifty-two years for South Sudan to gain its independence from North Sudan. However, she didn't want to leave Kakuma Refugee Camp, which has become her home.

The Hamar tribe is one of several who live in the Omo Valley in Southern Ethiopia.

Emmanuel eating a chunk of raw beef. Tera Sega is a favourite across Ethiopia.

One of my most vivid childhood memories is the Saturday school class that introduced me to ancient Egypt and the Pyramids of Giza. This is when I tell myself that a day will come when I discover the world beyond what I know of it.

Ibn Tulun Mosque is the oldest in Egypt. It was built by Ahmad Ibn Tulun from 870 to 879 AD. He was born the son of a Turkish slave and died the founder of the Tulunid Dynasty of Egypt.

These are some of the accessories ancient Egyptians adorned themselves with.
© Karim Hegab

A short walk from Lisamin Safari Hotel in Khartoum was an old woman with a simple coffee stall on the street. It was very basic: a small table, a couple of kettles to boil her water, drinking glasses and jars with coffee, ginger, sugar, and cardamom. I'd sit quietly with her and we would communicate with our smiles. It was such a tender and loving way to start my mornings.

Khartoum's skyline from the confluence of the White and Blue Nile rivers.

Old Dongola was founded in the fifth century. It was the capital of the Makuria Nubian kingdom.

XVII

Hearing Voices

March 2011

RWANDA IS AN ABSOLUTE pleasure to travel. Crossing over in
Gatuna from Uganda, I walk into officialdom and efficiency –
everyone and everything is where it belongs. There are no idlers
and hustlers and money is changed at a container that's been turned
into a bureau de change. We form a straight queue to wait our turn
at the immigration counter, where the customs official does his
job without asking or expecting a thank you franc note. When he
pages through my passport, poring over visas and stamps, his only
question is if I enjoyed myself. 'You're going to love Rwanda,' he
declares. I already love that my three-month visa is free.

Cars are in a designated parking lot and buses pass through
a searching station one at a time. Our driver stands at the door,
holding it open while an officer looks under seats and in overhead
compartments. A second officer does the same to our luggage. It
has been offloaded from storage, and we open our bags one person
at a time. 'Is this your bag, miss?' he asks. He follows my nod with

'may I please see what's inside?' He doesn't rummage through my things or invade my privacy by asking what my tampons are for. He does this to every passenger until he is satisfied that we meet a very important condition for getting into Rwanda. Plastic bags are not used in the country or allowed in. He takes the ones he finds and sends us on our way. There isn't a scrap of plastic or litter on the eighty-six-kilometre trip to Kigali.

The country lives up to its reputation as the land of a thousand hills. The villages are the quintessential picture of rural Africa, with fat brown cows that have long white horns flicking their tails while they graze in green fields. Farmers are bent over their land, pulling carrots, cauliflower and onions out of dark brown soil. There are no children on the farms; they're in school or walking home from school with books pressed against their chests. They wave at us and blow kisses our way.

Kigali is as perfect as everyone says it is. From our last stop in Nyabugogo terminal, I get a boda boda to the city centre. Even in the chaos of the bus station, with traffic streaming in from most parts of the country and beyond the border, the city is meticulously organised. The are no vendors darting between traffic to sell water and toys, and even though the matatus are as regional as ever with bodies that are splashed with pictures of Drake, Rihanna, Snoop Dogg, Shakira, G Unit, Beyoncé by herself and with Jay Z, and African soccer stars who play for European clubs, like Didier Drogba, Samuel Eto and Michael Essen, they don't blare with music. They only stop at designated stops, and boda boda drivers all wear helmets and keep a spare one for their passenger.

Boda bodas elsewhere in Africa pile in as many passengers as they can fit. Here, it's always one person on a trip. They also only stop at marked areas. Robots have timers that tells us when to stop and when to go, people don't jaywalk and only use pedestrian crossings and intersections. The city doesn't vibrate with music booming from shops and cafés, and there are no hawkers turning pavements into mini markets. When people say Kigali is clean, they mean that there is no litter anywhere and no weeds growing wildly on the road side. Kigali is also perfectly beautiful. I catch my breath regularly, amazed at the city's efficiency and the hills that envelope it.

I've been in the city for less than thirty minutes and I'm already bored out of my mind. It's not Kigali. It's me: I don't like sterile places.

The excitement I feel in Gatuna and on the way to Kigali turns into a flat line that I never recover from when I check into my hotel, the One Love Club. I choose it even though it's way out of my budget because it's also called Kwa Rasta. I imagine thumping raggae beats and a night spent on the dance floor. Needless to say, I have been to funeral wakes that had a more vibrant atmosphere.

I've been wanting to visit Rwanda since watching *Hotel Rwanda* in 2004: The true story of the heroic Paul Rusesabagina and the refuge he gives Tutsi people at Hotel Mille Collines instead of leaving them to die at the hands of Hutu militia. The movie makes me think of the genocide beyond simply knowing about it. I was a child in 1994. After watching the movie and revisiting the genocide that happens when I'm still a kid, my heart can't help but break over how sad it is that while I was high on the euphoria of Nelson Mandela becoming South Africa's first black president, my age mates in Rwanda were bearing witness to the greatest atrocity of their time. It makes 1994 the best and worst of times in Africa. I'm here to know Rwanda through experience instead of only through the memory of its most horrific chapter.

Destination Rwanda is still trying to establish itself beyond trekking mountain gorillas in the Virungas, and other than arts centres, museums and the market, there isn't much I can do in the city except experience its social life.

I make my first mistake within minutes of leaving the hotel when I start my day at the Kigali Genocide Memorial. The building looks like millions of dollars have been poured into it. The mansion with colonial architecture, stained glass windows and manicured rose gardens and flowers that dance to the morning breeze hides the horror it preserves. It's set on a hill and offers sweeping views of the city. Its looks help me explore the memorial without feeling any of the emotions displayed by other visitors. I cushion my emotions by pretending that I'm at a multimedia art installation, watching and listening to videos of survivors recounting the experiences while looking at pictures of the departed. It's curated history, and even as tears stream down their red faces, visitors stop to admire the windows and the view.

At the mass graves at the back, I sidestep what lies underneath by choosing to focus on the dark purple cloth that covers the graves. Purple is my favourite colour.

When I get to the name plaques of the murdered, their perfectly inscribed names allow me to further pretend that I'm at a show, even as sadness starts creeping up on me. It catches up with me at the children's room. It's the most personal room, showing pictures sourced from family albums next to their short biographies. David Mugiraneza, ten, wanted to be a doctor and enjoyed making people laugh. Ariana Umutoni was a four-year-old lover of cake, milk, singing and dancing. She was stabbed in her eyes until she died. Other than jogging with her dad, Nadia Channelle Ruterana, eight, also loved milk and chocolate. She was chopped with a machete. Fidele Ingabira, nine, was shot in the head. Sisters Irene and Uwamwezi Umutoni, six and seven, were killed when a grenade was thrown in their shower. They were daddy's girls who loved fresh fruit and playing with a doll they shared. Patrick Gashuyi Shimwira, five, was best friends with his sister Alliane. He loved riding his bicycle and eating meat and eggs. Aurore Kirezi loved playing hide and seek with her big brother. She was burned alive with one-hundred and ten other people at Gikondo chapel. When the militia reached Hubert Kirenya's house, the two-year-old watched his mother getting shot to death before the gun was turned on him. Thierry Ishimwe was too small for a nine-year-old. He was killed with a machete in his mother's arms. Fillette Uwase, two, was a good girl and best friends with her dad. She was banged against a wall until she died. Fabrice Cyemeza loved his cat and eating rice with milk. His favourite person was his aunty. He was fifteen months old when he was killed at Muhoro church. Sister and brother Yvonne and Yves, five and three, were a daddy's girl and a mommy's boy. They were hacked with a machete at their grandmother's house. I blink and refuse to let the tears fall.

I never recover from the children's room, and their dreams and habits follow me around town. I wonder if Patrick would still love cycling when I see a bicycle at a shop, and if Ariana's favourite drink would still be milk when I pour it into my coffee at Bourbon coffee shop. It makes me suspicious of people I meet, and something as basic as paying for my Coke Light at Nakumatt opens a flood gate of questions in my mind: What makes people turn on each other so cruelly that an estimated eight hundred thousand of the population is wiped out in a hundred days? Are people genuinely friendly when they smile or are they simply moving on from the trauma in a way that Africans do, when we pick up the pieces and rebuild life after violence without stopping to heal our traumas, glossing over the surface with new buildings and slogans of being open for business?

My simple pleasure of people watching and walking the streets to drop in on strangers and start conversations feel like a performance. Even looking at mosques, which usually fills me with peace, feels forced. I hate that I'm in Rwanda to get over the genocide yet my mind fixates on it. I'm scared to raise my voice in case I trigger someone. I feel guilty for hours when I catch myself with my butter knife pointing at a waiter. When I go out to sample brochette – one of Kigali's favourite things to eat – I decline joining a table of middle-aged men who invite me over to theirs. What if they were on the wrong side of the genocide and I associate with murderers?

After my night at Kwa Rasta, I move to Discover Rwanda Youth Hostel in Kimihurura, so efficient that their website has their address and directions to get me there from the business district: From the Union Trade Centre building you will approach the Kigali Business Centre roundabout. Continue straight on from this roundabout and beat left to the traffic lights and take your first right hand turn onto the cobblestone road. Continue along this road for approximately eight hundred metres, pass the Trattoria bar and restaurant and as the road takes a sharp bend to the left, you will find Discover Rwanda on this corner.

It has a more social atmosphere from overland travellers and backpackers who are on their way to trek silverback gorillas. Talk of experiencing the rare event takes over whenever the emotional effects of visiting the genocide memorial creep up. Still, the air is heavy. It gets darker for me when one of the residents takes his guitar to the garden, where he sings 'Kumbaya My Lord' over and over again, like he's trying to heal his soul.

Two nights in Kigali are enough for me to believe that Kigali doesn't float my boat. My escape is to Gisenyi, on the shores of Lake Kivu.

Like all trips around the country, this one is breathtaking. The thousand hills have an oceanic nature and everything looks green, like it has just rained. My faith in the existence of a God has been questionable lately. At best, I think of this mythical creator as an invisible superhero who lives in outer space; in Rwanda, I start thinking maybe there is a God after all because it's the only way to explain the mesmerising beauty, the clear blue skies and the mystical atmosphere.

My spirit becomes light again in Gisenyi from losing myself in its wide boulevards and my walks up steep roads flanked by banana trees. I'm smiling again, which last happened at Gatuna border, and even flirt with the uniforms who catch me stealing photographs of a military building. When I'm out for tea and chapati at a dingy café that smells like ammonia, I invite myself to people's tables and ask them to teach me Kinyarwanda knowing very well that like Portuguese, it gets stuck in my tongue, which turns my language tutorials into a joke that's on me. I order my meals of rice and fish, wali na sámaki, in Swahili and invite other diners to my table; amusing them with stories of my war with border officials and indulging their instinct to help me add more words to my Swahili vocabulary by translating everything they say to English to let them know that I'm keeping up with the conversation.

I radiate with happiness, as Remy, a man I meet at one of the restaurants, says. His left arm was amputated in the genocide but it doesn't bother me. It makes me respect this nation's ability to move on from horror without bitterness. When I visit the centre where Remy works with other people disabled by the genocide, I refuse to join the basketball game that's in session. 'Oh my honeys,' I say, 'Don't be fooled by this body that still has two of every limb; it can only walk, swim and dance.'

I'm still bored, but it's only because I feel restless without money to buy activities like cruises. There's only so much walking and watching the sunset turn Lake Kivu gold that I can do without wanting to escape to a more adventurous place.

I find it five kilometres from the beach when I see a signboard that says turning right will lead me to Goma in the DRC.

'Bella, I know you and I'm telling you now that you better not get up to your usual kak when you are in Gisenyi,' Heidi's words ring in my mind. While Heidi lived in Nairobi, she travelled around East Africa auditioning participants for her TV show. But she never took time out to explore outside of the few hours she stole to trek gorillas in Kigali. She knows I'll want to sneak into Goma without a visa for the fun of it. 'I promise I will behave myself,' I tell her, convinced that I will.

If I get in trouble in DRC, I will have to call the embassy and our ambassador and his wife Khanyi, the Mashimbyes, know me from our social life. They will know that I do it from boredom instead of a tale I'll spin to get out of trouble. So, no, I'm not going to Goma. Yet here I am walking past the beach front mansions to the border gate. I wait my turn to walk through the revolving gate and hand my passport over to be stamped out of Rwanda, secure in the knowledge that the country's strict adherence to regulations and Pan-African immigration policy of issuing visas on arrival for most Africans will not betray me.

I walk to the DRC side of the compound and join the line of people waiting to get their passports stamped. When my turn comes, I give the uniform my passport with the declaration that I don't have a visa in French. 'No problem at all, mademoiselle,' he says, 'Our embassy in Kigali will not give you any trouble at all, and you'll find me here when you return so I can welcome you to our country.'

As much as I want to visit DRC, the visa costs more than US$100. It's money I don't have. Or, as I rant to Siki, 'It's a fucking war zone, friend.' The least they can do is stop charging an arm and a leg to visit. 'My friend, I just want to spend a few hours in Goma to get a story that goes beyond the conflict in the area, and I'm broke. Please do me a favour,' I tell the uniform. He refuses.

'Darling Jean Pierre,' I say, changing tack to flirt. 'The truth is DRC has the best pagne in the world, and I want to shop.' He's wearing a shirt with an orange and blue print. 'I want to dress as well as the Congolese people.' It's still a no from him. I pretend to walk back to Rwanda and find a spot where I can keep my eye on Jean Pierre without him seeing me. When he leaves the counter, I walk behind one of the women who move freely around the border selling bananas and avocados from metal bowl on their heads. My plan works until I get to the exit. I mill among the mobile money traders and boys who sell SIM cards and airtime, plotting my way into Goma. This side of town is deserted. The few buildings are closed and there are no people around other than the vendors. A uniform comes over to ask me what I'm doing. 'Nothing sir, just looking for money,' I say and go back to Rwanda.

Take two of my trip to Goma happens a few days later when I discover Rubavu crossing at the other side of Gisenyi. Instead of reasoning with uniforms, I blend in with the masses of people pushing trolleys with fruit and vegetables. This is the DRC of my imagination; with snazzy dresses and women with pagne hanging loosely on their hips. The immigration office is crammed into a small yard with trucks and cars and melts into a street lined with vendors and restaurants. There's a butchery, kiosks, tailors and girls squatting next to buckets that overflow with palm oil. The ground is wet and muddy; it makes the man dressed in a white bazin tunic embossed with gold threads and matching slim-cut pants all the more resplendent.

More people pour onto the street from narrow alleys between houses. Out on the main road, Goma stops being the tragic town where, according to an Al-Jazeera special, two hundred women and girls were gang raped by the militia eight months ago. This afternoon, it's just another African city. People run errands, a shop that sells mopeds displays their shiny goods on the veranda. The streets blare with zouk music from giant speakers outside some of the shops. I pop into one that sells pagne and bazin and shake it up with a tailor who works outside it. I'm still debating if I should get a matatu to nowhere in particular when a truck with UN peacekeepers cruises by. Another one follows it; all soldiers have guns in their hands. I backtrack to the street with the immigration office and turn left into an alley that takes me through shacks that are jumbled together. Kids chase a worn leather soccer ball around, and a trickle of people walk towards Mount Nyiragongo. It becomes my new plan: I'll sit at its foot in honour of the privilege of knowing Goma through its sounds, sights and people instead of tragic news reports. Except, when I walk past the military compound, I spot a soldier at a watch-tower, scouting the area with binoculars and a machine gun. It's my cue to go back to Gisenyi.

When I leave for Kigali on Valentine's Day, the ATM's don't work, and I go to the bank to see if I can get money by any means necessary. I don't, but the gentleman who is trying to help me gives me a rose and a chocolate, and money to go back to Kigali, where I make a decision that will haunt me for years. I go to the genocide memorial in Ntarama, thirty kilometres south of the capital city.

The Catholic church is one of the seven genocide memorials in the country. It's a beautilful day to be out. There's a cool breeze and the sound of chirping birds mingles with the laughter from children at their school playground. The church yard has large, manicured gardens; it would be a lovely spot for a reading picnic.

The interior is horrific.

The walls are still stained with the blood of forty-five thousand who were killed while hiding in the house of God, given over to the militia by their priest. The victims' clothes are on the pews and their shoes are piled in one of the corners. The altar has a machete and more clothes lying around it, a rosary and picture of the virgin Mary and Jesus. It's dark and putrid, and light seeps through holes left by grenades. I follow the steps down to a small room with white-tiled floors and walls. There's a glass chamber shaped like a pyramid with a rosary, bangles and a mouldy identity card. My heart is cold, my mind clinical as I dutifully note the details like a diligent journalist.

The old man who works here asks if I need company. 'I'm fine,' I say, and make my way to the two mass graves at the back. 'You can go inside if you want,' he lets me know. This will prove to be my undoing. For now, with my notebook and pen in hand, I walk down nine steps. Lace and plain white cloth embroidered with a purple cross and purple ribbons covers the coffins. There are notes and letters with messages of remembrance and lists with names of some of the people who were killed and buried here: Rosalie Kabagwiza, Uwamriya Venerande, Uwizeye Mathieu, Uwimbabazi Rose, Mukayitesi Francois, Nyirigira Jean Bosco, Manzi Gele, Mahoro Senga, and Umuhire Giselle. I write, and climb down three steps to the right, where wood coffins are stacked on steel rails. One of them has Gakwaya Francois scribbled in black marker. My mind starts putting together a story I want to sell to a newspaper. I feel nothing and think in word count, headlines and blurbs.

The second grave has four bunks, three per row. They're stacked with skulls that have cracks from machetes and broken bones. Some remains look like the killer bashed people against metal spikes and other bodies are charred. There are skulls with cracked foreheads, skulls without jaws, skulls that have been broken into halves and others sporting holes that are as a big as a fist. A sign hanging over one of the remains remembers Ngenzi Emmanuel and Mukankwiye Patrice. I package my story – I'll call it 'Nine steps to hell' and my introduction will be delayed as I describe the remains before delving into the genocide and ending with its aftermath. 'Make the reader recoil with horror,' I write next to my descriptions of the grave. I don't believe in crying over history, no matter how harrowing, so what happens next shocks me: I collapse into a fit of tears and screams that make the gardener tap on the window to check if I'm fine. I can't breathe and I can't stand up. I'm not crying for the dead – they're gone. I'm crying from the guilt of reducing their life into a show-and-tell.

How dare I say 'never again' when Darfur is a killing field and Mogadishu still in flames sparked by the conflict that started in 1991 and is currently fuelled by al-Shabaab's bombing sprees? I'm worse than the militia because, unlike them, I pretend that I care about the lives they took away. Yet when I leave the mass grave I will go back to my life as usual, burying my despair in new, happy memories: I'm a sham, and my tears a performance put on to appease my guilt.

I compose myself and keep my eyes on the concrete pavement when I meet the gardener, and I tell the three guides that we don't have to talk any more as I had requested when I arrived: I'll only be collecting their stories of terror and survival, and asking them emotionally loaded questions to take them back to April 1994.

Then, I will leave them with their ghosts while I go back to my life.

When I get back to Kigali, I pop aspirins to quieten the lava bubbling in my head, then pack my bags to flee to Kampala to bury my guilt with its night life and waragi.

April 2011

My savings are depleted and I'm spending faster than I'm earning. I need a steady pay cheque to raise funds before getting back on the road. I leave Kampala by bus, stopping in Dar es Salaam for two days to visit my friend Tshepo, Violet's husband, for our long overdue catch up as members of a small but growing tribe of black South Africans who choose Africa before other parts of the world.

I arrive in Dar at night and decide to sleep at YWCA before moving to his house for the rest of my stay. When the dala dala conductor asks for my fare, I look for my purse in my bags and under seats. I've been robbed and my phone is gone as well so I can't call Tshepo. I check into YWCA and go to the taxi drivers who work along Maktaba street to ask for a phone to call my mom and ask her to send money via Western Union. One of them offers me a place to stay at his house overnight, but I want to be alone. He pays for my room and gives me a lift to Tshepo's the next day. I make my way back to South Africa by bus, retracing my well-worn routes to Lusaka and then Harare, where I get a bus to Pretoria and, in my mind, back to life as it was before my travels.

XVIII

LOSING MY MIND

April 2012

THE WORD FOR THE first five months of my life in 2012 is 'crazy'. I've always had a tumultuous relationship with sleep. Things hit rock bottom in 2012. I'm lucky if I get four hours of sleep and it's always interrupted around 2am as if someone has shaken me until I wake up. It takes me hours to fall back to sleep, and as a result I'm always wired on coffee and energy drinks during the day so I can function at work. I pump myself full of the Valium that I buy over the counter on trips that I still take to Tanzania, where I go around different pharmacies to get my stash. Outwardly, my life is great, even if all I do is go to work and hide out at home on weekends, claiming to friends that the distance between Pretoria and Johannesburg is keeping me from socialising, and telling family that my deadlines are the reason I can't visit.

When I do hang out, I'm on so much wine and Valium that I don't remember anything that happens after I sneak off to the bathroom to pop three or more pills, hoping to knock myself into a full night's sleep. When this happens, my mom says one morning, 'I wonder if you've finally killed yourself with these pills.' She thinks I take the occasional pill to help me sleep. No one knows about the storm in my mind.

One day at work, at a meeting to plan a new issue of *True Love* magazine, I fantasise about smashing the jug of water against the wall; I need a visual manifestation of what's happening in my mind. I excuse myself and call around until I find a psychiatrist who will see me before the day ends.

'What's troubling you?' he asks, opening floodgates I have been trying to control since March 2011. I want to scream, but everyone will hear what I'm saying. I whisper my words while bawling my eyes out. In the dreams that wake me up at 2am, I'm in a dark room with broken skulls and skeletons. I never feel afraid when I wake up, only guilty. Sometimes I cry but most times I pop a Valium and roll a joint, and still nothing works. The monsters follow me around even when I'm awake and off drugs. When I'm out for dinner, instead of enjoying my food, a voice whispers, 'Look at you, back to normal like nothing happened.' When friends take me out dancing at spots that play hiplife music, I dance to perform for them, while the voice says, 'You are a fucking sham.'

'I can't take it any more,' I tell the shrink, 'Please help me.'

He gives me anti-depressants and sleeping pills. I'm supposed to take one anti-depressant daily and half a sleeping pill at night, and still, like clockwork, I wake up at 2am to escape the dark room with skeletons; sometimes I see shadows, other times there is nothing. This also happens on nights when I take two sleeping pills.

I'm back at the psychiatrist's office two weeks later. He refers me to a clinical psychologist, who, truth be told, pisses me the hell off. She insists that I need to create a vibrant life, that helping other people will make me feel better. I've been volunteering to various causes since 1997, and still do. I may be hiding from it but I have a social life.

'Join a book club,' she says. I'm already a member of Amabhukubhuku.

'Look for a job that fulfils you,' she suggests. I love writing for black women, it feels like conversations with my sisters instead of a job.

'Perhaps what you need is travel,' she offers. I was in Zanzibar for Sauti za Busara a few weeks ago, I have a work trip to Washington in a few weeks and I'm planning a trip to Kampala.

'Please help me,' I beg her. We sigh and I walk away knowing that I'm wasting hers and the psychiatrist's time, and mine as well.

I go to the genocide memorials in Ntarama and Nyamata every night in my sleep. I'm haunted by turning tragedy into a show-and-tell. My salvation will come when I stop being a sham. I have to listen to the voice that I heard at the mass grave when it tells me that I don't have the privilege of saying never again. I have a duty to write Africa differently, to write life where others see death and take my position in the conflicts that still rage in Africa. But I'm afraid to obey.

XIX

BRAVEHEARTS

August 2012

I'M STILL FRIENDS WITH Angela, Pepe, Sandra and other people I
meet in Kampala in 2010 to write against David Bahati's hate bill
that wants gay Ugandans to be killed or jailed for life for their
sexuality. Angela has moved continents. I live vicariously through
her and spend a lot of time chatting with her on Facebook. One
day, she sends a message saying, 'If I were you, I'd be in Kampala in
the last week of July'. All she says for now is that something big is
brewing. She introduces me to her best friend, Michelle, whose real
name I can't reveal. It's still too early to let me in on the secret but if
I make sure that I'm in Kampala in July, I can stay at her house. My
features editor, Melinda Ferguson, says I don't have to take leave as
long as I come back with a killer story.

Michelle picks me up at Entebbe International Airport on the
first Monday of August. I keep my promise to her and Angela: I do
not tell anyone that I'll be in town, not even Pepe, whom I see in
Washington a few days before the trip to Kampala.

It's as if I never left. The road to Kampala still has convoys of trucks transporting matoke, vendors still sell slices of watermelon and chunks of pineapple from wooden wheelbarrows, and families of four still travel on one boda boda.

Michelle leaves me at her flat in Lunguja while she goes back to work and I catch up on my sleep. She comes back home with a bottle of waragi to fuel us for our night out. We hit the club scene and avoid places where we might run into activists. She hasn't asked her boss for leave, to avoid explaining her absence. We go to a meeting in one of the city's suburbs the next day, at the Freedom and Roam Uganda offices that are disguised to blend in with the houses around it. I finally discover what brings me to Uganda.

'Remember, if anyone asks what we're doing at any of the events, tell them that we are celebrating Kasha's birthday, are you hearing me?' Sandra, or Crazy as we call her, is standing in the middle of the room to address twenty people. Kasha, the 'radical feminist' and ferocious fighter for gay rights in Uganda and Africa, is the perfect person to throw under the bus if we run into trouble. She is indomitable.

The room remains pensive as Crazy continues with laying down the law. We must be on our best behaviour, be polite when people call us names and turn the other cheek if someone attacks us. 'I know we're all very happy but please, banange,' she says, using Ugandans' term of endearment for each other. 'More than anything, this is your moment – enjoy it.'

After they get over the shock of my sudden arrival when only the organising committee knows about Pride Uganda until a week before the event, Kasha points at my camera. 'You are the official photographer.'

The bravado that Michelle shows in the run up to Pride Uganda disappears on our way to the inauguration night. Her mood keeps shifting between euphoria and the terror of being discovered by her landlord and boss. The only thing that stops her from making a u-turn back home is the gridlocked traffic. The hotel owner is an ally and gives us a conference room that's far from the main building. There is no need to disguise the event. The room is decorated with rainbow flags and banners, and even though there are thousands of people in the gay community, around one hundred and fifty show up. LGBTI Ugandans still pay a very high price for their sexuality, they can still lose their jobs and homes if they are found out.

The mood is electric. A lot of people I know from my stay in 2010 are here. Bob, the man who breaks his rule to never speak to journalists to meet me and introduce me to Pepe, is here. He finally tells me his real name. There's an Ebola outbreak and, to contain it, we should not kiss, but we do anyway and spend a lot of time in each other's embraces. There are new faces as well: Lipstick lesbians in tight miniskirts and high heels, butch queens, femme boys, preppy boys, people dressed so plainly you'd think they're running errands. Pepe arrives in a white kanzu; his voice has become deeper. His transition is almost final. Didi's face now has stubble, and Stosh is in baggy clothes and a cap.

We move inside to get the formalities underway. They open with a prayer and a performance of The Kuchu Anthem by a band called Talented Uganda Kuchus, or TUK for short. I'm one of few people in the room who don't sing along to lyrics that assert that we are gay and proud and here to stay.

We are in church with hands stretched out to the heavens. Spirits remain high as speakers take their turn on the mic. Dr Frank Mugisha, the executive director of Sexual Minorities Uganda, says he still can't believe that Pride Uganda is happening. Kasha wants to be pinched and Bishop Christopher Senyonjo, who is expelled from the Anglican church for his tireless work against homophobia, says he's happy to see people who turned to him when no one would care for them, smiling. 'Even though tomorrow life will go back to fear and the struggles of being LGBTI in Uganda, I want to remind you that your struggle is justified – there are no gay or straight people. Human beings are made sexual, and we should all celebrate our sexuality.'

When she introduces *Call Me Kuchu*, the award-winning documentary about Uganda's LGBTI community, our MC Cleo holds her tears. 'I remember the hate and rejection from my family and how they called me a freak for wearing makeup and women's clothes.' She is a transgender woman. 'I remember how I was called a big mistake by my father and how badly it hurt when my friends and family turned against me. It hurts when you have no sense of belonging, but tonight I belong.' Kuchu is East African slang for gay. *Call Me Kuchu* is filmed against the backdrop of David Bahati's hate bill and the life and murder of David Kato as the coming-of-age tale of Uganda's LGBTI community. David finds his belonging in Johannesburg, where he lives for six years before coming back home to become the first openly gay person in Uganda. As the film follows David's life, we also meet other people and hear their stories. Growing up in Rwanda, Naome Ruzindana's mother thinks she's possessed by demons, and kicks her out. Stosh's rapist infects her with HIV after she comes out and her family forces her to abort the resultant pregnancy. We also celebrate a long-term couple's tenth anniversary and watch Long Jones put on a drag show.

Even the fun parts of the film hurt. David is attacked and killed with a hammer at his house and Long Jones has fled to the West. Tonight is the first time that people whose lives have been shown in film festivals across the world see their story. The film is banned in Uganda. The organising committee has snuck a copy into the country for Pride. The film's sound is drowned out by our tears. But this is Kampala, where hard-partying is a national sport. We warm up outside after the screening with a live show from TUK, and other entertainers who lip sync pop hits. The after party is at a club in the same area as the hotel. We take over one section of the outdoor club, and do not hold back. No one tries to disguise themselves. Girls are in each other's arms, boys are flirting and grinding up against each other on the dance floor. It's pretty obvious that we're at a queer party, and other revellers don't care. This wouldn't have happened two years ago when I first met queer Uganda.

Pride Uganda starts in November 2011 as a persistent idea in Kasha's room at a hotel that's across the street from Amnesty International headquarters in Amsterdam. Thinking about the places her activism has taken her to, she gets angry that she can be free anywhere except at home and that, unlike her, many people in her community don't have the privilege of experiencing a gay pride event.

She reflected on the possibilities and thought: 'Why not have a Pride Uganda?'

A Facebook page is set up, funds raised and history made on Thursday 2 August 2012, as the first Pride event is held outside of South Africa, where activists Simon Nkoli and Bev Ditsie led the first-ever Pride event in Africa in Johannesburg twenty-two years ago. The event has a film festival every day to incorporate aspects of gay and lesbian film festivals. Friday's main event is the fashion and rock show organised by Michelle and the parade happens on Saturday at the Entebbe Botanical Gardens. Staging Pride anywhere other than at the botanical gardens would be irresponsible when people still pay with their lives. We arrive in matatus, cars, boda bodas and hordes of minibuses.

Pepe and Didi are in black kanzus. Frank's black skin glows against his white sailor's uniform. Crazy adds a rainbow-coloured head umbrella to her uniform of shorts, a T-shirt, sneakers and socks that are pulled up to her knees. T-shirts and posters bear declarations like 'get something straight – I'm not', 'gay and proud', 'African and Gay, not a choice', 'marching for those who can't' and 'killing gay people solves nothing'. Shoulders are in rainbow fairy wings. Chests have rainbow sashes, rainbow flags are tied over shoulders like capes and national flags wave in the air. Faces are painted in red, yellow and green stripes, others are covered with paper bags. Instead of following floats, we follow a bakkie with a sound system, taking our place behind Jamaican gay rights and HIV activist Maurice Tomlinson, who is leading the parade. A growing crowd of onlookers joins us. It's mostly old people and the children they smack on the head to stop them from joining us. 'What's this?' one woman asks me. 'Freedom, sister,' I tell her. I blow her kisses when she sniggers. The parade ends with hugs, kisses and high fives. Frank bounces around the stage and the catering committee fires up pots with rice, matoke, beef stew and chicken.

I don't know when or how the commotion starts, only that trouble knows where to find me. Crazy, Kasha, Maurice and Dr Stella Nyanzi, another formidable defender of human rights, are arrested. Some people run in the opposite direction. I go to the van, and yell 'stop touching me' when a cop tries to stop me from taking pictures. 'This is so stupid, man, are you going to arrest all of us?' I ask. 'No, but you're coming with them.' He holds my hands to help me into the truck.

'What doesn't kill you makes a killer story,' I remind myself, already plotting how I will work my arrest into the feature I'm writing for *True Love*. I'm excited about the twist in my story even, until we get to the police station and reality hits me. Our ambassador is Jon Qwelane, a venomous man who hates gay people. 'How soon before some idiot demands to "marry"' an animal?' he asks in an opinion piece, renouncing gay rights as human rights. He is not going to help me.

We stand in line while officers book us in. My turn to get an international criminal record is three people away.

'On your marks,' I mumble when I'm second in line.

'Get set,' I say under my breath when the uniform asks my name.

'I'll only tell you when I know why I'm arrested,' I reply. I insist on it and start screaming for him to pinpoint my crime. Two officers come over. A tall female uniform orders me to shut up.

'And if I don't?' I increase my volume and rattle off curses in Xhosa for effect.

'Ready?' I murmur to myself. She loses her cool and threatens to take me to the cell if I don't stop.

'Gosh, you are so clueless, you don't even know how to do your job – you need to book me in first and it's not happening until you tell me what I'm doing here.'

She grabs my hands. We wrestle for a few seconds before she pushes me. I hit the wall.

'It's go-time, bitches,' I hiss, before I remember the day we buried my maternal grandmother. It's the most painful moment of my life, and part of my arsenal in my fight against uniforms.

I turn on the waterworks. When I feel bad for using her death to get out of trouble, I take myself back to the mass grave in Ntarama. I sound like demons are escaping my body. The male uniforms are the first to break.

'You need to calm down,' one of them says, making me wail louder than ever. The second uniform tells me to go outside.

'Aren't you arresting me?' I ask.

'Not any more,' he says.

'Thank you,' I say, composing myself so he knows my distress is an act. I should have saved my drama for another day as everyone who is arrested is released before making it to cells after contacts from the American embassy show up. The detour to the police station ruins Saturday night. People are rattled and, even though we go to the after party determined to not let the police ruin the day, spirits are low. It's the first time I'm home before 3am.

The crowd's still thin at the closing event the following day at a café in Kabalagala, my old stomping ground. A power cut puts an end to the planned performances and film screening. We hang out and reflect on the four days. 'Even though Pride Uganda was small in numbers, the rest of the world's homosexual communities will be inspired by this event. They will look to you and say "if they could do it, then so can we",' Maurice says in his closing speech.

'My bravehearts, we have done it. It has been a long journey but we will not be intimidated. In fact, the police did us a favour when they arrested us because they put us on the world map. Now everyone will know that we had Gay Pride in Uganda,' Kasha says, 'I keep dreaming about freedom.'

This moment, that the world will only know about next week, is one of the biggest acts of defiance against homophobia in Uganda, Africa and many parts of the world where LGBTI people dare not reveal themselves. I think of lesbian women who are slaughtered in South Africa while the powers stand and watch, and about the countless people around Africa who have been attacked, jailed or killed for their sexuality and gender identity. I refuse to remain silent while Africa keeps writing its history in blood.

XX

Small Country, Big Heart

September 2012

My high and pride at being the only African journalist actively writing against homophobia in Uganda at the moment and being the official photographer at the historic Pride Uganda keep me going in Johannesburg. My sleep is still restless but I don't have my dreams any more, even though my guilt has become my second skin.

I decide to get back on the road in October, starting in Burundi. My fascination with the country turns into an obsession when a friend whose journeys around Africa fuel my wanderlust, Thapelo, beguiles Mahlatse and me with tales of his adventures in Bujumbura. I leave on a one-way ticket to Kigali.

South Africa is one of the worst places in Africa to organise travel administration. Burundi doesn't offer visas on arrival and the US$90 fee is only payable in American currency. It means going to the bank with paperwork I don't have as I haven't applied for a visa and I won't book my flight without it. Exchanging currency in Kigali and many other places I have been to around Africa is as easy as walking into a Forex bureau; no questions, no paperwork, no hassles. My two days in Kigali are fun, and I even enjoy myself on a night out at Hotel Mille Collines, the setting of *Hotel Rwanda*. The South African embassy has put on an exhibition of women who fought in the struggle against apartheid. The live band put on renditions of Khadja Nin, Brenda Fassie, Lucky Dube and Mafikizolo; keeping me on my feet all night. I start warming to Kigali, even though I still find it sterile. I leave for Bujumbura a day after getting my visa.

I know I'll love Burundi at Kanyaza border, when I see a life-size cutout of a traditional drummer and his ngoma. Like the picture I find on Google, he's wearing red and white robes. In my picture, a dancer's body is curled high in the air in front of a semi-circle of drummers. It makes me want to feel the vibration of the beat that turns a man into a bird. I act like a child looking for approval, telling the uniforms and everyone within earshot how happy I am to be in their country. When a uniform asks if he can search my bags, I open them and ask him to get on with his job while I take pictures of the cutout of the drummer.

A uniform at a roadblock smiles sweetly when I tell him that I'm too lazy to open my bags. 'I don't mean to disrespect you, but I really am not in the mood to unpack,' I tell him. 'Welcome to Burundi, sister,' he says, 'You are going to love it.'

There is nothing not to love about Burundi. The seven-hour trip from the border to Bujumbura goes through villages and towns that are surrounded by mountains and hills that come in every shade of green. Banana trees lean into the road and when one of us buys fruit, grilled mealies or brochette, we get enough to share with people in the seats around us. It's impossible to drive a few kilometres without seeing the national flag waving from poles made with sticks. When we stop to load and off-load people, young boys selling bunches of onions and carrots, beef kebabs and roasted corn stick their hands into the minibus.

Rural Burundi bursts with colour; fields have autumn shades, people walk with umbrellas and all of them are red, green, blue and yellow; old women wrap their hips in pagne with neon red, green and orange prints. Long walls and the fronts of small shops are painted with the signature bright red of Leo mobile network. Leo is the Swahili word for today. Once in a while, we stop at road blocks where uniforms mostly start a short, laughter-filled conversation with our driver before circling the minibus and waving us off. When they do step inside the minibus, it's to greet us and wish us 'safari njema'. It's always said with wide smiles, and they wave at us until they disappear from view.

I'm the only foreigner in the minibus, and everyone wants to know what I'm doing in Burundi. When the driver sees me dancing in my seat when he plays Lucky Dube's 'Together as One', he wants to know if it's my favourite song. 'I love all his songs,' I say to high fives. The driver plays the *Best of Lucky Dube* CD. Someone else wants to know what we eat in South Africa and recommends local dishes to try. 'Start with ndagala,' someone says. 'No, no, no,' someone adds, 'Try mukeke first.' They also want my phone number. I don't have a local SIM card yet. They write their numbers and home addresses in my note book. 'You're welcome to stay with my family,' they all assure me. When we get close to Bujumbura, a girl who has been quiet since coming in asks me if I have a hotel, and insists that I come to her house until I tell her that I have friends I met at Couch Surfing and that a Kenyan friend I met on Twitter, Timothy, is expecting me. I outsource looking for accommodation to Timothy.

Winding down the hills, boys on bicycles hitch rides on trucks by holding onto their bumpers. With the thick, grey rain clouds, green forests and mountains that wrap themselves around the horizon Bujumbura is breathtaking. The city is covered in mist and smoke, and all I can see is its flat zinc roofs, a grey Lake Tanganyika and the mountains beyond it, in the DRC. Bujumbura has indigo hills with jagged tops that are shrouded by tumbling grey clouds.

As a destination, Buja, as its people call it, almost doesn't stand a chance of getting attention, bordered as it is by Tanzania which has the Serengeti, Ngorongoro Crater and Mount Kilimanjaro among a long list of other destinations; Rwanda and DRC which have the Virunga mountain and its populations of the only mountain gorillas in the world, which are also found in Uganda. The only thing Burundi has at the moment is a travel advisory, warning tourists to stay away or visit at own risk.

When we get to the bus station that connects Bujumbura to the rest of the country, as well as Uganda, Rwanda, DRC and Tanzania, the driver asks me to stick around. He doesn't want the taxi drivers that are already waiting outside the door to overcharge me for the trip to the city centre.

'We love visitors, but cab drivers will always try to rip you off if you don't know the city,' he says. I expect him to find me a cab. Instead, he takes me to a room at the corner of the compound, where passengers register their names and passport numbers to confirm our safe arrival. He gives me a lift to Club Havana, where he waits with me until Timothy and his friend Anthony show up. They've taken the afternoon off work to help me settle in. This only happens eight hours after my arrival. We walk across Boulevard de l'Uprona, into a shopping complex with a supermarket, a restaurant that turns into a club at night and a pharmacy. Every third shop in Buja is a pharmacy.

We go into a salon and barbershop for me to meet Veronica and Martin and ask them to look after my bags. Timothy hasn't found a hotel yet. 'It's not like finding one will be difficult in Burundi,' he assures me. We spend the afternoon out on a Primus beer-drenched lunch of brochette and chips at a run-down local joint with a one-room restaurant crammed with three tables and and a fridge. We sit on plastic chairs in the courtyard they share with a mechanic. We go on a joyride around the city afterwards.

The magic of travelling Africa is always on cue. On my first night, it happens when the driver plays 'Mapenzi' by Kidum and

'Sambolera Mayi Son' by Khadja Nin; one of my favourite love songs and a song that I used to sing along to wholeheartedly when I was kid, not knowing that Africa was putting itself in my heart in ways that will make me want to know my continent like the back of my hand. Kidum lives in Nairobi and Khadja Nin in Belgium. Their music is my first encounter with their homeland.

There's interrupted development and then there's Bujumbura. My first three days in town are a test of endurance. The incessant rain turns me into a prisoner in my hotel room. It has thin walls that let in conversations from other rooms and the sound of grinding steel from the welders next door. Our street, Kanyosha Road, runs over with mud, turning walking into a balancing act of avoiding slipping while walking in such a way that water doesn't get into my shoes. The power cuts drive me nuts. We have five on my first day, three on day two, and six that last between thirty minutes to an hour on day three. There are multiple power cuts every day in the two months I spend in the country. When the power is on long enough for me to work, the internet connection is slow, Skyping is impossible and phone calls have static.

There is also the money situation, with only two ATMs that are on the Visa and Mastercard network. They don't work on the first few times I go there. Luckily, in a rare display of being organised, I have dollars and francs to tide me over for a week. My arrival coincides with the Tabaski, which celebrates the sacrifice Ibrahim offers to Allah when he obeys the instruction to offer his only son Ismail's life as the ultimate sacrifice. Their generosity and hospitality is a Burundian trait that endears me to their country.

Timothy and Anthony's colleague, Hassan, has invited them over for lunch. I tag along to his house on a street that's getting electric poles. Furrows have been dug out, and the soil has turned into thick slush that keeps tugging at our shoes when we walk. The dark grey clouds are still pouring rain.

When we get to the house, our host offers me water to wash the mud off my feet and shoes. Hassan and his wife Fareeda have slaughtered two sheep for friends and neighbours who visit in trickles throughout the afternoon. We eat the lamb with spicy white rice. The rain makes our visit long, and I start feeling cold. Fareeda tells me to move to their bedroom when I fall asleep on the couch.

Before coming to Burundi, I ask friends who've been here to connect me to their networks in the city. Lupi, who has been keeping up with my travels on his radio show and off air, introduces me to his friend Christine, a Burundian who lives in Joburg. She hasn't lived in Bujumbura for years, but she knows people in her circle who have moved back home. One of them is Martin. We meet at Aroma café, where the crowd is a mix of middle-class locals, expats and aid workers. Everyone sits behind their laptops in the morning to enjoy the only source I know of an internet connection that doesn't take fifteen minutes and three attempts to attach a Word document.

When I tell Martin that I'm looking for a house on the beach, he says it doesn't matter where in the city I stay, I will not be more than fifteen minutes away from the shores of Lake Tanganyika. I leave Aroma with Mike's number, and meet him at my hotel the following afternoon when he comes to take me to my new home. There's just one problem: I still haven't figured out how to get money without involving Western Union's downright criminal transfer costs. He says rent will come when it does, and takes me to a lovely corner house next door to the Egyptian embassy on Nzero Avenue, where the gate is opened by one of two guards who are posted here day and night.

The front yard has a gazebo at the corner. The backyard has a guards' room and weeds that grow faster than anyone can pull them out. It's been raining once or twice a day in drizzles or downpours. The three-bedroom house belongs to Mike's friend and his aid worker girlfriend who is home in Europe to give birth. They share the house with Christian, a student from Kinshasa. His brother and cousin also live in the city. The sink in the kitchen has piles of dirty dishes and pots that someone has to wash because, looking at the dark wooden table that seats six in the dining room, Christian, his family, Tim and Anthony are going to be my lunch guests when I cook the seven-colour lunch I have been missing. Christian smiles when I tell him to save a date. Little does he know that nine out of ten times, my cooking belongs in the trash can. The watchmen are Joseph and Jean.

Joseph catches me near tears three days after moving in.

I haven't seen a laundromat and, unlike at the hotel, where I had the guard on laundry duty as well, I feel bad asking Joseph to wash my clothes. They are security, not domestic staff. Well, Joseph finds me cursing as I sort through my clothes, trying to figure out which ones will be clean after a dip in the water.

'Is there something wrong?' he asks. 'Wallahi, Joseph. I swear to Allah that He didn't make these hands for hard labour,' I moan. He offers to do my laundry.

'Mashallah,' I declare, before adding, 'The dishes are dirty as well. Actually, do you mind taking care of the house and my laundry? I'll pay you.'

Add Mike and Christian, and his brother as my occasional chauffeurs, and life is somewhat colonial.

On afternoons when I'm home instead of at the swimming pool, or out of the city, I sit on the porch in the backyard, listening to chirping birds as they settle back in their nests. A cup of tea in hand, I close my eyes and shut out the sound of traffic until I find the sound of drums beating across the neighbourhood.

My wake up call is the call to prayer; I feel at home in Buja.

Mike's a hot dude about town. He's tall and lean with a complexion that looks like brown milk chocolate. He likes running his beautiful, long hands through his thick shoulder-length locks. His smile makes girls swoon over him when we walk into clubs. His swag makes dudes buy us beers as a passport to hang out, and be cool by association. Barmen make our doubles stronger and offer tequila shots on the house.

My Friday evenings in Bujumbura start with a boda boda ride

to Bora Bora beach and Saga Plage. It's the rainy season and, even though the sun comes out, the weather is mostly overcast and sunsets are never bright and fiery, so the lake looks as blue as the mountains. It adds an air of mysticism that keeps me coming back to the lake's shore.

In these moments, the soccer games and laughter from the restaurants quieten – or maybe I block them out – and being here feels like a spiritual encounter. I now understand people who are drawn to mountains.

I'm walking along the beach when a man I don't know runs towards me with arms stretched out for an embrace we fall into, and hold onto for a long time. I have been here long enough to know that affection is the people's life blood. His name is Dudu. He's here with his girlfriend, Linda, and his best buddy Jimmy. It comes up in getting to know each other that Jimmy is travelling to Ngozi in the northern part of the country in two days. He wants me to come along.

We're in Ngozi to witness the biggest dream of Jimmy's life coming true. Along with several childhood friends, he is turning an old house into Hope Restaurant. More than getting a slice of the booming hospitality industry in President Pierre Nkurunziza's home town, Hope has moral significance. Between the effects of HIV and a civil war that raged for twelve years, Burundi is home to thousands of orphaned children who Jimmy believes he needs to account for by giving them a shot at a future that's brighter than their current poverty and helplessness. The way Jimmy sees it, after turning them into chefs and equipping them with business skills they learn in the afternoon, the children will be able to use cooking to get more than jobs.

'They can work anywhere in the world.'

He is speaking from experience. When he was looking for a new start in Europe to escape the war at home, he became a cook. It's given him a house in Bujumbura and his dream car. For now, the restaurant is an idea that's taking shape.

Jimmy normally walks like a tortoise. He's restless on our morning visit to the house that's becoming Hope Restaurant. He moves between the six rooms, issuing instructions to builders and engineers. He goes to the backyard with the architect, Emile, and draws invisible lines to show him where he wants the 'modern kitchen' to go.

'We are going to offer world-class service,' he tells Emile.

A group of old women in fading pagne dresses sit under a tree. Put them on a street corner, and they'll pass for the old women who beg around Buja. They're here to remove weeds and turn the space into vegetable gardens. The restaurant will buy their produce from them. There's a lot of land in the yard, and there will be more produce than Hope can use in a day. The rest of it will be sold at the market and other restaurants. Jimmy is making sure than no one is left behind.

He chooses Ngozi because he spent his school days here at his grandmother's house and it's also a stop-over for trucks that move fuel and other goods between Burundi, Rwanda, Uganda and Kenya. In the Kigarama quarter, where the dream is taking shape, there are hotels from the top of the main street to the market, about four kilometres away. The hotels have names like Jambo, Belvedere, Just, Come Again, Star and La Residence. Jimmy isn't worried about competition.

'People in the hospitality industry don't understand service,' he says impatiently over lunch at Star Hotel's restaurant. The rice is undercooked, the meat in the stew is tough, and overcooked vegetables turn into mush when my fork touches them.

'Burundians are hospitable but we don't know how to apply it professionally. Our restaurant is going to change it all.'

At the house that afternoon, the lounge is filled with plastic chairs and teenagers armed with yellow notebooks. Their eyes are glued to Jean Baptista Ciza as he plasters the wall with notes on cooking spaghetti bolognaise; the dish features on many menus in Burundi. There are notes on seasoning, working with and taking care of kitchen equipment, cooking plain rice and pillau, how to cook vegetables properly. The set up is informal but everyone is giving their full attention to the chef.

Like it is for Jimmy, cooking is Jean Baptista's passport. He trained in Doula, Cameroon, where he received his chef's certificate in 2000 before working in the Democratic Republic of Congo, Uganda, Gabon and Tanzania. He gets paid a 'modest salary', but there's nothing he'd rather do.

'I get my satisfaction from doing something good. I want to be able to help them with skills that give them a better future. It's a noble dream but it will come true. These young people are getting skills they can sell in their communities and around East and Central Africa. This is going to change their lives forever,' he tells me.

Training to work in the hospitality industry is one aspect of the project. Jimmy's team includes a social psychologist called Cynthia Ndayisaba and her assistant counsellor, Nadine Niyonizigiye, who also runs the two houses where the students live.

There's also Eddy Ndingani, who teaches professional skills like writing business letters, proposals and winning professional CVs. Eddy's role is to make sure that, once graduated, the students will be able to look for work anywhere they want to because their free training and accommodation comes with no strings attached. Jimmy and his associates spread the word about the project at churches, mosques and by word of mouth in Ngozi and surrounding areas to find trainees. They're between fifteen and twenty years old. They all have one thing in common: The trauma of seeing their parents die from AIDS or in the civil war, and the violence of their poverty. This is why the programme includes group therapy, individual counselling and life skills classes. They don't want to dictate terms to the trainees, but they hope that some, if not all of them, will go back to school. If they want to, they will be funded, just like graduates who want to open businesses instead of becoming employees.

Hope Restaurant is a powerful example of what happens when Africans looks inwards, instead of outwards to international aid, to begin our healing. It becomes an all-encompassing journey that puts people at the heart of all ideas and decisions.

Out of all the wonderful memories of living in Bujumbura, the most precious one is the echo of drums thumping from somewhere everywhere in the city. As a parting shot on my last day in Burundi, my buddy Valentine has, for US$100, gathered a group of traditional drummers to put on the finest show there is to catch in Burundi. Drumming here isn't just a song and dance, it's a source of national pride and a spectacle that combines powerful, synchronised drumming with dancing, heroic poetry and traditional songs, as UNESCO points out.

The spectacle starts months before a performance when the trunks of imivugangoma – which loosely translates into trees that make drums that speak – are carved into drums that rise as high as the waist and weigh up to fifty kilograms. The trees have to be at least one hundred years old. The hollowed trunks are then covered with ox hide that's been left to soak in water for a day. Wooden pegs stretch the hide over the drum.

Sixteen drummers wrapped in green, white and red cloth file onto the stage, an open field in front of a school, with drums on their heads. They move in sync. An elder dressed in a raffia robe leads the troupe. His regalia symbolises what the king wore on occasions that called for traditional drumming. He's also wearing a band around his arm, which the king wore on hunting trips, a bone and calabash around his neck, and a raffia bag the king used to carry his dearest personal belongings in while travelling.

The performance transfixes the audience with its energy, agility and perfectly synchronised harmony, even the man covered completely in a cloth, who curls his body into a ball in the half circle, does so with a head that nods along to the rhythm. There's humour and depth, songs and dances that make us smile and laugh, and songs that make us clasp our hands to our chests, silent and immobile lest we miss a beat that takes between two to six months of practice to perfect. It's a fitting way to spend my last day in Burundi; the small country with a big heart.

I leave by bus to Kampala, where I spend three days catching up with friends before visiting Arrot and David in Nairobi, then reuniting with author Zukiswa Wanner, who has moved from Joburg to Nairobi. I also meet journalist and literary blogger James Murua. We throw ourselves into the night, fuelled by Tuskers and his VIP access to industry events.

My next stop is Ethiopia.

XXI

WEIRD PRIVILEGE

January 2013

I KNEEL IN FRONT OF THE young man and hold his hands for a few seconds. I need a bit of time to fix myself. I wrap my netella, the linen shawl that covers the heads and shoulders of many Ethiopian women, over my body; careful to not leave any stray strands of my cheap human hair piece on my face.

'Don't be scared,' Neyan says as he puts his hand in the basket that's next to us to get intestines he wraps on a twig. The twenty-two-year-old has been coming to the outskirts of Harar every night for the past eighteen months to perform the nightly ritual that the Harari believe keeps them safe from the two hundred-plus hyenas in the city and the green hills that surround it. Legend has it that a drought befell Harar in its medieval days, driving the hyenas from the mountain to the city, where they developed a taste for humans.

The town's people make a special porridge they feed to the king of the hyenas, who in turn orders his subjects to change their menu from flesh to porridge. This starts an understanding between the

Harari and scavengers; they will live to see another day for as long as they make sure the hyenas are well-fed.

Like the men and boys whose job it is to keep the animals happy, Neyan has inherited his role from his father. The only thing that has changed between medieval times and today is that instead of porridge, the animals now get whatever scraps of meat and bones their feeders can get from butchers. Neyan puts the end of the twig that doesn't have meat in my mouth. My nostrils flare from the pungent smell.

'Aiii Tika, Butta, Mehai, Jimba and Jimta, nahi nayi,' he yells, calling his pack of hyenas using the names he gives them. Two of them stand behind me, their gasps warm my skin. They take their place at the end of the twig. I stay like this until all five have had their turn; feeding them from my mouth to theirs.

Visiting Harar is the highlight of my travels in Ethiopia. After spending four months here, being in Harar feels like waking up from a series of nightmares that involve food that tastes the same no matter who cooks it and hospitality that's downright hostile. People in Harar mind their business and leave me alone. Kids don't run after me yelling the Amharic word for foreigner, ferengi, and most importantly, people respect my boundaries. Here, I'm an adult with autonomy and an individual with her own preferences, a concept that's foreign to Ethiopians.

Harar is the fourth holiest city in the Muslim world after Mecca, Jerusalem and Medina. Islam shuns vice. Harar has a brewery and a lager named after it and the right time to drink is when you feel like it, even at 8am. In the morning when the town wakes up, women line the streets with sacks of qat that people buy in large bundles before starting their days with buna, as coffee is called, machiatto or beer. The main gate at the Juma mosque isn't crowded with people selling Qurans or prayer mats. They're here to sell or chew their favourite drug.

Walking around the old walled city that makes Harar a world heritage site, I'm astounded by the pastel blue, lime and salmon pink houses with white flowers and geometric patterns, and by how pervasive qat is. Even when I don't see the plant in people's hands, I see faces that have formed balls on one side of the mouth with jaws moving slowing like grazing animals – the telltale sign of someone who has been chewing for hours. People who don't have teeth grind leaves into fine powder to get their highs.

Every day after lunch, men empty out into the streets, closing shops and businesses to spend their afternoons chewing through plastic bags' worth of qat, including Girma, the affable manager and handyman at Teodros Hotel where I'm staying on the outskirts of the ancient town. I sit in the courtyard with him and Addis, my new friend, chewing until my temples become tense. Another man comes over to buy bottles of beer on his way home. He has two bags of qat, and jokes that he hopes everyone behaves because he's off to chew with his friends. He is the police commander, and although the police station is open, everyone has effectively stopped working for the afternoon.

Madness, a language I'm most fluent in, is also one that Harar speaks well. Take Addis. He shows up at my door after our chewing session. He pins me against the wall when I let him in and starts kissing me. He thinks I'm playing hard to get when I try to push him away.

'Addis please stop,' I beg him between dodging his wet lips. He comes in for another kiss.

'Addis. Listen to me – I'm not playing hard to get. You have to stop.' He doesn't.

I pull him to my bed and pin him down with my ass on his small beer belly. I plant kisses around his face and neck, anything but his lips, and slowly unbutton his shirt. 'Is this what you want?' I whisper. He grabs my ass. 'Slow down,' I purr and run my finger down his body. 'Oh Addis,' I say breathlessly, 'O mo masepeng.' This silly boy is knee-deep in shit, as I warn him in Setswana, and getting a hard on over it. I kiss his chest and run my tongue around his nipple. I open my mouth until I can't stretch it any more and bite his breast so hard, it moves with me when he tries to push me off. I only let go when my temples get tired.

'What the fuck? Are you trying to kill me?' he whimpers, 'You're crazy.'

His eyes shine with tears.

'Not crazy Addis, mother-fucking-crazy,' I tell him.

One of the effects of being a woman in South Africa, where rape and gender-based violence are a pastime, is that I've had this conversation with myself for years. Just as we tell ourselves to not fight thieves, I always tell myself that I will not try to fight any man who tries to rape me. I will teach him a lesson he'll never, ever forget. When I see Addis the next day at the office where he runs his small transport business, he unbuttons his shirt to show me a ring of dark red teeth marks. 'You should thank me for not biting into your dick,' I say, laughing while he stands a safe distance away from me.

The crazy follows me to the minibus I take from Harar to Addis Ababa. Our driver speeds through roadblocks no matter how much we beg him to stop playing with our lives. He has unpaid fines and the traffic officers have set up roadblocks along the way to try and catch him. He drives through them at high speed, causing people on the road to run for cover. I ask him to stop so I can get out, but he refuses. The cops are onto him and call colleagues to tell them to create a roadblock that closes all the lanes; they use two trucks.

Eastern Ethiopia is in the highlands. Instead of stopping, the driver goes through the pavement on the edge of a hill. We scream, and the woman next to me starts crying. This is the kind of move where a mistake always ends fatally, with the car rolling down to sure death. I always have a knife in my bag so I don't have to worry about peeling my fruit. I put it on his neck, 'I said, let me out now, or I will kill you'. He drives to the police station and tries talking his way out of paying for the fines. I still get off the taxi and wait for a safer one to Addis.

I'm shaken but I'm not shocked. My life in Ethiopia has been a series of bizarre moments that have made me love and loathe the country in equal measure.

My obsession with Ethiopia runs deeper than any country's hold on me. It has nothing to do with being the only African country that was never colonised, or the awe I feel whenever I think of the Battle of Adwa, fought in 1896, when the Ethiopian army won over the Italian one. Although Rastafarianism is an influential aspect of my identity, my fascination has little to do with the fact that in this land lies the Rastafari manifestation of repatriating back home to Africa, two hundred and fifty-one kilometres away from Addis Ababa in Shashamane, or that, according to the religion, Haile Selaisse I is the manifestation of the return of Christ. I don't question or deny his lordship because, according to Rastafarianism, God is black and African – I am God.

I seek out Ethiopia around Johannesburg, Pretoria and East Africa, and find it in downtown DC and Harlem. I eat Ethiopian food more than other cuisine, I know where in Johannesburg and Pretoria to find Ethiopian honey wine, tej. My fascination goes far beyond obvious differences like using the Coptic calendar, which has thirteen months and according to which Christmas falls of 7 January and New Year of 11 September. The Ethiopian clock also ticks to its own standard. They start counting time at 6am, which is midnight to the rest of the world; so 8am here is 2am elsewhere.

This sense of Ethiopia being a world of its own is something I perceive long before my visit. Experience doesn't prove me wrong.

It starts on arrival at Bole International Airport. Visas are issued on arrival but the US$20 fee must be paid for with American currency. The ATMs in the customs area don't work and the seat of the African Union doesn't trade African currencies. I can exchange dollars, pounds, dinas and euros; not the stack of Kenyan shillings

I have. It takes a long time and a massive tantrum for the uniforms to understand my dilemma and let me out so I can look for an ATM in the city.

An air hostess comes over to ask why I'm sad, and shows me another ATM at the airport that works. She is the only person who hasn't been cold and dismissive in the first hour in a country I used to refer to as 'Her Majesty' in my first travel journal.

My bitter first impression infuses itself into many moments as my three-month stay turns to six after my passport is stolen. In the end, when I get onto a flight to Johannesburg, I realise that Ethiopia is my weird privilege for strange and sometimes harrowing as being in the country is, it's wonderful to experience its landscape, heritage and the unrivalled pride Ethiopians have in their land and their ways; even if it almost drives me insane. What matters, I suppose, is that Ethiopia evokes strong emotions. It makes it an unforgettable destination; I love it as much as I hate it.

My visit comes five months after the death of Prime Minister Meles Zenawi and the country is not over his passing. Along with paper triangles modelled after the national flag that hang on lamp posts to celebrate Jesus' baptism, called Timkat and held on 19 January, comes posters with Meles's photograph. The driver makes the sign of the cross over his face and chest whenever we drive past Meles's face. The storm of my arrival has made way for rays of sunshine I feel from how authentic Addis is. Everything is written in Amharic and the blue and white Lada cars add a vintage element to the modern city where skycrapers are going up faster than in any country I've been to. I'm in a shared cab to Piazza neighbourhood, and the last person who will be dropped off. In some areas old zinc houses are neighbours with newly built mansions, and the road we use on our way into one neighbourhood is closed for construction on our way out. There are more coffee shops and massage parlours than I can keep count of.

My spirit is soaring by the time the driver drops me off at hotel Taitu. It's run down with toilets that put me off shared bathrooms for life, but it is the oldest hotel in the city, in the oldest neighbourhood of the capital.

Even in their current grubby state, the hotel and its neighbourhood are charming. Taitu was built in 1898 by emperor Melenik II's wife, Taitu Betul. It has a mix of backpackers, overland travellers and cosmopolitan Addis Ababeans who grab a bite or sundowners on a patio that overlooks tour company offices. Boys who take their chances as touts huddle at the main entrance next to an old man who sells loose cigarettes and sweets under a worn-out blue umbrella.

Being in a new destination makes the old and broken seem exciting. Around Piazza, it's the boys who sit on low stools with foamy buckets of water to wash shoes, and the hawkers who walk along Churchill Avenue to sell dirt-cheap punnets of strawberries; they make up for the begging children who cling to my arm until I give them birrs and the piles of human crap I keep sidestepping.

Other than its museums and the connection they give me to Ethiopia's rich heritage, I love Addis for its ornate cathedrals, and the sense of wonder I get at how Ethiopians worship with ritual and pride. Ethiopians are Orthodox Christians. As with everything that defines life here, the religion's authenticity is untouched by time. Scriptures are written in the ancient Ge'ez script. At the Holy Trinity Cathedral, where Haile Selassie and Empress Menen Asfaw's remains are in granite tombs next to the altar, men and women use separate entrances. Everyone leaves their shoes at the door and only the priests are allowed to go beyond the altar, just as it has always been.

I love Ethiopia because it is true to itself. At its best, it makes my trip to Holy Trinity Cathedral start with confusion when I ask for help getting there using its English name, and only find it when someone realises that I'm looking for Kidst Selassie, as locals call it. At its worst, this authenticity takes the pleasure of eating Ethiopian food out of me. I discover that it tastes the same whether I eat at a restaurant in Harar, Awassa or Lalibela or as a lunch or dinner guest, when I'm forced to eat chunks of raw beef, called tera sega. It's the pièce de résistance of any meal. Ethiopians love it. I eat my meat so well done, chefs leave their kitchens to beg me not to let a good cut go to waste. It offends people who offer me tera sega when I tell them that raw meat makes me gag, and because Ethiopian mothers rarely accept no for an answer, I have to eat it whenever it's offered. There is also a point during any meal when someone feeds me with their right hand. This tradition is called gursha, and is considered an ultimate act of affection. I now use it during my own meal times.

Another upside of my bewilderment that food tastes the same no matter who cooks it is that eating is not only about feeding the body. It has traditions and rituals that everyone observes without fail, whether it's at home or at a restaurant. Wednesdays and Fridays are fasting days. On these days, even restaurants only serve vegan meals.

'I'm not an Orthodox Christian,' I complain to a friend one afternoon, tired of eating shiro wot, a powdered chickpea stew.

'We are on a fast,' she says, before telling me that there are seven fasting periods per year. Some periods last a day, like the night before Epiphany, and others, like Lent, go on for fifty-six days.

At first, it seems to me like being overly prescriptive, but I soon realise that it's a sign of reverence. In any case, it's not like the fasting period takes the joy out of eating. As a traditional standard, lentil and meat stews are cooked with a blend of herbs that include basil and rosemary, and spices like chillies, cumin and cardamom called berbere. When I'm in Addis, I go on a joyride around the Arat Kilo neighbourhood in the afternoon, when the smell of the berbere hangs in the air. It makes every breath delicious.

More than anything, I love Ethiopia for the simple coffee cafés called buna bet, where women sit on their stools to brew coffee traditionally by roasting the beans in a pan before crushing them and boiling them in a clay jar. There's an alley in downtown Addis that smells like roasting coffee beans from the buna bets that line it. All of them are small with floors that are covered with grass, bamboo chairs and zinc walls that are decorated with posters of women brewing buna against backdrops of popular tourist destinations like the seventeenth-century fortresses in Gonder, the Blue Nile waterfalls in Bahir Dar and the fourteenth-century obelix in Axum; where Ethiopians say the Ark of the Covenant, which has the remains of the slabs on which Moses wrote the Ten Commandements, is found after king Solomon gives it to the Queen of Sheba, Makeda, who is the mother of his son, Menelik I. The story of this liaison between the King of the Israelites and the Ethiopian queen finds its way into many conversations. Buna is only brewed by women and, in keeping with tradition, they wrap a shawl over their heads. Even in people's homes, Buna is brewed traditionally.

I know very little about the transatlantic slave trade beyond its existence, the crimes committed against the slaves and the racism and exploitation that did not end with abolition in 1816. What I know and feel very deeply is the yearning for home felt by Rastas, evoked by listening to the music of Bob Marley, Peter Tosh, Morgan Heritage, Burning Spear, Culture and Capleton and reading Marcus Garvey's work. Other than their black nationalism and the influence their religion plays in my personal politics, I respect Rastafari people because they live with conviction, self-assured and unshakeable in their belief that Africa is a spiritual home. In Shashamane, the dream came alive in 1948 when His Imperial Majesty Haile Selaisse donated some of his private land to the descendents of slaves.

I arrive from Addis at night after being in bed with a fever for several days. The first thing I hear when I get out of the minibus is 'Summertime' by Vybz Kartel. I follow it to McKenzie Bryan Hotel. It's like living next to a dancehall nightclub. I feel at home. It doesn't hurt that hanging out at the bar is the quickest way to start meeting some of the repatriates. The hotel is owned by Sister Wendy, who relocated from Manchester, and an Ethiopian-Jamaican boy whose dad is among the first group of people coming back to this patch of the Motherland.

There are between two and three hundred people like Sister Wendy. Some have been here for four decades, others are new in town or visit for weeks at a go with one foot in the West and another in Africa. It has added some Caribbean touches to the town. The lingua franca in Shashe is patois when I'm at Sister Joan's and other Rasta-owned restaurants. It's Amharic elsewhere. Some gates are painted in the red, gold and green of Rasta colours or black, green and yellow after the Jamaican flag. While Shashamane may seem like a meaningless dream for this very misunderstood religion, to me, it is one of the greatest affirmations believers can receive. Why else would anyone leave their life in the West and the Caribbean to build a new life in a barely developed town that tests their faith daily?

The closest ATM is twenty-five kilometres away in Hawassa, there is scant economic activity, power cuts are frequent and there are days when the taps are dry and the jojo containers used to store additional water remain empty. On these days, I use a litre of bottled water to wash myself from head to toe, including brushing my teeth. My days are planned around the brief periods between power cuts. One of my first articulate sentences in Amharic is, 'mababrat yelemi?' Is there electricity? Often, the answer is 'ayi', no.

Whenever I ask repatriates if moving to the promised land is worth it, the answer is a variation on the fulfilment of no longer living with a spirit that feels restless and homeless no matter how dreamy their former life is to onlookers. Take Julian. He used to live in New York and enjoyed the kind of life that comes with being Peter Tosh's tour manager, among many other reggae luminaries he has worked with. His life felt superficial and empty until the day he arrived here, where he spends his days working on his farm. Brother Levi is from Trinidad and Tobago. Like everyone who resolves to move here, he started preparing for his African life long before he arrived. Sitting with him in his leather shop, I note how much he references Haile Selassie in our conversations. When he offers me a drink, and I ask what my options are, he recommends sour sap. 'It was His Majesty's favourite fruit,' he says, before telling me to visit to the hot water springs in Wondo Genet, sixteen kilometres from Shashamane. 'It was His Majesty's favourite holiday spot.'

Setting up homes and businesses is not always easy. For a start, some passports have long expired, leaving their holders neither Ethiopian nor Caribbean in the eyes of the law. It still hasn't stopped people from creating a permanent life and their social hubs. There's a Manchester House for people who used to live in that UK city and other properties that belong to the twelve Tribes of Israel, Bobo Shante and Nyabinghi sects of Rastafari.

After His Majesty's birth and coronation day, the third most important date on the social calender is 6 February. Bob Marley's birthday is big. It starts a week before the date with fliers and posters reminding us to save the date. There will be live music, food and drinks.

A power cut kills the mood on the day of the party. Even so, whatever happens, people are simply enraptured to be in their promised land, living a lifestyle that's close to nature and the environment and, most importantly, living a dream that many of them nurture from when they are teenagers and spend their life working towards.

Away from my interest in Rastafarianism, Shashamane gives me the opportunity to observe everyday life as lived by Ethiopians. At the moment, this life includes finding myself in the strange position of being friends with Tsega. The eighteen-year-old is from Addis, and here to live with her teen boyfriend. Her mother thinks she is getting an education while Tsega is really occupied with playing the real-life version of house. They are not the only ones. There's Chachi and Peter, Berek and Genet and a couple who work at McKenzie Bryan. Watching these teens spend days looking into each other's eyes tests my ability to bite my tongue. I fail with Tsega and implore her to go on birth control before an accidental baby happens. The more serious couples in the mix start building their lives together, starting with a spaza shop. Tsega and Yared go from renting a back room and living off the money she makes selling shiro wat to opening their first business. To keep it afloat among the six others within a kilometre radius, they sleep in their shop. The teen couple who work at the hotel moves out of their room to the new spaza as well. It's the first business many people start with.

My first stop after Shashamane is Arba Minch, named after the forty springs in southern Ethiopia's biggest town. About six hours from Shashamane by minibus, Arba Minch is a typical big town that's not a capital city – a bit broken by time but still awe inspiring for the endless green hills and valleys it's set around. Life on the streets looks like a mass evacuation. I'm in Arba Minch to find transport to Konso, from where my trip to Lower Omo Valley starts. Omo Valley is the picture of tribal Africa, with naked bodies painted in white chalk and scarified, bottom lips that are slit and discs put in, earlobes that are elongated, and hair is shaved into patterns or twisted into thin strings that get their colour from red clay and their shine from some of the butter churned for eating.

In Konso, I discover that travelling in this part of the country requires a lot of waiting. Transport is scarce and passengers scarcer. Journeying in southern Ethiopia feels like a road trip to the ends of the world. The road our minibus uses to leave Konso joins a long one that spans kilometres through the savannah landscape. It has been raining, and vegetation and acacia trees are bright green. Occasionally, we drive past trucks, forklifts and other tools of construction that are turning the road into tar. For the most part, it's just the expansive savannah and the small villages that dot it, as well as the villagers and livestock.

Life in Omo Valley revolves around market days. I plan my visit around them, starting in Turmi on Monday, but not before the waiting game turns into an event. Jinka is the main town and the only place where getting transport is guaranteed. It's also at the end of the route that covers most of the villages. Hoping to find a lift to Turmi, I end my trip in Key Afer. Their market day is on

Thursday. On this Sunday afternoon, the town and its streets are empty, and the only time I see a person walking around is when they go into a café for buna or beer. I don't find transport to Turmi until mid-morning on Monday, and even then, I force my way into Yohannes's car. Whenever a car parks at the restaurant next to my hotel, I walk over to ask for a lift. Yohannes and his friend Tesfaye are the only people on their way to Turmi. I leave them to their buna and breakfast of injera with scrambled eggs, and follow them to their car when they leave. There, I open the door and take my seat with the suggestion that they loosen up because only one of two things will happen: They are retracing their steps to Jinka, or moving forward to Turmi with me. Our trip is icy at first. Yohannes's cheeks are swollen from all the sulking he is doing. Nonetheless, they are calm by the time we get to Turmi, going as far as helping me find a hotel and introducing me to their friend, a tour guide called Emmanuel, who runs Explore Omo Valley tour company.

The market is dissipating when we arrive in the late afternoon. Some of the traders have packed their goods. Many of them live in the villages outside Turmi. Some of them have more than thirty kilometres of walking ahead of them. In the evening when Emmanuel is certain that his village family has had ample time to walk back home and settle into their evening, we follow them on his moped. They are already sleeping when we get there. Instead of meeting them I smell their cows and goats in the cleanest air I have ever breathed. We hang out under the darkest of skies, with the brightest stars, and listen to the shrill of insects. In the morning, we join the family for coffee, which they make by boiling the husks instead of using coffee beans. My gift is a token goat. Receiving it teaches me that the Amharic word for goat is fiyel.

The biggest con of my life on the road starts as innocently as any random conversation between strangers admiring a piece at the museum. The pieces in question are the two gold sculptures at the entrance of the Ethnological Museum, the former palace of Haile Selaisse. The boy follows me inside to ask for a favour. His name is Mehari. He is a first-year student at the University of Addis Ababa, the woman he is with is his aunt Leila and her visit is the first one by family: Would I mind photographing this special occasion? I do and we spend the afternoon together. Leila wants to know how much their pictures cost.

'I don't charge people for pictures,' I say.

'That's kind of you. If only there were something we could do to repay your generosity,' she says, 'Perhaps you can stay with us when you visit Lalibela.'

It just so happens that Lalibela is my next destination. I'm going to Ethiopia's Holy Land for Easter. I decline the invitation to stay with Leila but promise to visit her and meet the rest of Mehari's family. I rue the day I meet them, because knowing this family turns into the biggest inconvenience of my life in Ethiopia.

The bus trip from Addis to Lalibela starts around 4am at the bus station in Merkato. Ethiopians move in a swarm. The station is heaving with people and hissing buses. After months of prayer and fasting, the Holy Week is about to start. I settle into my seat for the long journey ahead. It takes more than twelve hours to travel north to Lalibela. As we get closer, the landscape and people turn into the Ethiopia from traditional music videos that the national broadcaster plays all day every day; the Ethiopia of traffic jams that are caused by camels and fat cows with long horns, of men dressed in blue or green shorts and matching shirts that look like a safari uniform, and sticks they carry on their shoulders. We arrive in Lalibela in the early evening. My first stop after check-in and a shower is to the churches that have turned this town into Holy Land. Legend holds that one night in the twelfth century, the angels came down from heaven to chisel red volcanic mountains into twelve churches, carving Lalibela into a world heritage site. The windows, pillars and doors are built from the same rock. Walls have faded paintings of saints and angels with round faces and almond-shaped eyes; floors are covered with worn red and faded Persian carpets where bishops and deacons stand. Behind the thick curtain in all of them lies a replica of the Ark of the Covenant, where only church elders are allowed to go. The most known of these rocks is the St Georges, or Bete Giyorgis as Ethiopians call it. It's shaped like the cross and named after the country's favourite saint. He also has a beer named after him. In the two weeks when the fasting season draws to an end, prayer becomes even more important. On days that commemorate Jesus' final journey to the cross, church becomes a second home.

The Friday of my arrival marks the end of the first of two weeks of Easter celebrations. All the churches are in the same complex. Celebrations are held at different ones, and typically at the ones that are close to the entrance. There is a service, but people are also here to spend time with God without being in a group. Tucked into some enclaves of the buildings they pray or read scriptures in solitude. Everyone is dressed accordingly in shawls and robes and the monks' heads are in wraps. Some people wear rings made from palm leaves, while some others are adorned with palm crowns made by tying a leaf around the head and fashioning it into a cross that sits on the forehead. Feet are bare and heads bent in prayer. There's chanting, clinking bells and murmurs. The smell of incense permeates the air.

Saturday is the main market day. I start my day here, moving around thick crowds of sellers, shoppers and – at the livestock market – goats, cows and sheep feeding on dry grass. Those that have been sold are being dragged home on leashes or beaten with sticks so they don't stray. Around the town – which still has mud houses with grass roofs and yards that are fenced with sticks – women sit next to round fire pits topped with wide black pans into which they pour a mixture of fermented teff flour and water to cook injera. I go to Leila's house to meet her son and husband as promised and then walk up the road to see her sister, Mehari's mother Miriam and her family. I meet her husband and two daughters, Fassil, Martha and Gete. Martha, the eldest, has a boyfriend, Teshome, who works as a tour guide. He joins my domestic life when Miriam tells him to show me around Lalibela, the hilly town on the edge of bare mountains and green hills. The only person missing from the happy mix, his mother says, is Mehari. Miriam wants me to move in but I pass: I have been to their toilet and still have a week in town. I promise to move in two days before leaving Lalibela. In the meantime, I spend a lot of time with the family after Miriam and Leila insist that I should come home for meals daily. I do, and learn to keep a straight face when all I want to do is yell 'stop it already.' Ethiopian mothers are pushy.

Mehari's mom and aunt are not different. They also enjoy introducing me to the Habesha way of eating some things, for instance, putting sugar on avocado, offering me a piece of raw chicken liver and serving me litres of tej and a bitter black drink called tella. Three days before I leave, I move in with Mehari's family as promised and feel as loved as I always do whenever people let me into their homes, often sharing their already small space. Mehari's house only has one bedroom. I share the lounge with his sisters, taking over one of their sleeping sponges while they share another. Miriam insists that I have to 'look Habesha' for the main church service. This means getting a local hairstyle and wearing a traditional dress called kemi, which she lends me. She pouts and sulks when I tell her my beauty ideal doesn't include silky hair, so off to the salon we go, where bouncy human hair is added to my cornrows. I feel like I'm cheating on my Pan-African gods. I also feel ugly whenever there is a lot of distance between how I look naturally and how I dress and style myself. However, the compliments I collect around Lalibela with my Habesha hairstyle, with everyone calling me konjo – Amharic for beautiful – are worth the slight guilt of wearing silky hair.

My happiness is short lived. I wake up with a swollen face that keeps getting bigger by the minute. My features melt into one grotesque mess. I have an allergic reaction and the only thing new on me is the human hair. The gods are clearly teaching me a lesson on why I must never distance myself from how I look naturally, I think as tears stream down my face: Vanity is the deadliest sin in my life.

I hide my face behind my netela at the church service. It's already in session when we arrive. People sit on benches in the courtyard, next to the main entrance. Unlike on my other visits when some people look ashy or dress in dirty shawls and wraps, everyone is clean and the women are in various traditional dresses. A handful of people stand away from the crowd to worship in solitude. If there are people beyond us, in the other buildings, the crowd at the entrance is too large for me to find out. I join people who are standing behind the circle of priests who have formed a human wall around a group of their colleagues in the circle, who are walking from one end of this section of the yard to the other in step with the beat of three drummers walking behind them. The human wall sways to the beat while chanting and clapping hands. Afterwards, deacons who were standing under cloth umbrellas with gold tassels form a procession, their hands carrying brass, gold and silver crosses with intricate designs on their left shoulders. They smile at me when our eyes meet.

Gete takes me to the clinic after the service and the doctor gives me blue pills that knock me out for hours. I'm sleeping on what has become my sponge in the lounge when the voices of Martha and her man wake me up. I'm too groggy to even open my eyes fully, much less talk or move my body. My camera bag doubles as my purse because it's always on me. Except now. It's on the table and Martha and her man are digging through it. They separate my money into two bundles. One goes back to my bag and the other into his pockets.

Miriam is aghast when I tell her and begs me to not tell her husband while she deals with her kids. She calls a meeting and, of course, the couple denies swindling me. What happens next shocks me. Miriam turns on me, and says I'm lying. Her children are neither thieves nor liars. I don't know about you, but where I come from, when you invite someone home, you don't steal from them, and if your children happen to be little pieces of shit, you call them out. I'm somewhat disappointed but not shocked – I've come to expect that something weird will happen just when I think I'm having the most wonderful moment of my life in Ethiopia. Miriam protests when I move back to the hotel, complaining that people will gossip about why I move out of her house.

I leave Lalibela for Addis, then Harar, a day later.

25 May 2013

The African Union is turning fifty years old today. Addis Ababa has been in a party mood all week with clubs throwing parties in the name of African unity with soundtracks that feature Mafikizolo, original and Amharic dubs of 'Chop My Money' and 'Nwa Baby', Ethiopian stars Jah Lude and Teddy Afro, whose hit 'Tikur Sew' is one of my favourite songs, and, of course, Bob Marley. The official celebration is at the Millennium Hall in the airport area. Streets around the hall have been barricaded and the gates into the complex equipped with scanners. I take my place in the line of women waiting our turn for the female security guard to pat us down. On any given day, the capital city is a never-ending parade of African presidents, political VIPs and a small group of political aides. Almost all of them are in Addis this afternoon. It turns the main entrance that has been reserved for VIPs into a parade of expensive cars, and the red carpet they walk on to get to the hall is turned into a fashion spectacular of flowing grand boubous and intricate ankara ensembles that are complete with head wraps rising up to the heavens. The crowd, mostly Ethiopians, is also dressed to represent Africa, in ankara, bazin, kente and other African textiles. I'm in a red kemi.

I'm too short to see the stage from the front so I spend most of the evening backstage or outside the hall, where an exhausted Somizi Mhlongo, with bloodshot eyes, spends most of his time, relieved that his mission of choreographing the biggest party in Africa is almost complete. His calm demeanour doesn't inspire one of the women who run the stage to take it easy.

I find her screaming at the event director for his oversight; never in her diplomatic life has she come across the ignorance that makes a person overlook political protocol 101 – presidents speak in the order of their country's liberation. It's sacrilege that President Armando Guebuza speaks before President Idriss Deby. 'Who doesn't know that Chad's independence comes before Mozambique's?' she screams, storming off to the VIP waiting room to line up more presidential speakers. It's only then that the event director stops holding his breath.

A pair of black moccasins shuffles by. Their owner sits next to me. Looking up, I find Kenneth Kaunda's face. I kneel and greet him like the elder he is and go back to minding my business. When his speech is over, and the slow shuffle walks past me again, I get to lock my arm into his and walk him down the ramp, and when photographers ask for his picture, I kick the aide to the curb and issue instructions from the side lines. Mzee is eighty-nine years old – there'll be no flash lights.

'Thank you for my freedom,' I say, patting his forearm.

I'm a journalist, so technically I can meet anyone I want to. However, this moment comes into my life because I give it to myself instead of waiting on fate and professional perks. When I go back to my seating area, I find Uhuru Kenyatta holding court with Kgopedi Liloke, whose frequent trips to Addis Ababa are my respite from cheap hotels and a chance to get whatever I may be missing from South Africa.

Uhuru has swagger. It makes everyone swarm to him for a picture. I do like everyone and wait my turn. Unlike other speakers, he doesn't keep to himself and he makes small talk. 'Sasa Uhuru?' I say, using the Nairobean greeting. I catch my faux pas, and greet him again. 'Excuse me. Good evening, your excellency,' I say.

'Good evening, just call me Uhuru,' he says, reaching out to shake my hand.

'Okay, Uhuru. Is that your speech?' My hand is pointing at a stack of papers in his hands.

'Yes,' he says.

'We don't have the whole night, you know,' I banter.

'It's not a long speech. The font size is big so I can see properly,' he explains. The president of Kenya is the coolest political VIP I've ever met.

I leave African Union's party to have dinner with Dr Zakes Motene, whose regular trips to Addis are another source of comfort along with Kgopedi's. The predictable, inevitable turn for the bizarre happens when we try to get back into the hall for Salif Keita's performance. The security guard has decided that the party is over for the small crowd gathered at the entrance and he refuses to let us back inside. I miss Salif Keita but I also start a party at the gate with Papa Wemba's dancers. The guard's weirdness gives me the privilege of dancing with people whose liquid hips have been my entertainment for years; this is why I call being in Ethiopia a weird privilege. This is why I cannot hold on to my bitter experiences here.

The biggest mystery of my life in the country is how lightly someone steals my passport in Shashamane. I only realise days later that it's lost. The uniforms at the police station refuse to take my statement when I tell them I don't know who took it, only that I last saw it on the day I went to the bank to withdraw money. I try reporting the loss in Addis Ababa and get the same story: I can't get an affidavit unless I know exactly what happened. In the meantime, my visa is about to expire. I take my problem to the immigration office, and walk out without a solution. I apply for a temporary passport but without proof of when I came into Ethiopia or an official document from the police, there is nothing I can do except travel around the country and try my luck at all the police stations in the areas I visit.

I finally get an affidavit in Addis in June after I barge into the police commissioner's office, refusing to leave until he helps me. He writes a letter that I take to the police station in Arada. Armed with an affidavit, I make my way back to Immigration, where I'm sent to court for staying in the country with an expired visa even though, as I point out to the uniform, they know my hands have been tied since March.

All court cases are in Amharic and I need a translator.

I show up with my friend Galila, who is a tour guide with Balehageru Tours. She warns me to keep my mouth shut and admit guilt without letting my sarcasm get in the way. I retrace my steps to Immigration once again and walk out with a visa; except, when I go to Balehageru's office to buy my ticket to Johannesburg online, my passport is nowhere to be found.

I go back to the embassy to apply for another temporary passport. The Ethiopian lady who works there rolls her eyes at me and thinks there's more to the story than what I'm telling. In the end, it takes a favour that Kgopedi calls in for me to get a replacement.

This is Ethiopia, where strange things know where to find me. The driver of the taxi from the embassy to Piazza tells me to sit in the front. He makes small talk before opening his cubby hole; he has my passport but he refuses to give it back unless I pay him. 'But I'm broke,' I complain.

'It's not my problem. Do you know how much money I spent trying to find you? I even went to your embassy,' he lies.

'Will you drop me off at the hotel then? I'm sure my friends will lend me some money,' I claim, and wait until we're stuck in traffic before I suddenly find birrs in my bag. He reaches for my passport, my hand sneaks to the door handle, I grab my stolen property and jump out without giving him any money.

When I get to Balehageru's office at Taitu hotel to tell them the latest instalment of my crazy life in Ethiopia, the owner and now dear friend Teshome Ayele locks my passport in the safe, and offers to drive me to the airport in the morning. 'This is the only way I can be sure that there'll be no more drama,' he says.

I never miss South Africa when I travel and always feel sad when I land at OR Tambo International because it means an adventure has come to an end. On this occasion, I join everyone who claps when we hit the tarmac; happy to escape the madness of Ethiopia.

I don't want to live on the road any more, not in the foreseeable future anyway. My spirit is weary from the intensity of the highs and crushing lows of living like a vagabond and I miss sleeping in one bed for days on end and the cleanliness of a home toilet that I wash with Domestos after every flush to make sure that it lives up to my obsession with clean sanitation facilities.

I watch my Kilimanjaro-sized backpack going around the conveyor belt several times, like I do on 24 June 2008 in Dakar, my heart hurling itself against my chest as it did then. My steps to the exit are heavy and slow: I'm closing the most important chapter of the story of my life, when a three-month break to West Africa turns into five years of living and travelling around the continent.

XXII

EGYPT

June 2017

I ACHE FOR FARAWAY places when I listen to Khaled sing 'Aicha'. This Friday morning is no different as he begs Aicha to cast him a glance and accept the pearls and gold he wants to give her. I want to walk the streets of a city that was just a dot on the map until my feet carry me around it with the familiarity of home. I picture myself swaying to a song I don't know until the moment it plays on the radio; to walk hand-in-hand with strangers in dimly lit streets and haggle with market women. I haven't lived on the road for four years, and even though I still travel, around Africa, I'm yearning for an experience I have never had before, a place that's unlike any other I have been to, where people speak a language my ears have never heard.

It's Ramadan. My destination has to be a Muslim country.

By the time Khaled stops singing, I've booked my ticket to Cairo. I have never been to North Africa.

The action starts as soon as the plane lands at Cairo International

Airport. Families push trolleys with high stacks of suitcases. I do like the men I find huddled around the ATMs at the banking centre and shove my way to the front. Queues mean nothing in Cairo. Neither does order; I force my way through the exit where scores of people surround it so loved ones walk into their arms. My Arabic goes as far as Salam Alaikum and my Uber driver's English ends at good morning. I give my phone to a lone old man to tell the driver where to find me in Arabic.

Billboards on the highway wish us Ramadan Mubarak. A goofy smile plasters my face as the small waves of euphoria grow: I'm in Egypt, as I keep telling Mohammed whenever we drive past signboards and mosques.

'You grew up in a city the world is obsessed with. How does it feel, knowing that your ancestors are the most fascinating the world has ever known? People pay thousands of dollars in the best universities of the world to unravel your mysterious heritage,' I add.

He smiles and plays Arabic love songs. He gets off the road and walks to my door to open it. 'Come out,' he says, using his hands instead of words. 'Kneel,' he tells me. I'm lost until he points behind me. 'Kneel.' He smiles. We're at the Nile River. It's pronounced like kneel. He grabs my phone as my cue to pose for a picture. 'Welcome,' he smiles.

My jaw hits the floor when we drive into Giza and I see a pyramid. The shops on my right sell Samsung and Apple gadgets; I'm on my way to the side where Giza existed long before it was a sprawling modern city.

I'm at the Guardian Guest House that I choose for its rooftop views of the Sphinx and two pyramids. I have a few minutes to go before my tour guide picks me up at 8.30am. I shower and adorn my body with a purple and white kanga I turn into a shift dress. It's from Stone Town. I stack my neck with three Maasai necklaces from Nairobi and drape my chest with a purple and yellow kanga from Dar es Salaam. Giza is going to know that Madam Afrika has arrived.

I'm around eight or nine years old when our Saturday school teacher shows up with an armful of posters for a lesson that plants a seed that has grown into my life as a vagabond. I still remember it more than twenty years later, as flashes of a picture of King Tutankhamun's gold death mask, lesson sheets with hieroglyphics on them and a poster of the Great Pyramid. One memory is very vivid: I stay behind over lunch break and stare at a poster of the Sphinx, transfixed by the face of a human on the body of a lion. This is the first time I discover that the world is bigger than what's around my corner, and it's older than I can fully understand. I vow to know this world.

The site of my first travel dream is a sixteen-hectare complex on the edge of the Sahara Desert. The crowd is sparse. I stand at the entrance for a long time looking at people climbing the base of the Great Pyramid. Others are on the backs of camels decked out with rugs, and plastic flowers on the heads.

'Please don't say anything,' I ask my guide Osama. I want to be in tune with my emotions and the realisation that my adult life is the perfect manifestation of my childhood fantasy. I'm also getting over the shock of people showing up at *the* Great Pyramids dressed in chinos and tie-dye harem pants. An old man walks over to sell postcards of the only one of the seven ancient wonders of the world remaining.

What I think of as my guided tour is actually Osama's one-man show. He rattles off facts and anecdotes with pride, like he's telling me news I have not known for years. 'Many people think the pyramids are buildings but they are, in fact, tombs,' he says. 'I bet you also thought there was only one pyramid, huh? That's because people only know the big one,' he continues, pointing at King Khufu's tomb. 'It was the tallest building in the world until the Eiffel Tower went up in 1889 CE. It's made with two point three million limestones that workers carved into bricks. Can you believe it, huh?'

His sons, kings Khafre and Menkaure, commission the other

two large pyramids, and the three small ones belong to his queen and daughters.

Nothing I have done and will do can compare to climbing the base of the Great Pyramid. The guards at its entrance repeat the only instruction Osama gives me. 'No picture,' he says, before telling me how sad he is that South Africa's national soccer team exists as a memory of its long-gone days of glory.

'You used to be the best in Africa,' he sighs.

A few steps into the tomb and I'm already breathless from the steep walk. A man I meet along the dark, narrow passage smiles awkwardly when I pass him. 'I'm generally fit,' he heaves. My calves sting and the beads of sweat on my face are turning into a stream.

The king's burial room is built with granite. His body is no longer in its chamber. The room is quiet apart from the excited teenagers taking selfies. Two women kneel in front of the chamber, moving their lips silently while the rest of us lean or sit against the wall. More people go into the chamber. I wrap my kanga over my head and shoulders when I take my spot next to it, and lead the adults into breaking the rule against taking pictures. 'Please forgive me,' I whisper to King Khufu's spirit and head back outside to join Osama.

I've experienced Africa on boats, bikes, trucks, trains, donkeys and just about everything except a camel. They terrify me. At five feet tall, even sitting on a bar stool makes me feel out of balance. Nevertheless, I march ahead of Osama to a group of four camels lying next to their minders. The first one I go to refuses to stand up. At the second camel, I swing my right leg over the camel while Osama and two minders push and pull my body until its lodged on the saddle. The camel jerks its head to make its unsteady rise. I sway to the right and freak out. My minutes-old fantasy of exploring the compound on a camel comes to an end, and Osama takes me back to the air-conditioned car. We drive around the complex in a rush. The country is in a Ramadan-inspired standstill and all attractions will close around 3pm. Also, Osama has fasting fatigue and is still recovering from a fainting spell. I become one of millions of tourists I've always wanted to be, posing for photos that make it seem as if I have a pyramid in my hand.

Our next stop is the Sphinx. 'Please don't say anything,' I tell Osama again. I close my eyes and travel back to Saturday school, where I stand next to the door to stare at the poster of the Sphinx. When I open my eyes, I go wild with pictures, making it look like I'm kissing Khafre's image, putting sunglasses on him and holding my phone against his ear; my happiness is childlike.

From Giza, we drive twenty-four kilometres to Sakkara. Buildings and street lamps are decorated with neon plastic triangles for the holy month. Street corners have fruit vendors whose wares include cherries, my favourite thing to eat after watermelon, and even though this is a part of Africa I have never experienced, it triggers memories of my time in other countries with butcheries that hang animal carcasses out in the open, and overcrowded, beat-up taxis. I roll down my window and offer my Salam Alaikum and Ramadan Mubarak to people we drive past.

Ancient Egypt has ninety pyramids. The first one, in Sakkara, was designed by Imhotep, the commoner and architect-turned-chancellor to Pharaoh Djoser and the high priest of the Sun God Ra, who I first meet in my mom's much-loved crossword puzzles. The stone and clay structure was built around the twenty-seventh century BC as Pharaoh Djoser's tomb. It's also the resting place of his eleven daughters. It's being renovated and has been closed off with scaffolding. We walk around the complex to explore the temple ruins; where I run my hands on smooth limestones and pillars that are shaped like lotus flowers. I'm on holy ground; where the great Imhotep, the African who gave the world the practice of medicine, once stood. Tears of gratitude mingle with the sweat streaming down my face.

From here, we speed off to what used to be the city of Memphis, and the seat of power in ancient Egypt. It still stands, as a museum set in a yard with artefacts that include an alabaster Sphinx, and kiosks that sell alabaster curios. The granite statue of Ramesses II, who is considered the most powerful in the exhaustive list of rulers from the Egyptian Empire, is the centrepiece of the collection. It lies on the ground floor at the museum. His ankles are broken and crown chipped, but he is carved to withstand time and all his features are still visible, even the fingers curled around a rod and the bracelets on his wrists.

I'm in awe of the foresight that makes ancient Egyptians preserve their world so we never forget that Africa is the cradle of civilisation. They are the reason I walk with my head held high and proudly challenge anyone who says Africa would be nothing without colonisation.

Osama and I part ways after he takes me to a papyrus museum in Giza, where the curator shows me how the 'paper of our ancestors' is made. He peels a lotus stalk with a knife and cuts the spongy white flesh into thin sheets that he beats flat with a hammer. He flattens them with a roller. 'We leave them in water for six days to remove the excess sugar,' he says, laying out leaves that have been soaking for days horizontally and vertically. The low sugar content in the plant binds them naturally. He leaves them in a pressing machine for just over a week, after which the papyrus paper will be ready to use; the process hasn't changed since 3000 BC.

I go back to the hotel to shower and change into a little black dress I wear with a red shuka from Kampala and Maasai earrings. I layer my lips with red lipstick. Cairo by night turns into a party zone that features its West African community. My plan is to let the men who will surely swarm to me pay for my entertainment. I remember that it's Ramadan and suspend sundowners in keeping with my rule of assimilating into the culture of the places I visit. Besides, Eid is only four days – it won't be long before I can drink again. I go to Cairo Tower to watch the city at sunset, when the horizon looks hazy from the thick layer of smog and dust that hangs over the city. The Nile River snakes through its endless sky-scrapers and apartment buildings; traditional boats called felluca floating below me. I can barely see the pyramids through the smog.

I struggle to find a cab to Khan el-Khalili bazaar, and no one I meet on the tree-lined street I walk down speaks English. A security guard at a building I walk into goes inside to find someone who does.

After bemoaning Bafana Bafana's misfortune on the soccer field, he takes my hand in his and helps me cross a busy street. He flags a cab and tells the driver to charge me like a local. 'She's African,' he says, 'One of us.'

At seven hundred years old, Khan el-Khalili is a cultural institution. It can barely contain people who are out tonight. Its narrow alleys spill over with food vendors and tiny shops that sell yards of cotton. The brass shops and coppersmiths add a medieval atmosphere. No matter the corner I turn, the air is laced with hookah and incense. The bazaar hums with the sound of hundreds of dinner conversations.

I find the perfect spot to watch people while I eat. The menu has a picture of Queen Nefertiti's bust. I order sweet, thick guava juice that the menu spells as 'guafa' and bissap juice, called karkade here. Sipping it takes me back to my first trip to West Africa in 2006 when Accra inspired me to start travelling around the continent. A young girl comes to sell prayer beads. She blows kisses at me when she walks away.

The cab ride back to Giza starts off fine. The driver is also an Osama. 'But I'm not the terrorist,' he laughs before making me regret the decision to not use Uber. He drives like he wants to kill us, and comes within an inch of bumping other cars. 'Slow down man,' I say. 'My friends call me Rambo,' he laughs, and tells me to put my hand on my heart for good luck. He puts his hand on a copy of the Quran on the dashboard before pumping up the volume. He removes his hands from the steering wheel to clap to the beat.

I'm walking down Abou Al Hool Street mesmerised by my surroundings. To my left is the complex with the Sphinx and the pyramids that peer out from behind flat rooftops. On my right, squeezed into a corner, are KFC and Pizza Hut outlets that are still closed. For now, the scooters for the home deliveries are parked in a row outside the shops. Along the street, donkey carts and horse-drawn carriages are side by side with Ubers, tuk tuks and camels. The supermarket opposite KFC only sells airtime vouchers in twenty-pound units, and while the tea shops next to it are quiet, at night they will buzz with men and boys out in groups for hookah and tea; some of them overflowing from the shop and its stoep to sit on chairs across the road. The baker piles the tables outside his shop with cakes, cookies and pastries for Eid.

The walk to El Malek Fouad Street should take ten minutes but every third shop on Abou Al Hool sell papyrus art. It turns the short walk into a social event. The hook is always an invitation to tea. The end result is always a sales pitch. At shops that sell papyrus art, the pitch always includes switching off the lights so I can see pieces that change objects and glow in the dark. The art is displayed on every surface of the walls and varies from poster sized to large pieces whose presence will dominate the walls they will end up hanging on. There are paintings of the Sphinx, the Great Pyramids, Tutankhamun's death mask, Queen Nefertiti's bust, the plethora of gods worshipped by the ancient Egyptians and some with scenes from the lives of royals, like weddings and funeral processions. Personalised birthday art with signs of the zodiac and names in hieroglyphs are made on the spot.

Tahrir is the Arabic word for freedom. I learn this word in 2011 when the second wave of the Arab Spring revolution comes to Egypt, and sit-ins are staged at Tahrir Square. There are no people other than the traffic officers at the boom gate and the tour bus drivers in the square's parking lot.

Even without its recent history, it would still have an impressive stature, what with being the location of the Nile Ritz-Carlton Hotel. I'm here for the peach colonial building across Tahrir that's one of the most important heritage sites in the world, where the largest collection of ancient Egyptian artefacts is housed. At last, I'm at the museum of my dreams. It's just after 8.30am. Other excursions I've been on had thin crowds, but here the line to get into the museum is about three hundred metres long. The gates only open at 9am. Until then, people who are in tour groups have spirited and happy conversations. Cameras are slung on necks, phones are on selfie mode and Egyptian pounds are already in our hands waiting to pay our way in.

Even just through the gate, the Museum of Egyptian Antiquities tantalises with its contents. The yard is scattered with imposing statues. We form an orderly line going through the gate and the scanners to the ticketing counters. We fall into a frenzy shortly afterwards. Everyone spreads around the yard taking pictures; wandering off around the building, where there are more statues.

Egyptians call their land the mother of the world. I'm not one for labels that countries give to themselves, but it's hard to not call Egypt mother. The old world has left behind art, literature and architectural monuments. Ancient Egyptians preserved every aspect of their life from their fashion, diet and makeup techniques to pottery, tombs, decor pieces, their jewellery – everything, really.

The variety of artefacts is astounding and their details dazzling. They immortalise rulers from all ancient kingdoms and their dynasties. The theme of perfection I first experience at the pyramids is still carried over. The section dedicated to King Tutankhamun drips with gold: A leopard head, a funeral figurine called unshabti, left on tombs to do any work the departed might be called to in the afterlife. There's also a wooden board game called Senet, played by moving different pieces across square boxes with hieroglyphic symbols. Among the glittering collection is what's considered the most known artefact of the pharaonic era – eleven kilos of gold inlaid with glass and moulded into the elaborate death mask worn by the king after death; covering him head to shoulders. It features a plaited glass beard, a head dress crowned with a cobra and a vulture's head and hieroglyphic inscriptions at the back.

More than the gilded life and what's considered one of the greatest civilisations in the world, I'm most impressed by the royal mummy room, a level up from the ground floor. Vanity may be a deadly sin now, but it has also ensured that the kings and queens who created ancient Egypt live forever. In their quest to start the afterlife looking good, they are turned into mummies. Several of them lie in glass cases. Their skin has become jet black and leathery, hair fine, and nails and teeth yellow and brown.

Satisfied that I have at last had a personal encounter with the buildings and artefacts that planted the first seed of my wanderlust, I leave for Luxor in Southern Egypt.

On the drive from the Luxor airport, through wide palm tree-lined boulevards surrounded by green farms, to the East Bank, there is no sign of the city's reputation as the world's biggest open-air museum. The town is quiet on this side. It turns into a loud mix of hoofs and beepers at the corniche. My cab driver, Assad, gets off the road to show me the avenue of sphinxes; a three-kilometre walkway that used to connect the temples of Karnak and Luxor. It's still lined with some of the one thousand three hundred and fifty sphinxes constructed by various dynasties of the New Kingdom. An obelisk at the Luxor Temple, built by Pharaohs who include Amenhotep III, Ramesses II and Tutankhamun, looms over the area.

I'm at the Bob Marley Peace Hotel; chosen for being named after the man whose music has been the soundtrack of my life since the mid-1990s. The purple swing doors fling open violently. The entrance is taken over by a motorbike, and I stumble on the step and almost fall. The receptionist lifts his eyes from the counter for a second, and goes back to ignoring me as I take my careful steps to the reception counter. The room hums with Egyptian music and smells like ganja and incense. His words drawl out, like he's high. He winks and says the only thing burning here is incense. This is the only time he comes close to being friendly. He badgers me about about my safety and impending danger in Luxor.

I shouldn't trust anyone outside the hotel as they're all con men who lure travellers to their homes with a lunch invitation that turns into a robbery. I shouldn't wander off by myself lest I get robbed. I thank him for the warning. He asks what my plans are, and repeats his dreadful 'welcome to Luxor' speech when I tell him I'm off to wander the streets he just warned me about. He pouts when I refuse to let him organise a guide to accompany me.

Walking out of the hotel onto Mohammed Farid street for my first exploration of Luxor. I smile so much my cheeks start hurting. Men who run one of the kiosks motion for me to come into their shops where they 'invite' me to buy water or cool drink from them. At the tea shop, I decline an offer for a drink and promise to visit before I leave Luxor I enjoy a slice of watermelon offered by a boozed-up old man who sells the fruit in piles on a dusty stoep that turns into his home when he pulls a blanket over his body to sleep. Even with the few people out, the street is quaint, with hotels, restaurants, and a juice bar. I stand at a corner waiting for the cabs, minibuses and horse carriages to pass. There's a fish shop and restaurant ahead on my right with a menu handwritten on the wall; two boys sit on the steps of the building opposite the restaurant. There's a mule not far from them with a visible rib cage. This carriage, unlike the gleaming ones lined along the corniche, looks like it will fall apart any moment now.

A man at the stall behind me fills the air with the smell of the fried liver he sells with bread. Even though the shops I can spot from where I'm standing look old, they're charming instead of broken down; even with the dust and stains on their walls. I hire a horse and carriage from Ahmed. We start at the mosque next to the temple, where the Imam takes me around before asking for a donation. Across the street from the temple, mules jostle for space with hooting cars and minibuses. A McDonald's sign glows in the fading day light. We explore the West Bank's sandy alleys and side streets before stopping for hookah and tea.

On the way back to the Bob Marley not-so-peaceful hotel, Ali returns from a shawarma shop with a plastic bag with kushari. It's a mixture of macaroni, spaghetti, rice and lentils topped with tomato sauce made with up to twelve spices, chickpeas and crispy brown onions. My appetite finally joins me in Egypt.

I pace around reception the next morning seething that the tour company is running late for our 3.30am pick up time. The clock is ticking towards 4am. At this rate, the sunrise will find me on the ground. When the minibus arrives, it has eight other people in it who are as sleepy as I am. I make small talk with a Brazilian guy who backpacked here from South East Asia, via Jordan, on a seven-month trip that still has a European leg left, and a Mexican mother and daughter pair on a detour from Greece. We drive to the river for a felucca across the Nile River to the West Bank. I drink three cups of lukewarm Nescafé and hope we make it on time.

The ten-minute drive to the launching point of our adventure features avenues dotted with statues. The fields glow with orange flames from the burners that are not loud enough to muffle the Brazilian fellow who complains about our group being hard done by by the tour company. Not only are we late and currently watching people float above us while our flame keeps dying, our balloon is washed out and grey. The others are bright citrus colours. Our balloon keeps deflating; further delaying our ascent.

Luxor is truly a wonder to behold from the air. The soft light falls over rows of flat-roofed apartments that turn into green fields that eventually turn into bare rocky mountains and desert. Nothing

I've experienced compares to the romance of soaring over the Nile River as it runs between the city's East and West Bank, and the mountains that hide the tombs of King Tutankhamun and Queen Nefertari, among other rulers who become immortal with time. The artefacts and tombs they built when the city was called Thebes have turned Luxor into the biggest outdoor museum in the world, as the city punts itself.

Back on solid ground in the West Bank, streets are overrun with people celebrating the first day of Eid al Fitr, dancing to blaring music as they follow its sound to Luxor temple and beyond. I follow tour groups around the courts of Ramessess II and Amenhotep III and strolling along the Avenue of Sphinxes, the three-kilometre alley flanked by ram-headed sphinxes. One of the greatest wonders of ancient Egypt is that new artefacts are being discovered as you read this.

Thebes is woven into life in Luxor, the monuments and temples are simply there. In one of the streets, houses built in Luxor have sphinxes of Thebes at their gates.

In the afternoon, I meet Tayeb, a tour guide, to sail along the Nile River in a felucca. We sail with Mustafa the boatman, who brews karkade tea. Our boat is in a reflective silence – Tayeb reminisces about the days when he could barely keep up with demands for trips, and my head rings with 2Face Idibia's 'African Queen'; floating on the Nile like he sings. I'm living a lyric in one of my favourite songs. Once again, I realise why I can't stop travelling Africa – this continent is fantastical.

Later, in the evening, Ahmed and his horse meet me a safe distance from the hotel and the receptionist's ongoing warning to stay away from locals to take me to his house for Eid celebrations with his mom, three sisters and six nieces and nephews; the youngest is a toddler who cries whenever they put him in my arms. Ali, their neighbour and Ahmed's father figure, is also here. His hospitality is more hostile than an Ethiopian mom's.

My visit starts off well. I sit in the lounge with Ahmed, his eldest sister who is visiting from Cairo and Ali, who shows me the family albums and pictures of him and his mini-me Ahmed, and the tourists they met years ago when Ali was still a tour guide. Ali plies me with sweets, bottles of Sprite and Lays while Ahmed's mom finishes preparing our meal.

It comes on a large tray with plates that have fried fish, a whole chicken, potatoes fried in cumin, raw tomato and onion, kofta in tomato relish, stacks of pita-like bread called aish baladi. It's dinner for three, with the rest of the family having had their meal already. Every piece of fish, kebab and chicken that we put on our plates is replaced minutes later with a fresh tray bearing more of the same. Ali feeds me with his own hand when I try to stop eating, and only accepts that I'm full when I tell him that if he forces another morsel into my mouth, the lunch I'm due to have with the family tomorrow before I leave Luxor will be cancelled. My threat gets me out of eating the cake I bring for dessert.

I spend my last day in Luxor in Thebes, at the tombs in the West Bank. I visit the Valley of the Queens, the final resting place of seventy-five queens, their sons and daughters and other royal family members from the eighteenth to the twentieth dynasties. A guide follows me into the tombs to make sure I don't take pictures – not without giving him baksheesh. The tombs are all designed in the burial tradition of the time, with walls covered with drawings of gods and depictions of the afterlife. The two tourism police who guard Queen Nefertari's grave follow me to the entrance, demanding to see my separately bought ticket into her burial chamber. As I stand outside her tomb trying to bargain a free entry, I can't help but wonder if she has been turned into the whore of Luxor; the pleasure of her company costs 1000 Egyptian pounds for ten minutes.

The infrastructure at the Valley of the Kings is made for tourists. Along with shops that sell alabaster curios and replicas of famous artefacts, the site comes with a cart that drives us to the remains. By this stage, I'm soaked with sweat and my feet have pins and needles. Everything sort of looks the same: Tombs dug out in the mountains with the paintings and carvings of kings and gods on the walls protected by a glass wall.

And so my day goes, with more statues, falcon heads and dazzling stories of empires and conquests. Sometimes, I give up walking and watch them from afar. At the burial grounds of the royal workers, I hide in a tomb with a tourism police officer, drinking tea and water, and charging my phone in the electric plug that's been added to the tomb and go on social media; the Old World meeting 2017 and beyond. I end my visit at King Tutankhamun's tomb that, although small, is decorated as vividly as the others.

I fly back to Cairo to connect to the one-hour flight to Dahab, a small town in the Sinai Peninsula that overlooks the Red Sea coast on one side, and imposing rocky mountains and escarpments that eventually turn into desert on the other. As much as I love journeys back to ancient Egypt, my mind can't take it any more. I need sun, sand and sea; and other than being my wild card that I pick by closing my eyes and running my pencil on the map of coastal Egypt to go wherever it stops, Dahab also comes with a reputation that I love. It's known for being bohemian.

The one-hour drive from the airport in Sharm el Sheikh to Dahab is through barren jagged hills that remind me that this part of Egypt is the setting of biblical stories that star Moses as the leader of the exodus. The driver drops me off at Tarbouche House after several trips in the small city centre to look for an ATM that works.

I pick Tarbouche House based on raving online reviews about

its close distance to the waterfront, and its helpful owner and manager. The man is in a bad mood when I arrive and greets me by launching into his house rules: My door and windows must always be closed when the air con is on, I must put my soiled toilet paper in the basket provided for this purpose, the gate must always be locked and anyone who isn't a paying guest is not allowed onto the premises. He disappears to his office to make copies of my passport while I fill in the checking-in form. It lists the rules and warns that anyone who breaks them will be kicked out. I discover two days later that this is not an idle threat.

The strict rules don't match the town's relaxed atmosphere. Even though it's predominantly Muslim, Dahab carries itself like a real coastal town. The dress code in the business centre features tunics and burkas but clothes are optional at the waterfront and the streets around it. Hot guys with sun-kissed brown skin walk along the promenade topless, flexing their gym-honed bodies and groomed poodles. Women are in bum shorts and bikini tops, and divers turn heads with bodies that look like marble sculptures under their wetsuits.

It's not a walk at the promenade without people who own perfume and curio shops making a sales pitch that starts with invitations for Bedouin tea that's made with dried wild sage, cardamom pods, cinnamon bark and black tea.

I follow a Bob Marley song, 'Zimbabwe', to Planet Café, where I park myself on a lounge chair next to a young couple who's either kissing, puffing on a splif or sipping on beers. The people in the water swim with their dogs and hang out at the water's edge to smoke hookah and joints; Dahab's relaxed to the point of being hedonistic.

The night-time bustle comes from seafood restaurants with names like Nemo, Shark, Fresh Fish and Ali Baba. Their entrances have page-by-page displays of the menu, while their ingredients – lobster, tuna, crab, red snapper, calamari and a host of other species I don't know – are displayed on ice in glass containers at the door. They're weighed and sold per gram. My dinner of two hundred grams of lobster starts with a meze of a brinjal dip called baba ganoush, tahina sauce and hummus served with warm puffed pita bread dished from oven to plate. Mains are lobster with salad, grilled vegetables and a subtly spiced rice cooked in tomato paste called sayadeya. Dahab's plate is local and international, with a choice between several Indian, Korean and Thai dishes. The selection covers vegans, diner-style menus and a German bakery.

Like other tour companies, King Dahab Safari sells its business on placards and boards with pictures pinned on them of the highlights of the many experiences on sale. Most of them have a day trip to the Dead Sea and a hike up Mount Sinai. The desks in King Safari's office have albums with frame-by-frame photos of their tours and activities. The walls are also covered with pictures of people trekking up mountains on camels, divers surrounded by exotic fish, exhausted but satisfied hikers walking down rocky mountains, on 4x4 adventures in the desert, sitting around a bonfire. The message is clear: It's always playtime in Dahab. My playtime starts with the realisation that the town doesn't know how to keep time or its word.

Exhibit A: King Safari insists on picking me up at Tarbouche House at 8am for a snorkelling trip to Three Pools. My trip starts at 10am after many unanswered calls make me walk to their office, only to find it locked. I bang on the glass door until someone comes out from the back of the room.

'We forgot about you,' he says coolly while we wait for a driver who shows up in a bakkie.

When we get to Happy Life Village, where the pools are, the private instructor who is supposed to snorkel with me turns out to be non-existent.

The white lies become part of my Dahab experience. Exhibit B is the trip to Jerusalem. All companies say they go there once a week, another says they make daily trips and I can still go even though I have a single-entry visa, says Salim the tour guide. He swears that he knows the border officials and they will not stamp me out of the country. When I try to book, he tells me that they only travel with a Russian group, so essentially I will just be coming along for the ride. I decided to give it a miss.

I book an overnight trip to a Bedouin village in the mountains with Salim for a night of traditional food and music. The mountains turn out to be the rocky escarpment close to Happy Life Village; the village is a beach with camping facilities, dinner is the fish we buy in Dahab and roast on the fire with tomatoes, potatoes and carrots. He sings folk songs his grandmother used to sing for him when he was young when I ask about traditional music. He smiles and chain-smokes the night away, waiting for the sunrise.

Staying up all night under the stars watching Saudi Arabia shine so close to me, I revisit my wish to one day travel there to follow Prophet Mohammed's footsteps. It makes up for my improvised night in the mountains.

When I book my snorkelling trip to Ras Abu Galum, I know that what I'm paying for is not what I will get, so I'm happy that the private trip includes four other people and become even more excited when we collect a group that makes us travel in three bakkies to Ras Abu Galum. However, I'm shocked to discover that all the snorkelling gear that's included in the money I pay for the trip is old. My flippers have holes at the toes and my goggles are held together with strings and rubber bands.

The biggest lie anyone tells me is that it's easy to hike up Mount Sinai. I book a trip and stock up on water and energy drinks. Our 11pm departure to Saint Catherine's Monastery at the foot of the holy mountain starts after midnight, and we arrive there with less than four hours left before sunrise. The 'easy' climb to the mountain top is up almost four thousand steps. I finally face my fear of camels, and spend my trip praying silently that I don't topple over and fall down the mountain whenever it walks on the edge of the rocky path. The camel's minder scolds me when I ask him to make it walk in the middle of the road. 'This is not a car, you can't control it.'

He tells me to lose weight when I point out that his camel is so slow, others that start the journey after us catch up and disappear from view. 'You're too fat,' he says.

'Please repeat your words when I'm back on solid ground so I can smack some respect into you,' I tell him.

My group of two Cairene friends, five American students and a mother with a son and daughter, who is dressed like her in Juicy Couture, wedge heel sneakers and fully made up faces have already started their final climb to the spot where Moses collects the Ten Commandments when I arrive at the camel's final stop. The only way up from here is up seven hundred and fifty steps. Our guide Aziz is annoyed with me for being slow. He sizes me up before saying, 'You won't be fast enough. I'll find you here.' He takes my phone. 'At least you'll have pictures of the chapel,' he says, running up to rejoin the group. I'm not fit but, given time, I can keep up. It's the late start that steals my time. If the trip didn't start on African time, I'd be able to take in sights like a chapel built on the spot where Elijah spent forty days and nights waiting to meet God.

'You're lucky I know that the sixth commandment says "thou shall not kill", otherwise, I'd bury you with my words,' I hiss back at him to have a last word in the conversation.

I know by now, after nine years of travelling the continent that, 'this is Africa,' as seasoned road hags love saying. In my case it means inconvenience and things that are annoying always precede incredibly rewarding experiences. In this case, it's the perfect peace that overcomes me sitting on a stoep, watching the darkness disappear and camels munching on watermelon while their minders nap inside the café.

The group returns with minor scratches and a twisted ankle for the mom; she looks wild with runny makeup and her ironed hair has become frizzy. I walk down on foot and still too slow to catch up with the group and other people who walk past me. One of the camel minders stays within view to help me make my way down.

Often when we talk about Islam and Christianity, it's about conflict, and although it's true that religion has caused havoc in Africa, I also stumble upon places that remind me to never take anything at face value, especially when it's about Africa.

Saint Catherine's Monastery stands as a testament of harmony between Christianity and Islam. The story of its origin dates back to 530 CE when its grey granite walls went up. They're still standing. Islam and Christianity have always been entwined at the monastery and, at one point, the monks turn to Prophet Mohammed for protection during invasions. The Prophet has also been to the monastery, and the mosque that was built in medieval times still stands on the grounds.

Aziz is in a hurry to end our trip and runs us through the visit, taking us to the tumbling green plant that's believed to be Moses' Burning Bush and into the church. He says he's doing us a favour when I complain that I need more than ten minutes here. The group complains that they're tired and the majority wins; we head back to Dahab. This moment is the reason I prefer travelling alone; places have different meanings to all of us and the person who doesn't have numbers on their side gets overruled.

On the trip back to Dahab I think about the few Sunday School classes I went to, and how alive the stories become in Egypt, from visiting the compound where Jesus and his parents stayed in Cairo, and drinking water from the same well they used to drink from, to walking in Moses' footsteps and the realisation that in the rocky region of the Sinai, it could very well be true that water was drawn from rocks because they are the only things around.

I started travelling to know Africa through its sights, smells, tastes, sounds and textures. I now do it to honour my experiences in West Africa, so that time never turns them into fading memories in other journeys my life takes me on.

XXIV

SUDAN

December 2017

ON PAPER, GETTING A Sudanese visa is as easy as submitting an application form in person or by courier to the embassy in Pretoria and paying R700 for a two-month single-entry visa. I hate travel administration that involves more than showing up at borders, and getting a Sudanese visa is tedious: I need two recent passport pictures, proof of flight reservations, confirmed hotel bookings, a copy of my passport, a three-month bank statement, a letter of employment and a yellow fever card. I buy my ticket to Khartoum on a whim six weeks before my travels and only apply for a visa a week before my date of departure.

The application form is rather amusing, with the usual questions about nationality, gender and passport number, where and when it was issued, when it will expire; and questions I have never encountered before, like my blood group, my mother's name and my religion, which I answer as none. I'm a socialised Christian with a strong affinity for Rastafarianism, slight guilt that I increasingly need to keep a God in my life doesn't include becoming Voodoo even though Mahu is a feminine spirit, and I've been thinking about Islam a lot and realising that I subconsciously travel to Muslim countries, and feel like something is missing if I don't spend Ramadan in one of them. Writing 'none' is easier than 'it's complicated'.

I submit my paperwork with an email asking for the application to be fast-tracked so I don't miss my flight even though, as I discover, I'm supposed to book a flight after the visa has been granted. I pack my tears in case I need them when I get a call saying the counsellor would like to meet me. I shouldn't have bothered because, as it turns out, the Sudanese people, including officials, believe that guests should feel at home, no matter who you are.

Mr Masjeed's first question is about my religion. I tell him the complicated story, he assures me that even though his country is predominantly Muslim and conservative, people with and without religions are free to express themselves. He wants to know what I want to experience and whether I have a host, then gives me his friend Bashir's number.

Bashir is a Sudanese-South African, so I will not feel like a complete stranger. 'It's a pity you are arriving two days after his son's wedding; I'm sure he would have loved it if you were also there.' I show off my limited Arabic when I drink tea with thlath, three sugars. The ambassador also wants to meet, to offer me bissap tea and let me know that he knows I'm not being honest when I say I'm staying at one of the most expensive hotels in Khartoum.

Even with travel apps and Google, it's hard to plan my logistics and when I call the cheap hotels I find online, receptionists don't speak English. He refers me to a cheaper hotel he knows and tells me to never turn down an invitation, whatever its nature.

'You're going to be pleasantly surprised by Sudan, even with your experience. The Sudanese people are very different,' he says. I'm already off to a great start because officialdom usually wants to meet to ask questions that leave me wondering why I'm so attached to a continent that's not always the easiest to travel.

The eleven-hour flight from Johannesburg to Khartoum includes a stop at Bole International in Addis Ababa, the city of my dreams and nightmares. I arrive in Khartoum switched on to the person I become on the road, greeting the uniforms with 'salam alaikum', thanking them by saying 'shukran'. The first person I ask for directions to the ATM points towards the door. The next person says there are no ATMs and the third tells me that there are ATMs but I can't use them because Sudan is still under sanctions that keep them out of the Visa and Mastercard networks. I'm screwed.

I have no money other than a thin stack of Kenyan shillings and Egyptian pounds left over from my trips there at the beginning of 2017. I exchange them for enough Sudanese pounds to tide me over the Christmas holidays at home. My plan to get money via Western Union falls flat when my cousin Oageng discovers, at the third outlet he goes to in Pretoria, that they don't transfer money to Sudan. My partner steps in and calls a Joburg-based outlet first to find out if they send money to Sudan, only for the story to change from "yes we do" to "only if it's going to a resident". I'm really screwed now.

Plan B comes from Mahlatsi, who offers to ask his network of Somalis to transfer my money from South Africa. For now all I can do is wait. I use the time to visit the confluence of the Nile Rivers at sunset, to peruse the main shopping districts in Khartoum and in Omdurman, the country's second largest city, and to take evening joyrides that end at the restaurants along the river bank, from where I watch the city lights twinkling on the Nile.

Plan B fails. My sister takes US$1000 to Mr Masjeed, who sends a Khartoum-based banker to my hotel with a suitcase filled with Sudanese pounds. It's not the ideal way to access cash, but it becomes yet another way I'm made to feel at home.

I have been wanting to come to Sudan for years, but I've been afraid that being here would rattle the ghosts I buried. Before my trip to the mass graves in Rwanda, visiting Sudan was about going to the pyramids in Meroe and exploring the ancient Nubian history that predates that of Egypt. After my breakdown in Ntarama in 2011, a trip to Sudan needed to feature Darfur as part of the instruction to write wars and conflict. Unlike the voices that tell me 'Africa now' in 2007, the word in Ntarama scares me and I run away from the instruction until 2017 when Sindi, a friend of almost two decades, loses her fears and emboldens me to think about my calling to places like Darfur, Bangui and Mogadishu. I'm now ready, and even though this trip doesn't include travelling to Darfur, I use being in Khartoum as a start; forming social networks with people who live or work in Darfur.

Being in Sudan feels like a sigh of relief. My spirit is light and I find the simplicity of life here restorative. Other than waking up to the call to prayer and hearing the muezzin bounce around the city five times a day, I feel transported back to a gentler, more innocent time when trusting strangers was second nature instead of a dance with danger.

I'm at Lisamin Safari Hotel in Al Amarat. Flags of Sudan and Kenya wave at the entrance and the lobby is decorated with swathes of kente cloth. The wall behind the receptionist has a mural of two minions, only they're dressed traditionally in a purple hijab, and a tunic and turban for the male minion. Being in countries that are authentic to who they are is one of my greatest joys of travelling.

The receptionist refuses to tell me how to use public transport to get to the national museum. She doesn't want me to get lost or be frustrated by the language barrier and doesn't care that getting lost is part of the magic of being in a place. I hang around Street 41 looking for someone to help me, but it's too early and the restaurants, ice cream shops and kiosks in the dusty square behind the hotel are still closed. Only the mechanics and old women with simple coffee stalls are open for business.

I go to the old woman hidden behind zinc sheets put up around a construction site, and sit under the tree with her greasy, mechanic customers for my morning cup. Her quiet grace draws me to her.

She sits on her stool under the baking sun with a toothless smile glued on a face shrouded by a delicate black cotton wrap. She wears thick socks with flip flops to keep the dust off her feet. Her work station is a small red wooden table topped with jars of sugar, coffee, cinnamon, star anise and ginger powder. It also has short drinking glasses. The rest of her equipment includes a small brazier, a small plastic bag filled with coal, several kettles and a plastic bottle she's cut in half and uses to rinse used glasses. We can only talk with our smiles and by clasping our hands. It's a pleasing way to start the day.

I relent and go back to the hotel for the receptionist to order a ride to Nile Street on Tirhal cab app.

Despite being on the Cape to Cairo route that has inspired adventurers for generations, Khartoum treats tourism like a side event, even with talk of rising visitor numbers. Signs are in Arabic and there is scant information about its attraction or the artefacts at the museum. It makes what should be an enlightening time at the double-storey building underwhelming; leaving me with more questions than answers about the ten thousand leftovers from ancient empires. Instead, I hark back to my visit to the Cairo museum, recognising the granite columns, statues and remains from the temples of Kemma, Semma and Buhen by the details I associate with ancient Egypt instead of information plaques. I'm the only tourist among different groups of school children and sparse families on a Sunday outing.

Three girls follow me around the floor until their ring leader gets over her giggles and greets me. They'd like to take selfies. Their classmates join us, and phones are passed to the security guards and teachers for photos.

The first floor of the museum houses the religious exhibition. The security guard leaves his chair next to the fan to follow us around and make sure we don't take any photographs. Most of the collection has chips and faded spots, but their colours are still bright. The tenth-century depiction of Daniel and three of his friends being saved from the furnace by the archangel is a reminder that, contrary to idle thoughts, Christianity didn't come to Africa with our colonisers.

Khartoum is famous for being the location of the confluence of the Blue and White Nile rivers that flow from Ethiopia and Uganda and onwards to Egypt. It's on my to-do list after the museum.

My plans change when I get a call from Yusuf. Mr Masjeed has given him my number, and he wants to take me out for lunch. We meet at a food court across the road from the airport for a meal that's as African as any featuring grilled meat that's sliced off fatty animal carcasses that hang on hooks at the butchery. Yusuf has an easiness that defines the character of the Sudanese people. Being with him feels like being home. When he drops me off at the hotel later, he tells me to call him the following day to tell him how I'm faring with my cashless situation, and he buys me airtime that doesn't run out in the two and half weeks I spend in Sudan.

Just as I sensed in 2006 that the trip to Accra would turn my life around, I send Mahlatsi a text message to tell him that Khartoum is under my skin in a way that will never leave me, and that experience tells me it will make me live on the road again. This realisation hits me when I go shopping for a local plug so I can use my laptop. I start my search at the hotel, where the receptionist tells one of the cleaners what I'm looking for and asks him to take me to the hardware store and speak Arabic on my behalf. They don't have what I'm looking for and even though they know where I need to go, they can't communicate the information.

My salvation comes when I see a man wearing a beaded wrist band in the colours of the Kenyan flag; I pull his hand without even talking to him first. He overlooks my invasion of his privacy, and uses his perfect Arabic to tell the tuk tuk driver where I'm going. The shop is closed for Maghrib, the sunset prayer. I sit on the stoep to wait for it to open again. Another shopper arrives but unlike me she doesn't have time to wait. She gives me her mobile number and asks me to call her when shopping resumes. When it does, I send her pictures of frames and their price tags, and the easiness of how we relate seals my destiny with Sudan: I belong here.

It's an affirmation that I get in every moment of my stay here. I get it from Osama on my second morning. He's the complete stranger who calls on me from the hotel lobby while I'm out for coffee. He doesn't speak a lot of English but it's enough to let me know that being with me is an errand from Yusuf; Osama will take me around the city on public transport so I don't get lost in translation.

We're like a painfully awkward blind date for the three days that he shows up at the hotel to take me around Khartoum, but I feel loved and cared for that he puts his life on hold for a few hours a day to make sure that I'm settling in. While I wait for money that I'm making plans to get via Western Union or the Somali network that Mahlatsi is trying to link me with, I visit the confluence of the Nile at sunset, the main shopping districts in Khartoum and the country's second city, Omdurman, and go on joyrides around the city that end at restaurants on the banks of the river on Nile Street, where I watch the city lights twinkling on the water.

Bashir is the next person to call me over, for tea at his house in Omdurman. Three things stand out about his visit. The first is how his son spends the duration of my trip on the phone with the taxi driver to give him directions so we don't get lost. The second is that my hosts pay for the trip. Walking into their yard, I find it odd that it has two narrow woven beds next to the door. The are two more beds in the room we walk through to get to the lounge. A section of it has more of these beds, called angareeb, that are a feature of private and public life in Sudan. They are for sitting and sleeping on; in bus stations, outside shops, in people's yards and their lounge rooms. We sit in the lounge for tea that's served with dates, chocolates and an assortment of butter cookies.

I meet his family in trickles. First, it's the new bride and groom who still have henna tattoos from their wedding day. His is black ink at the tips of his fingers. Hers is an elaborate pattern inside and outside her hands, running up to her arms. I also meet Bashir's wife and daughter, whose feet, like everyone else's, are always between Khartoum and Pretoria. Our conversation is one that I enjoy more than all others – always a favourite – a world I will only know from the records of history. Bashir works with Dr Mathole Motsekga through Sukara Heritage Society to preserve ancient Sudanese history. At the moment, they're examining the origins of Sudan as it's explained in the book of Genesis as the land of the children of Ham, Noah's son.

On the biblical map Bashir shows me, the land covered Egypt and Ethiopia, while Noah's other sons lived across North Africa and parts of the Middle East. Any narratives that position and acknowledge Africa as the origin of mankind and civilisation have a ready believer in me. I leave Bashir's house with an open invitation to visit whenever I want to and a tin filled with enough dates, biscuits and chocolates to last a week, even when I share them with everyone I meet on my journey.

My trip to Port Sudan starts at the bus station in Almin Albenie, where I follow an old man to one of the small offices packed into the alley with even smaller cafés selling bread and fried meat; as always, there are old and young women with tea and coffee stations. Our bus looks like a grandmother's sitting room with velvet seat covers and silk curtains that are decorated with gold tassels. The overhead compartment is draped with red silk. The aircon is set on freezing and the TV on an Imam's teachings. They add another word, shabab, to my Arabic vocabulary. It means youth.

Buildings become smaller and the landscape sparse when we get out of the city. Most of the trip is through vast stretches of flat desert, with snapshots of towns that turn street corners into second-hand fridge and tyre shops. No matter how desolate the location, there's always a mosque around.

We stop for lunch and the afternoon prayer, Asr, at a roadhouse with a mosque at the back and coffee stalls at the front. A butcher stands behind a zinc counter at the door. One of the passengers from our bus refuses to let me pay for my lunch, and the workers call me over to chat in broken English and pose for pictures.

In other parts of the journey, the desert is punctuated with bare mountains and villages where herds of camels are left in kraals next to the main road. The women in this part of the country wear large hoop earrings in their septums; all of them drape cotton shawls over their bodies and all the men are in tunics and turbans. Their complexion is jet black and their hair silky. Sudanese people are breathtakingly beautiful. I have to stop myself from staring.

Port Sudan on New Year's Eve

Being here on the biggest party night of the year seems like a mistake. The bus station is on the outskirts of the city. The streets are dead on the tuk tuk ride to my hotel. The only living things around me are the flocks of sheep left on the railway grazing on piles of dry grass. This side of Port Sudan needs cardiopulmonary resuscitation.

The mood changes when we get to the Bohein Hotel in the area around the corniche. The streets spill over with crowds from cafés, everyone is enjoying fruit juice, tea, coffee, ice cream and sodas. There is alcohol, apparently, but it's not a feature of social life. I haven't been drinking since my trip to Cairo, when I forget to resume my daily sundowners at the end of Ramadan. It looks like everyone – young, old, men, women, teen squads, couples – the whole population of Port Sudan is out. Pavements have become picnic spots with people sitting on plastic mats and concrete benches. Buildings and lamps glint with fairy lights. I mill around the streets, following the sound of music until it leads me to a group of musicians surrounded by an impenetrable crowd. I follow folk songs to an outdoor auditorium and spend the final minutes of 2017 at the edge of the stage, where some band members form a circle around me, gazing into my eyes, singing and clapping like they're putting on a private performance just for me. The sky explodes with fireworks.

I'm only here for three nights. The hotel owner gives me a discount I don't ask for, and never lets me walk past his office on my floor without inviting me over for coffee, like the people I sit next to at coffee shops and stalls. New Year's Day is also the country's Independence Day. I celebrate it at a mushy lagoon with throes of people who arrive on buses, taxis and tuk tuks, and picnic on full meals brought over in pots.

Other than the angareeb, another ubiquitous feature in public spaces are the clay pots that are several feet apart from each other. They're filled with water and a jug is left next to them so that anyone who wants to quench their thirst in one of the hottest countries in the world doesn't have to buy it or ask for it. Another common feature is plastic jugs and prayer mats left on the streets so that anyone who wants to pray can cleanse themselves and face Mecca wherever they are.

This innate generosity is the highlight of my travels in Sudan. People just care for each other. They do so patiently, giving their time and hearts to each other. When I look for my bus ticket out of town, Ahmed the tuk tuk driver doesn't just drop me off at the station. He goes from one company to the next until we find the first ticket out. Some companies write destinations in Arabic and Amharic to accommodate the Eritrean community, and all cashiers put the piles of pounds they collect from us in boxes they leave on the counter, knowing that no one will steal from them. It reminds me of another hotel in Khartoum, which uses a ribbon to keep the gates closed at night.

The trip to Meroe retraces the road I take to Port Sudan from Khartoum, through the now-familiar jarring peaks of granite mountains, the long stretches of desert, the occasional herd of camels and mosques, even when there are only a few houses in the area. This part of the trip ends at Atbara.

Like the highways around the country, the station looks like millions of Sudanese pounds have been put into making it look modern. There are designated parking zones for buses, tuk tuks and cabs. The large building is kept cool with air conditioning that's always set on freezing. There are mini supermarkets and waiting area with benches. The bus companies have demarcated ticket offices and different exits depending on where you are going. I'm the last passenger in the minibus to Meroe.

I've been on buses, taxis and tuk tuks decorated with curtains, mirrors, lace trimmings and plastic flowers. This mini bus takes the prize as the most tricked-out public transport in the country, and believe me, they decorate them like it's a competition. Every surface of the interior is covered with a brown and gold suede cloth. The curtains have frills, the roof has round and triangular mirrors and plastic tear-drop chandeliers that shake all the way to Meroe. The trip is uneventful until the driver stops and tells me to get out in the middle of nowhere. I may not know where I'm going, but I'm not going to be left by the roadside. The day light is fading; I'd rather end up at the last stop with other people. No one speaks English, so the minibus waits until a car that's going to Meroe finally shows up. I call Bashir, who has become my translator, so he can tell the driver where to take me. He chooses Meroe Tourist Village, which has a mosque on its grounds, a culture museum that's never open, and a restaurant that looks like a school dining hall and a patio with views of the palm tree forest that stretches endlessly.

Meroe is not as famous as Giza but it's possibly one of the most important sites in Africa for the two hundred-plus pyramids left behind by Nubian kings and queens. The earliest date back to the sixth century and while they are small compared to the famous ones in Cairo, they have the cachet of being the first to go up. They're scattered around the former heartland of the Nubian kingdom, and much like other experiences and relics from Sudan's glorious past, there is barely any information about them at the site. The information black out is frustrating but the lack of tourists turns being here into an experience that's not marred by throngs of people; it makes exploring them a private tour of sorts.

I waddle through the sand while my cab driver stays behind and catch a lucky break when I meet Ibrahim and Mohammed and the two Chinese friends they're taking around northern Sudan. They give me company, someone to take pictures of my bucket-list moment and a crew to trek to the pyramids in Nuri with.

Meroe has two sides; the near-desolate sites of the desert, and the vibrant town that sits on the banks of the Nile. In this part of town, houses and buildings look like a box of Smarties with colourful walls. The muezzin for Isha, the last call to prayer in the evening, finds me at the viewpoint at the hotel. I walk back to my room to repeat a ritual I've seen countless times in the past nine years, when believers rinse their right hands three times, followed by the left, then the face and feet. After my improvised wudu, I go to the mosque, where I kneel and make my head touch the ground, declaring: 'Laa ilaaha illalaah, Mohammed ar-Rasool Allah'; there is no God but Allah and Mohammed is His messenger. I first say these words in August 2009, when one of the passengers in my taxi from Conakry to Bamako writes them in my journal. This time around, I say them to mark my conversion to Islam. The other people in the mosque are the manager, Mubarak, and the two staff members he's leading in prayer. When he's done, he shows up at my door to tell me that seeing me pray is the final sign he needed to tell me that he wants me to be his second wife.

I find him camping outside my door the following morning. 'I have spoken to an Imam who has agreed to marry us before you leave for Dongola,' he says hopefully. He backs off when I promise to think about his proposal. I block his number a few minutes after I check out to travel to Dongola.

At the bus station in Dongola, I show a driver the picture of a jellabiya-clad man walking into a mud hut shaped like a beehive. I want this scene to be my last experience in the north before I trek back to Khartoum. Within seconds, a group of other people, all men, has gathered around us, passing my phone from hand to hand to figure out where I need to go. I'm excluded from a conversation that's become spirited, and sounding like it has stopped being about getting me on a taxi to the place in the picture.

Whenever someone joins the chatter, the conversation goes back to arguing about where I'm going. Someone calls a friend that speaks English. In what's turning out to be the story of my travel here, he doesn't just tell me where to go. He drives to the rank to meet me in person and offers to help me look for a hotel when I come back from my trip. In the meantime, he, along with the group, agrees that Mohammed is the best person to take me there. He speaks English and he is a police officer. The guard will open for us if they're already closed for the day. Another plus with Mohammed – he's the only person who will drive me there and back for three hundred pounds.

Mohammed speaks good English on the hour-long drive through desert towns that add pops of colour to the earthy tones with pastel purple and lime walls with white borders, dots and pin stripes. I may not know where I'm going but forests of palm trees don't match the barren landscape in the picture Mohammed keeps assuring me we are on the way to. My picture doesn't have other buildings around. The trip ends in a sprawling compound housing a peach-coloured building. We've walked into a family day with families picnicking on the sunburned grass. Children take a break from chasing each other to get ice cream, which they always do with a smile, and to join their families for food, which they sulk over. The guards know Mohammed. They laugh and catch up with each other, and let me through without charging me. I show him the picture again. He says starting at the Kerma Museum is part of the experience.

Kerma Museum has the largest collection of Nubian relics. It's an ancient site with ruins of what used to be the royal burial grounds and temples. The collection of relics here is even smaller than the one at the national museum in Khartoum. It still gives a rounded impression of life at the height of the Nubian kingdom. The collection includes granite statues of kings from the Nubian dynasty, ceramic vases and jars, figures and models of village life then and a burial site with a grave and skeleton. Through a gate at the back of the museum are grounds with some of the tombs from Kerma's golden age between 2500 and 1500 BC. Without context, they are just solid lines of sand in blocks and spherical shapes.

Mohammed stays on the ground while I climb heavily up the steps to the top of one of the three deffufas left over from the Kingdom of Kerma. Deffufa is derived from the Arabic translation of pile. It's an apt name for the mud building. Its previous use is unknown. It's now a viewing point for sunsets that sink into the forest of palm trees. After the ritual rounds of taking selfies, I show the beehive huts to a boy I find hanging out on the steps. I ask a boy who speaks fluent English if he knows where I need to go, and if he can tell Mohammed how to get there. We're not just at the wrong place. We are at the opposite end of town. Worse, with the sun starting to set, it's too late for me to trek there. I have been keeping myself in check from the beginning of my trip as people send me on wild rides around town because 'no' seems to be a forbidden word in Sudan. I tell myself to chin up, and enjoy the moment for what it is. But this is enough. I'm leaving the country in three days. I can't afford to lose any more time.

I storm off with a trail of young girls chasing after me. The leader of the selfie gang holds my hand and starts telling me about her family. I have to meet them. Her mom will love me, her baby brother won't touch me but that's how he is. He'd rather crawl around than be coddled. I need a few minutes by myself to calm down, and dig deep for a crocodile smile that becomes genuine by the time we are back among the families. She shows her mom and dad our pictures, tells them I'm from Johannesburg and passes other morsels of information until her mom tells her to let go of my hand. I'm still a little pissed at Mohammed, and don't really feel like talking. He buys me ginger tea and tickles me until I laugh, and my temper goes away without leaving a trail of blood on the floor: I need to live in Sudan.

We stop at his sister Amina's house on the way back to Dongola. The first thing I notice walking into the house are the beds from Bashir's house in the lounge. Amina offers me a seat on one of them and tells me to lie down. She puts a mink blanket over me to protect me from the cold night air. While her husband makes tea, she brings out a plate full of sweets she leaves in my hands. Her tenderness reminds me of Jilly and Astou from my life in Bamako.

I still haven't found a hotel. Mohammed offers me a place at his house. When we get home, he leaves the car at the gate for the night. It doesn't fit into the yard. 'It's not as if someone will break into it,' he says.

The yard is even smaller than what I imagine when he says the car doesn't fit into it. It has a bathroom at the left corner and space that can fit five people at most. A paint bucket with a satellite on top of it occupies the left corner of the yard. The house has two main doors next to each other, the one we enter opens into a lounge with a small passage that leads to the main bedroom and a small TV room with three angareebs. His wife and daughter, Fatma and Iman, have already dozed off. Fatma rises from her sleep to welcome me and to serve the take away dinner we pick up on the way home. Mohammed gently coaxes Iman out her sleep and tells me to 'relax' when I sit on an angareeb. When a Sudanese person tell you to relax what they mean is take your shoes off and sprawl your whole body on an angareeb; they are the homeliest people I've encountered in my travels.

In the morning, after my shower and coffee, Mohammed takes me to the dining room, which has its own entrance. There are two angareebs next to the door, and one at the back of the room next to the dining table. He takes out three photo albums and takes me through snapshots of his life since boyhood. One of the albums has an Ethiopian Airlines boarding pass from his first and only trip out of Sudan to Delhi. He was there to visit his sister in hospital.

In Amina's pictures, she's a dark-skinned girl who turns into a pale woman from using Hydroquinone. I've seen the change, marked with red blotches against unnaturally white skin, on a number of faces. The wall on one side of the room has framed certificates Mohammed has collected in his life as a police officer. I'm on my last hours in Sudan. My hugs are tighter and longer than usual, and when my eyes tear up when Mohammed leaves me at the door of the bus, I'm surprised by how deep my sadness is. It's going to be hard for me to get over the peace I feel in Sudan.

Mohammed introduces me to the other passengers and asks them to show me where to get off. A man who happens to be an English teacher takes over the trip. He tells the driver where to drop me off, and assures me that I will know I'm at the right place when we reach a T-junction with a police station and road block. There, I wait at a restaurant for a bakkie to the banks of the Nile where I join a group of others waiting for a boat to take us across the river. Everyone gets off except for me. After seeing my picture, Moussa the boatman sails up the stream to drop me off next to vegetable gardens.

I drop to my knees and crawl up it. The only living beings around are the old man watering the garden and a white mule grazing on weeds. When I get to the top and back on my feet, it's to views of an empty desert with granite pillars and columns and pieces of vases, remains from a seventh-century church, peeking out of the sand. There's a fort a short distance away on what locals would call a hill, but is in fact a high sand dune with stones. The ruins of the city are scattered across the area, mostly as ruins of houses. Less than a kilometre across the road are the mud huts. There is nothing else around me. It makes being here feel like walking into the moment in the picture that brings me to Old Dongola until I see a bakkie, then a bus and other, occasional traffic on the new tar road between the tombs and the earth-coloured hills – again, actually dunes.

While royals were buried in pyramids, Sufi saints from the medieval kingdom of Makuria were mummified and left in tombs adorned with inscriptions. In a nine-hundred-year-old tomb whose existence goes international after a Polish archaeologist's trip in 1993, walls have verses from the gospels of Mark, Matthew, Luke and John.

There are around twenty tombs. Most are in near-perfect condition, others have lost their walls and beehives. Walking to the first one to start working my way around the group that's here, I notice that there are small piles of sand with pebbles and flat headstones. I ask God and the gods to forgive me for stomping on their resting place. I'm a little nervous about being here, but it's not because of the Muslim graveyard I walk carelessly around; graveyards are one of my favourite places.

The tombs are completely dark, even with the round opening at their roofs. There is no way to tell what's inside unless I walk head first into the darkness. The air is stale in the first hut. There's nothing inside it. The walls have inscriptions, including graffiti carved by previous visitors. I hear animal sounds that I think are from rats at the second and third tombs, and take it as my sign to walk past. And so goes my visit; with me marching boldly to an entrance and being scared to be in the dark by myself. When I remember that fear is an irrational emotion best dealt with through physical confrontation, I stand a few feet away from the entrances. One hut has an old wooden bed and cloth over it. It could be a net over a deathbed. They could be whatever is left after mass excavations when Western archaeologists 'discover' world heritage.

I call Moussa to pick me up before my phone battery dies. Going back to Khartoum, I take my chances and wait for transport at the T-junction. One of the uniforms says he has called a bus that's still in Dongola, telling them to reserve my seat. They'll be here in an hour. The sun sets, darkness settles in with cold air and still no sign of the bus. I wait until my shuka is no longer enough to keep me warm. There's an office with a bed, where I'm charging my phone. The old man doesn't invite me inside no matter how many times I pop in to check my phone, and complain about how cold it has become. Everyone else is welcome, though. I go across the road to the twin-cab van where the uniform looking after me is sitting with two others. After fourteen days in Sudan, I'm used to being a pampered princess who never asks for anything, from food to hailing my cab or a minibus. I let myself in and ask them to help me find food. We drive off to get bread and grilled meat. The clock is ticking towards midnight; I make peace with the possibility of sleeping here until the morning, when I'll go back to Dongola when, finally, a minibus to Khartoum arrives with space for one person between the driver and another passenger.

I sleep until we stop for fuel, where I remain in my seat while others look for food and fruit. The man in the seat next to mine buys me a bag of oranges. I wake up again when we get to Libya, on the outskirts of Khartoum. The driver wants me to pay six hundred pounds for the trip to Al Amarat. Public transport will start running again at 6am, according to the man we find to translate for us. He tells me I'm better off waiting at the bus station. His wife has a tea stall in front of a row of angareebs. He finds me a blanket and tells me not to move until 6am.

Buses that will be leaving for long distance trips start revving their engines, and passengers leave their angareebs to wash their faces and their mouths, filling the area with the guttural sounds of phlegm being pulled out of their nostrils. They stop for tea and legemat on their way to the buses. Getting into the taxi to Khartoum, I understand why Masjeed and Bashir laugh when I tell them I'll be using public transport; people push, pull, shove and step on each other to get into minibuses in Libya.

I spend my last day in Sudan at the Sheikh Hamed al Nil shrine in Omdurman, where the nineteenth-century Sufi leader's remains are. Today is Monday and the throes of Sufi muslims who gather here on Friday have turned into a handful of people who are at the shrine to pray, or park themselves under a makeshift veranda. I'm here with Nusaiba, the twenty-year-old student I befriend on my trip to the confluence of the Nile. She should be in her lectures but wants to spend my last day in Sudan with me. She gives me pink faux pearl teardrop earrings and a necklace.

At the airport, I discover that travellers need to register their presence with the Ministry of the Interior within three days of arrival. This information is on my visa but I never read it. Without any money to pay for my fine, I ask the head of immigration at the airport to help me. My flight is leaving in a few minutes. He makes a call to Ethiopia Airlines, asking them to remain grounded while someone prints my boarding pass. 'I hope this won't happen again the next time I see you,' he says, hugging me.

I have been travelling Africa since 2008. While I know only too well that there are ways of arriving in a new country, like knowing where I'm going and where I will be staying, I will never be this person, and it's okay because I'm home in Africa.

AFTERWORD

I NO LONGER LIVE ON the road but I still travel around Africa. I want to see other parts of the world too but whenever the moment arrives when I have to spend the money in the saving account I have for my travels, my spirit whispers: 'You have only scratched the surface of Africa'.

I often wonder about the hold this continent has on me. Perhaps it is that every new place I go to also has a familiarity from a lived experience in any of the countries I have been to before: The certainty that I can walk up to a complete stranger and be held with love like we have always known each other, the invitation I will get to join in a communal meal even with a plate of my own food in front of me, the unshakable faith that I will never lack for anything because everyone around me will hold my hand as I turn their home, a place that was a speck on the map, into mine as well.

It has been eleven years since those three months in West Africa turned into five years, and now my life, because I cannot think of a better gift to myself than that of knowing the continent that defines my identity intimately. As I write this, the main reason I started travelling – writing the continent beyond our strife – seems like a fluke. The Timbuktu of 2009 is gone. In its place is instability and milltary attacks, yet Abdul is still the same resilient hustler and now has a tour company, Timbuktu Camel Tours, that specialises in trips to Niger, Mauritania and Burkina Faso.

When I stood among Southern Sudanese refugees in Kakuma, crying tears of joy with them on the last day of voting to secede from North Sudan, I didn't for a second think that the independent state would end up as another humanitarian crisis. I expected people to leave Kakuma refugee camp instead of escaping there like they have been doing since 1990. Against stark realities that keep increasing the number of people who seek refuge here, the camp made world history in June 2018 when it hosted TEDxKakumaCamp and a gay pride parade; no other refugee camp in the world has done this. There are endless examples of how this continent keeps surprising me by how closely hope lives to our despair; as if it's a coin that can be flipped in a second to reveal its other side of love, faith and fortitude.

Not so long ago, the thought of going to Mogadishu used to fill me with dread. Now, I cannot wait to go there and write the country beyond news stories of al-Shabaab because the Somalia of five years ago – of bomb blasts – no longer exists; certainly not as a daily reality. Africa proves my conviction correct daily: The continent is always in a state of metamorphosis. We pick ourselves up over and over again, and come out of the fire more determined than ever to assert that we are greater than the clichés that reduce us to death and despair.

Pressed to pinpoint why I cannot stop exploring Africa, and why I have been planning to go to so-called war zones and conflict areas, I guess my answer will always be that I still hear voices telling me 'Africa – now'. It's more urgent than before that I find my way to Mogadishu, Darfur, N'Djemenna, Bangui, Malabo, Niamey and Juba to honour the instruction I received inside the mass grave in Ntarama; to spend time traipsing the Sahara and swimming around the Mediterranean coast, to be a hijabi and explore my conversion to Islam around the Horn of Africa and offer my sincerest gratitude to Allah at the Sahaba mosque in Massawa and around North Africa. Not because I have to, but because I live on a fantastical continent that has given me my heart's desires and made my wildest dream come true.

Acknowledgements

It took a village for my dream to come true, from my publisher Thabiso Mahlape and editor Megan Mance to my family, friends, colleagues and hundreds of strangers who opened their hearts, homes and purses to help me make it through another day – some without even asking for more than my name because we didn't have a language in common. Their presence in my life was fleeting. Time has turned them faceless but the gift of their generosity endures.

While living as a vagabond and thereafter, many people who read about my journeys in *City Press* and *True Love* and later followed my adventures through social media would send direct messages or stop me in my tracks to high five me or urge me to keep going. On days when wanting to travel Africa while earning a pittance reduced me to rage and tears of desperation, your encouragement kept me together. I was alone physically, but emotionally, I was travelling with a tribe – betam ameseginalehu, thank you very much.

Writing *Vagabond* made me remember childhood memories that I realise were planting a seed that would one day grow into my life. My mom, Dikeledi Miemie Mogoatlhe, wasn't a fan of saying yes to everything, not even with my tears and tactics. What she never said no to was buying me books and music, or letting me hang out with her on Sunday afternoons when it was meant to be her alone time whenever I had seemingly random questions to ask, like 'Mom, who is the Egyptian sun god?' My first encounters with countries that would become the story of my life started with literature and music, and there was never a moment when asking for these was met with anything but, 'I'll do it tomorrow'. Thanks, Mommy, for feeding my lust and gluttony for all things African. To my paternal family, ba ga Mogoatlhe: Lesego, Vincent, Mapolo, Sebati, Maphalane, Grace, Leah, Dinaane, Isaiah, Matlakala, and my maternal family, ba ga Malebane: Dr Matlhogonolo, Matheko, Thabo, Esther, Oupa, Mangaka Ngubane. Ba ga Seabela: Mapula, Mpho, Tebogo, Oageng. Ba ga Dube: Ndu, Portia and Boitumelo.

For the rolls of Randelas wedged between my cleavage, the expressions of faith that became my sustenance and the phone calls, social media chats, messages, and emails that came in like clockwork to check that I was indeed fine: Tebogo Mothoa, Dr Khumisho Moguerane, Kgopedi Lilokoe, Heidi Uys, Babalwa Shota, Adam Levine, Norman Mekgoe, Sarah-Jane Boden, Nicole Gazard, Sikelewa Geya-Mdingi, Nonzwakazi Cekete, Dr Sindisiwe and Marinus van Zyl, Lerato Molele, Voilet and Tshepo Maila, Tsakani Shibisi, Dr Zakes Motene, Dr Cephas Chikanda, Tiny Bikitsha, Vukani Lumumba Mthintso, Lucas Ledwaba, Arrot Iramisi, Ceasar Pirs, Khuthala Nandipha, Thapelo Mokhathi, Mathata Tsedu, Mahlatsi Maredi, Tokiso Mbatha, Maikano Mokoka, Matshidiso Masebe, Thabiso Sekhula, Thami Kwazi, Carl Collison, Mapula Nkosi, Sonia Motaung, Nokwazi Mzobe, Adrien Dawans, Manana Monareng, Lerato Legoabe, Teshome Ayele, Mokgadi Seabi, David Odhiambo, Kwelagobe Sekele, Celuxolo Nhlengethwa, Neo Maditla, Ramathabathe Muroa, Siphiwe Ndaba, Neo Merafi, Dineo Rabaholo, Pepe Julian Onziema, Gelila Yehualashet, Souleymana Sene, Abdoulaye Alitunine, Ceaser Pirs, Nana Ama Afrakoma-Todhunter, Liphumileilanga Goduka, Joshua Mudau, Noletu Moti, Joe Correia, Dr Sithembile Mabaso, Lungi Mlotshwa, Nosipho Jiyane, Lebohang Maphasa, Sello Nzama, Omphile Raleie, Melinda Ferguson, Ali Naka, Lefa Mokgatle, Angela Lang, Lebo Mashile and my beloved Maetheng Hlalele, for keeping me sane and inspired when it turned out that writing a book is easier said than done and supporting me through other challenges that come with the process of working on a manuscript.